AT HOME IN SHAKESPEARE'S TRAGEDIES

For David Bergeron

A fé é vida e a vida para mim é fé—S. Geraldo Majella (1726–1755).

At Home in Shakespeare's Tragedies

GERALDO U. DE SOUSA
University of Kansas, USA

ASHGATE

Published by

Ashgate Publishing Limited
Wey Court East
Union Road
Farnham
Surrey, GU9 7PT
England

Ashgate Publishing Company
Suite 420
101 Cherry Street
Burlington
VT 05401-4405
USA

www.ashgate.com

British Library Cataloguing in Publication Data
Sousa, Geraldo U. de, 1952–
At home in Shakespeare's tragedies.
1. Shakespeare, William, 1564–1616 – Tragedies. 2. Shakespeare, William, 1564–1616 – Settings. 3. Dwellings in literature.
I. Title
822.3'3—dc22

Library of Congress Cataloging-in-Publication Data
Sousa, Geraldo U. de, 1952–
At home in Shakespeare's tragedies / by Geraldo U. de Sousa.
p. cm.
Includes bibliographical references and index.
ISBN 978-0-7546-6886-2 (hardback: alk. paper)—ISBN 978-1-4094-0428-6 (ebook)
1. Shakespeare, William, 1564–1616—Tragedies. 2. England—Social life and customs—16th century. 3. England—Social life and customs—17th century. 4. Families—England—History—16th century. 5. Families—England—History—17th century. 6. Home in literature. 7. Families in literature. I. Title.
PR2983.S68 2010
822.3'3—dc22

2009050475

ISBN: 9780754668862 (hbk)
ISBN: 9781409404286 (ebk)

Printed and bound in Great Britain by
MPG Books Group, UK

Contents

List of Figures

Acknowledgments

As a meditation or memory exercise, I frequently revisit in my mind's eye my childhood home in the Brazilian highlands, visualizing every detail I can. Our house became the center of our family life and the source of our family's livelihood. Built when I was two years old, the house and adjacent buildings functioned as our family home, my father's road-side café, and an all-purpose Brazilian *venda*—a family-run entrepôt, retail shop, and general store. Such multi-purpose compounds can be found around the world, early examples of which include the housing compound in eighteenth-century Liberia, West Africa. Eighteenth- and nineteenth-century accounts of travel to the interior of Brazil include numerous references to similar *vendas*.

My family's estate was known as *Estiva*, a word derived from Latin, *æstivare*, "to estivate," to reside during the summer. In regional Portuguese, *estiva* also means a wooden bridge; and the verb "estivar" refers to the stowing, loading, and unloading of a ship. Although Estiva was my parents' year-round residence, far away from any fluvial or sea port, and had no bridge, the name seemed oddly suitable: my school-age siblings and I, who attended school in nearby towns, used to return home only on weekends, for school holidays, and during the summer. Buses, private cars, trucks, and caravans of pack animals, following ancient trade routes, would regularly make a stop at our home, which bridged many worlds.

Eventually, home became a cluster of associations revolving around a commercial center, family life, and the uncultivated, wild countryside. Whenever I was home, I wanted to explore Estiva. Perhaps against their better judgment, my parents always granted permission for me to organize and lead day-long expeditions into the surrounding areas, provided that at least one adult came along. Almost anything would serve as an excuse for exploration, although I often made a case based on my credentials as a student of science and on the uncontestable scientific significance of the expedition: to collect exotic plants and flowers, study geological formations and geographical landmarks, and watch the birds and wildlife. Frequently, however, I simply argued that I wanted to gather wild *mangaba*, the fruit of the *Hancornia speciosa*, everybody's favorite.

Estiva was my little corner of the universe. It afforded shelter, refuge, and security; yet it also seemed to abut not just the great unchartered wilds of the Brazilian interior but a mysterious, dangerous, sometimes tragic world, fraught with human drama. A close encounter with a rattlesnake in our own backyard, sightings of an onça-pintada (*Panthera onca*) or a very large *sucuri* or anaconda (*Eunectes murinus*), or reports of the dangers posed by the deadly venomous *urutu* (*Bothrops alternata*) were frequent reminders that a house can give us but a provisional sense of stability.

From time to time, a shocking event would dislocate our habits of mind and shake our sense of domestic security and stability. When I was growing up, I witnessed much suffering and poverty around us, but our home was a healing place, a place where those in trouble would stop for help, sometimes seeking transportation to the hospital in Patos de Minas or just to refresh themselves on a long journey. A complicated network of routes seemed to intersect our world, including the caravans of pack animals transporting merchandise to the deep interior, or the so-called *paus-de-arara*, truckloads of migrants who had left abject poverty behind and were following a dream of new life and opportunity in Brasilia, the newly-erected capital on the distant central plateau.

These childhood experiences, memories, and reflections have imbued the writing of this book with the passions of living. The anthropologist James Clifford must surely be right when he speaks of the roots and the routes of our lives. Estiva represents my deep roots but it also positioned my life in an intricate web of mysterious routes. With this childhood home, I associate solitude, introspection, and exploration of the natural world, as well as a vibrant sense of being part of a family, household and community. I am grateful to my parents for providing us the shelter, security and protection of a loving home and the comforts of life. Above all, our home was a place of rest, healing and rejoicing. I also thank all those whose lives intersected mine for a profound sense of spirituality, a love for story-telling, and the memories that still enrich my life and inform and guide my many pursuits.

In the process of researching and writing *At Home in Shakespeare's Tragedies*, I have incurred many debts of gratitude. First I would like to thank Xavier University, Cincinnati, Ohio, for granting me a sabbatical leave and therefore making it possible for me to begin research. My colleagues at Xavier were unfailingly supportive, and I want to thank Norman Finkelstein, Ernie Fontana, and Provost Roger Fortin in particular, as well as my friends in Xavier's Office of Spiritual Development and in the Society of Jesus, especially Leo Klein. At the University of Kansas, I want to thank Dorice Elliott, chair of the English Department (2004–2009), especially for her patience and kindness to me; Richard F. Hardin, for reading drafts of the manuscript and sharing his vast knowledge and experience; Mary Rieser Davidson, for her helpful comments and suggestions on the chapter on *Hamlet*; Paul Lim, for his friendship, generosity, and sharing his vast film collection; and Marta and Byron Caminero-Santangelo for their friendship and support. I also thank Margaux DeRoux, Alicia Sutliff-Benusis, Gaywyn Moore, Brian Harries, Keri Behre, Andrew Kuhn, Kristin Bovaird-Abo, and Ann Martinez-Villalobos for helpful suggestions and encouragement. Likewise, I want to thank the Hall Center for the Humanities, especially director Victor Bailey, the Hall Center staff, and the British Seminar, which provided a forum for the presentation and discussion of the chapters on *Hamlet* and *King Lear*. I profited a great deal from these discussions. I am most grateful to all of my students at Xavier University and at the University of Kansas, with whom I shared ideas while writing this book.

I also thank the following institutions, libraries, museums, art galleries and foundations for supplying illustrations and for granting permission to reproduce them: Longleat House; Houghton Library, Harvard University; Folger Shakespeare

Library; Special Collections, Spencer Research Library, University of Kansas Libraries; and the Nelson-Atkins Museum of Art, Kansas City, Missouri. I want to thank the following persons in particular for their kindness and generosity: The Marquess of Bath, The Trustees of the Longleat Estates, and Dr Kate Harris, the Curator, Longleat Historic Collections; Richard W. Clement, Dean of Libraries, Utah State University; Karen Severud Cook, Special Collections, Spencer Research Library; William P. Stoneman, Florence Fearrington Librarian of Houghton Library, Harvard University; Stacey Sherman, Imaging Services, The Nelson-Atkins Museum of Art, Kansas City, Missouri; and Auste Mickunaite, Permissions Office, The British Library. A generous grant from the Herbert and JoAnn Klemmer Fund, Endowment Association, English Department, University of Kansas, made the publication of these illustrations possible.

Chapter 2 incorporates ideas and materials from my essay "Unhoused in *Othello*," published in *Approaches to Teaching Shakespeare's Othello*, ed. Peter Erickson and Maurice Hunt (New York: The Modern Language Association of America, 2005) 133–47, herein republished by permission of MLA. Throughout this book, all quotations from Shakespeare's plays, unless indicated otherwise, are from *The Complete Pelican Shakespeare*, ed. Stephen Orgel and A.R. Braunmuller (New York: Penguin, 2002).

I presented sections of this book at the annual congresses of the Mediterranean Studies Association at the University of Cagliari, Sardinia (2009); Leuphana Universität, Lüneburg, Germany (2008); Universidade de Évora, Portugal (2007); Università di Genova, Genoa, Italy (2006); Università degli Studi di Messina, Messina, Sicily (2005); Universitat de Barcelona, Barcelona, Spain (2004); and Central European University, Budapest, Hungary (2003). I am grateful to the congress participants for their comments, suggestions, support, and convivial discussions, including Richard and Franziska Raspa, Anna Leider, Karen Leider, Bob and Mary Dudy Bjork, Caroline Jewers, and David Johnson.

The staff of the following libraries, where I conducted research, deserve my gratitude: McDonald Library, Xavier University; Spencer Research Library, Watson Library, and Art and Architecture Library, University of Kansas; the British Library; and the Folger Shakespeare Library. I want to thank Gwen Claassen, Digital Media Services, College of Liberal Arts and Sciences, the University of Kansas, for her expert assistance in formatting, design, and helping me prepare the manuscript and illustrations for publication. This is an invaluable service that the University of Kansas provides the faculty. In Britain and in the United States, I thank the staff of Ashgate, especially Erika Gaffney, Whitney Feininger, Seth F. Hibbert, Nicole Norman, Suzanne Sprague, and Lee C. Kemsley, with whom it has been a pleasure to work, and the readers who read my manuscript for Ashgate for wonderful insights, comments, and suggestions.

Several friends, colleagues, and scholars have been extraordinarily kind and helpful to me. I would like to thank the following in particular: Dick and Franziska Raspa, Heather Dubrow, Mary Thomas Crane, Fran Teague, Coppélia Kahn, Bruce Smith, Jeanne Addison Roberts, Misty Schieberle, James W. Hartman,

Judy Bissett, Marilyn Stokstad, Elise Goodman, Billy Joe and Susan Harris, William O. Scott, Laura Mielke, Jackson Boswell and Daryl Palmer. Elise Goodman read the manuscript in its entirety, helped with proofreading, and advised on art history in general and on Caravaggio scholarship in particular. Elise has been a faithful and generous friend, and I am much in her debt. Likewise, I would like to thank my friends and spiritual companions at Plymouth Congregational Church in Lawrence, Kansas, especially Rev. Dr Peter Luckey, whose sermons over the last few years seem to have intersected my work with amazing frequency. I also thank for their friendship and support Cliff VanBlarcom; Sister Mary V. Maronick of the Sisters of Charity, Leavenworth; Leon C. Bergeron; Judy and Gene Bauer; John and Ardith Pierce; John B. Timmer; Cindy West and Judith Galas; Marco Antonio de Sousa; and Ângela and Josafá do Couto.

Finally, I express my heartfelt gratitude to my friends Rick and Susanne Clement; my sister Rejânia Aparecida dos Reis Soares Araújo; and my faithful companion, David Bergeron, to whom I dedicate this book.

Introduction

> In consecrated earth,
> And on the holy hearth,
> The lars, and lemures moan with midnight plaint,
> In urns, and altars round,
> A drear and dying sound
> Affrights the flamens at their service quaint;
> And the chill marble seems to sweat,
> While each peculiar power forgoes his wonted seat.[1]

> Houses for Tragedies, must bee made for great personages, for that actions of loue, strange aduentures, and cruell murthers, (as you reade in ancient and moderne Tragedies) happen always in the houses of great Lords, Dukes, Princes, and Kings. Therefore in such cases you must make none but stately houses. Sebastian Serlio, *The First Booke of Architecture* (London, 1611).

For the ancient Greeks and Romans, Dionysus was the youthful god of wine, orgiastic god of fertility, and violent god of tragedy and of the maenadic cults; yet he was also "the mysterious god who comforts the dying and frees them from the fear of death."[2] Bacchus, an alternative name for Dionysus, means "the Frenzied One."[3] An encounter with Dionysus, through worship or in tragedy, dislocates habits of mind and disrupts or destroys households. In fact, Dionysus was known as a destroyer of households, and, ironically perhaps, also as "the liberator of women from their homes."[4] In their tragedies, Aeschylus, Euripides, and later Seneca depict the powerful effect of Dionysus's presence in a house, shaking or shattering sturdy foundations and transforming the residents. Longinus reports

---

1 John Milton, "On the Morning of Christ's Nativity," *John Milton,* (eds) Stephen Orgel and Jonathan Goldberg (Oxford: Oxford University Press, 1990) 3–10. All references to Milton, unless otherwise stated, will be to this edition.

2 Thomas H. Carpenter and Christopher A. Faraone, (eds), *Masks of Dionysus* (Ithaca: Cornell University Press, 1993) 1, and Richard Seaford, "Dionysus as Destroyer of the Household: Homer, Tragedy, and the Polis," Carpenter and Faraone 115–46. See George E. Mylonas, *Eleusis and the Eleusinian Mysteries* (Princeton, NJ, Princeton University Press, 1961); Rosemarie Taylor-Perry, *The God Who Comes: Dionysian Mysteries Revisited* (New York: Algora Publications, 2003); Gerald Else, *The Origin and Early Form of Greek Tragedy* (Cambridge, MA: Harvard University Press, 1965); and Albin Lesky, *Greek Tragic Poetry*, trans. Matthew Dillon (New Haven: Yale University Press, 1983).

3 Carpenter and Faraone offer a very useful "Glossary" of key terms associated with the cult of Dionysus (297–301). Bacchus is also the god of wine in Italy (297). Unless otherwise indicated, references to these terms come from this glossary.

4 Seaford, 115–46.

that at the appearance of Dionysus, in a lost play by Aeschylus, the palace of Lycurgus becomes "divinely possessed": "Then the house is in an ecstasy, and the roof is inspired with Bacchic frenzy."[5] Peter Hall, in his 2002 production of Euripides' *Bacchai*, recreates that effect. In this performance, Dionysus, played by Greg Hicks, made his entrance with the sudden, explosive igniting of gas burners that seemed to set the entire stage ablaze and momentarily scorch the entire auditorium.[6] Just as suddenly, the flames subsided, and the god stepped forward to justify his appearance in Thebes.

In Euripides's play (c. 405 BCE), Dionysus has driven his female worshippers into a wild ritualistic frenzy (*bakkheia*). Raising Bacchic shouts (*euhoi*), dressed in deerskin cloaks, and holding the thyrsus[7] or the ritual phallus in their hands, the women have run out of their homes to wander wildly or dance franticly on the mountains (*oreibasia*)[8]: "And I made them carry the emblems of my mysteries; and the whole female population of Thebes, every woman there was in the town, I drove raving from their homes."[9] Ignoring the prophet Teiresias's warning, the foolish and proud King Pentheus of Thebes belittles and defies Dionysus, who in retribution inspires Agave, Pentheus's mother, to dismember her son's body in a maenadic ritual (*sparagmos*), a wild fit of madness and delirious fury.[10] Upon this dismal sight, Dionysus warns the Thebans: "The royal house is overthrown; the city's streets are full of guilty fear, as every Theban repents too late for his blindness

---

[5] See Longinus, "On the Sublime," in *Classical Literary Criticism*, trans. by T.S. Dorsch (Harmondsworth, UK; Baltimore, MD: Penguin Books, 1965) 123. Presumably, this refers to Lycurgus, king of Thrace, who defied the new god. In revenge, Dionysus drove him mad and then had horses tear him to pieces. See reference to Lycurgus in Homer, *Iliad* 6.132, and other references to maenadism in Homer and tragedy (Seaford 115).

[6] This production, directed by Peter Hall, opened at the Olivier Theatre, the Royal National Theatre, London, on May 17, 2002 and closed on June 12, 2002. I attended the June 3, 2002 performance. See review by James Davidson, "Illusion versus delusion," *TLS* May 31, 2002, 10.

[7] Thyrsus—"wand or staff consisting of a fennel stalk (*narthēx*) with ivy leaves attached at the top; frequently handled by Dionysus and his followers in their processions and dances" (Carpenter and Faraone 301).

[8] Carpenter and Faraone 300.

[9] Euripides, *The Bacchae and Other Plays*, trans. Philip Vellacott (Harmondsworth, UK; Baltimore, MD: Penguin Books, 1954) 182.

[10] "The tearing apart of a hero, or his ritualized death in an analogous manner as represented in some tragedies or myths when it symbolizes part of the cycle of death and rebirth" (*OED*). See Carpenter and Faraone; and Northrop Frye, *Anatomy of Criticism* (Princeton: Princeton University Press, 1957), especially the discussion of the mutilation of the hero and ritual death (192–3). According to Frye, this pertains to the sixth phase of tragedy, "a world of shock and horror in which the central images are images of *sparagmos*, that is, cannibalism, mutilation, and torture" (222). He adds, "Any tragedy may have one or more shocking scenes in it, but sixth-phase tragedy shocks as a whole, in its total effect. This phase is more common as a subordinate aspect of tragedy than as its main theme, as unqualified horror or despair makes a difficult cadence" (222).

and blasphemy" (225). Likewise, in Jasper Heywood's 1560 translation of Seneca's *Thyestes*, the furies exact revenge by raising Tantalus from the underworld to set his nephews, Thyestes and Atreus against each other, and therefore to wreak havoc on the entire household. Heywood's translation is one of the main sources for Shakespeare's *Titus Andronicus*.[11]

Primarily through the plays of Seneca, English Renaissance writers were, of course, acquainted with Dionysus's association with tragedy. Ben Jonson, for example, pays homage to Dionysus on the title page of the 1616 folio of his *Workes*. Renaissance playwrights were also familiar with tragedy's destructive effects on great houses, families, and households.[12] As Aeschylus, Euripides, and Seneca illustrate, house and household, body and place—nothing can escape Dionysus's orgiastic fury; for tragedy ruins lives; rips families apart; shatters sturdy foundations of houses; reduces aspirations, dreams, and ambition to a smoldering heap of ashes. Such is the power of Dionysus; such are the familiar themes of tragedy.

As an adverb, "home" signifies a return "to one's home, house, or abode," and a movement toward "the very heart or root of a matter, into close and effective contact, so as to touch, reach, or affect intimately."[13] These usages, dating from c. 1000 and 1542, respectively, have remained current to this day. Home-bred or not, tragedy, however, tends to strike home or become something nearer home. As my title suggests, *At Home in Shakespeare's Tragedies* explores a cluster of phenomena and a web of cultural connections pertaining to domestic life and tragedy in Shakespeare's great tragedies—*King Lear*, *Othello*, *Hamlet*, and *Macbeth*. In particular, I explore the dramatic function of dwelling places in the

---

[11] Seneca's plays appeared in various English translations, culminating with Thomas Newton, *Seneca His Tenne Tragedies* (London, 1581). George Gascoigne translated and adapted Euripides' *Jocasta* (1566). See John W. Cunliffe, (ed.), *Early English Classical Tragedies* (Oxford, UK: Clarendon Press, 1912). For Seneca's influence on Shakespeare, especially Senecan elements in *Hamlet*, *Othello*, *Lear*, and *Macbeth*, consult Robert S. Miola, *Shakespeare and Classical Tragedy: The Influence of Seneca* (Oxford: Clarendon Press, 1992).

[12] In France, after the February 1553 performance of *Cléopâtre captive*, a tragedy by Étienne Jodelle (1532–1573), the playwright's friends captured a goat, crowned it with ivy, and led it to the hall, where Jodelle awaited the merrymakers. Apparently, this was done just for fun, but the detractors of the Pléiade spread the word that Jodelle and friends wanted to sacrifice the goat to Dionysus, and therefore revive a barbaric pagan ritual. King Henri II also awarded the playwright a prize of 500 crowns. See John W. Cunliffe, "Introduction," *Early English Classical Tragedies* (Oxford: Clarendon Press, 1912) liii. See Étienne Jodelle, *Oeuvres complètes*, (ed.) Enea Balmas (Paris: Gallimard, 1965), 2: 444–5; and Kathleen M. Hall's introduction to her edition of *Cléopâtre captive* (Exeter: University of Exeter, 1979): " … *les camarades d'université du nouveau dramaturge auraient improvisé une fête pour le couronner de guirlandes, tel un triomphateur ou une idole antique, en lui amenant un bouc qui, selon les ennemis de la Pléiade, lui aurait été sacrifié*" (v–vi).

[13] *Oxford English Dictionary*, "Home, adv."

tragedies, and the extent to which Shakespeare intertwines home and perception. In a broad sense, I am, of course, concerned with the materiality of the house, the staging of place, and theatrical issues such as setting, scenery, and spectacle. More precisely, however, my interest lies in how Shakespeare *imagines* home life and explores mediated, inhabited space in the major tragedies.

In *The Poetics*, Aristotle argues that spectacle, which for him subsumes stage design and special effects, functions as a mere "attraction," something unessential and unnecessary. Of all the tragic elements—plot, characters, diction, thought, spectacle, and melody—spectacle is, for Aristotle, not only "the least artistic" but "more a matter for the designer than the poet."[14] Aristotle recognizes the power of narrative: the recital of the plot of *Oedipus* suffices to generate the tragic effect of horror and pity. Yet, he adds, "To produce this same effect by means of the spectacle is less artistic, and requires extraneous aid" (*Poetics* 14.5–7). In other words, spectacle diminishes the power of tragedy. But, in fact, Aristotle also concedes that in performance "the spectacle must be some part of the whole" (*Poetics* 6.32–3). Without resolving the much-debated contradictions in the *Poetics*, I believe that in Shakespeare's tragedies, scenery, in the strict sense of lived space and living place, does indeed become an integral and indispensable part of Shakespeare's vision of the tragic experience. Dwelling places and images of places become intimately intertwined with the "passions of living."[15] Therefore, like Bert States, I propose to examine "scenery as our total impression of a play's world"; States adds: "We are not interested in scene design per se, as distinguished from other elements, but in seeing everything on the stage *scenically*: that is, as a shifting image in time and space, formed by the interplay of visual and aural events."[16] I submit that, in Shakespeare's middle tragedies, the tragic journey rests upon shifting images of dwelling places.

In *Defense of Poesy* (1583), Sir Philip Sidney argues for the effects of tragedy on the body: tragedy opens "the greatest wounds" and exposes "ulcers that are covered with tissues." Tragedy, according to him, also affects minds, for it "maketh kings fear to be tyrants, and tyrants manifest their tyrannical humors." For the audience as well as for those within the fictional tragic world onstage, tragedy elicits "admiration and commiseration," teaching "the uncertainty of this world," and the "*weake foundations*" upon which *"guilden roofs are builded.*"[17] In this passage, Sidney not only echoes Aristotle's tragic effects of pity and fear, but he

[14] *The Complete Works of Aristotle*, (ed.) Jonathan Barnes (Princeton: Princeton University Press, 1984), 2: *Poetics* 6:16–20.

[15] I am borrowing the term from Yi-Fu Tuan, in *Space and Place: The Perspective of Experience* (Minneapolis: University of Minnesota Press, 1977) 85.

[16] Bert O. States, *Great Reckonings in Little Rooms: On the Phenomenology of Theater* (Berkeley: University of California Press, 1985) 50–51.

[17] Philip Sidney, "Defense of Poesy," in *English Literary Criticism: The Renaissance*, (ed.) O.B. Hardison, Jr. (New York: Appleton-Century-Crofts, 1963) 122, emphasis mine. I have also somewhat regularized the original spelling.

also suggests that first and foremost tragedy exposes the weak structures of human constructions. Throughout, the tragic journey occurs in space, engages specific locations, and evokes architectural metaphors.

I am particularly interested in the house as a privileged *imagined* place—the material, yet imaginary locations, where Shakespeare's tragic characters dwell, or the domestic spaces they traverse to their destination. Key terms need to be defined. Douglas Pocock writes that "place relates to an area which is bounded and has distinctive internal structure, to which meaning is attributed and which evokes an affective response."[18] Consequently, place cannot be defined without reference to the emotions, memories, and experiences associated with specific locations. In "Place in Fiction," her seminal 1955 lecture at Cambridge University, Eudora Welty (1909–2001) argues that place refers to named, identified, concrete, precise location; yet in fiction, as in drama, it functions as "… a credible, gathering spot of all that has been felt, is about to be experienced." In other words, "location pertains to feeling; feeling profoundly pertains to place."[19] As I have argued elsewhere, "home," a specific kind of place, suggests both the house or dwelling in which one habitually lives or regards as one's proper abode and a place, region, state, or country to which one properly belongs and in which one's affections center.[20] "Home" evokes "the remembered field of familiar experience," and functions as "the loci of memorable personal events."[21] Indeed, if, as the medieval philosopher Roger Bacon (c. 1214–1294?) states, "place is the beginning of our existence," then, I submit, place also serves not only as the beginning but also the trajectory of the tragic experience.[22]

For Shakespeare, place is always virtual, always *imagined*, not based on exact observation and not represented realistically. Shakespeare invites us to form images and notions with regard to something not known with certainty.[23] The house as an imagined place suggests mediation through perception. Places come into focus, but then seem to fade from the characters' consciousness. Shakespeare treats such imagined places as phenomena of perception, therefore always partially concealed, and only partially revealed. The French philosopher Gilles Deleuze argues that

[18] Douglas C.D. Pocock, "Introduction: Imaginative Literature and the Geographer," *Humanistic Geography and Literature: Essays on the Experience of Place*, (ed.) Douglas C.D. Pocock (London: Croom Helm; Totowa, NJ: Barnes & Noble Books, 1981) 17.

[19] Eudora Welty, *Place in Fiction* (New York: House of Books, 1957) n.p.

[20] See my discussion of these terms, quoted almost verbatim here, in "Alien Habitats in *The Tempest*," in *The Tempest: Critical Essays*, (ed.) Patrick M. Murphy (New York and London: Routledge, 2001) 439.

[21] David E. Sopher, "The Landscape of Home: Myth, Experience, Social Meaning," in *The Interpretation of Ordinary Landscapes: Geographical Essays*, (ed.) D.W. Meinig (Oxford and New York: Oxford University Press, 1979) 136, qtd in Sousa, "Alien Habitats," 439.

[22] Roger Bacon, *The Opus Majus of Roger Bacon*, trans. Robert Belle Burke (New York: Russell & Russell, 1962) 1:159.

[23] These comments paraphrase the *OED*'s definitions.

the Baroque "endlessly produces folds"; this "Baroque trait twists and turns its folds, pushing them to infinity, fold over fold, one upon the other."[24] Deleuze adds: "Things jump out of the background, colors spring from the common base that attests to their obscure nature, figures are defined by their covering more than their contour."[25] In this mode of representation, "clarity endlessly plunges into obscurity."[26] Like contemporary baroque painters, such as Michelangelo Merisi da Caravaggio, who perfected chiaroscuro and tenebrist techniques, Shakespeare controls the representation of place as if it he were manipulating light, darkness, and shadows, which he also does, to produce startling effects. The middle tragedies situate the tragic characters against an unstable world, evoked with varying depth and detail, plunging into depths of obscurity. Perhaps, more significantly, Edward Casey reminds us, Bachelard, Braudel, Foucault, Deleuze, Guatari, Derrida, Lefebvre, and other philosophers of place believe that "place itself is no fixed thing: it has no steadfast essence."[27] In other words, for Gaston Bachelard and others, "The sense of place that counts here is not that of place as it contains and perdures but as it lights up with the sudden spark of a single striking image, like a shooting star in the dark abysm of night."[28] For Shakespeare, place becomes a fluid, malleable medium, which he evokes to convey interiority, reflect a profound dislocation of habits of mind, interrogate everyday life, and register the transformations attendant on the tragic journey.

In the Shakespearean theater, when actors, embodying their dramatic parts, walk onstage, they make their presence real "by claiming position in that field of force that the open stage represents."[29] G.K. Hunter argues that, in English renaissance drama, a character's entry and movement on stage create "the environment that is appropriate to his deeds," if the action so requires: "The actor did this by projecting upon the neutral or generalized diagram of stage space the shape of his fictional life, and the audience then supplied the visual particularities."[30] Therefore, "the landscape of Shakespeare's stage is a landscape of persons (creating appropriate environments around them)."[31] Likewise, Bert O. States sees this power of the actor

---

[24] Gilles Deleuze, *The Fold: Leibniz and the Baroque*, trans. Tom Conley (Minneapolis: University of Minnesota Press, 1993) 3.

[25] Deleuze 31–2.

[26] Deleuze 32.

[27] Edward S. Casey, *The Fate of Place: A Philosophical History* (Berkeley: University of California Press, 1998) 286.

[28] Casey 288.

[29] Hunter 21.

[30] Hunter 22. Contemporary theater directors, producers, and historians suggest widely divergent views about how engaging the architectural features of the theater into a production might affect the relationship of the audience to the performance. For a discussion of this debate, please see William Faricy Condee, *Theatrical Space: A Guide for Directors and Designers* (Lanham, MD: Scarecrow, 1995), esp. 17–19.

[31] Hunter 24.

to embody a part and to radiate the character's persona and life into the surrounding environment as the "basis of scenic illusion"; the stage thus "served as a tabula rasa on which the actor could draw the ever-shifting pictures of the text."[32]

To a large extent, characterization and place go hand in hand, as twin processes and functions of the early modern stage. In 1904, Bradley contended that "the centre of tragedy, therefore, may be said ... to lie in action issuing from character, or in character issuing in action."[33] In 2006, Henry S. Turner argued that "In a theatre that used no perspective backdrops, a minimum of stage properties, and rudimentary sound and lighting effects, the primary illusionistic tool for designating location *was* spoken dialogue, and the final power of the scene depends on this awareness of stage convention."[34] The late Victorian critic and the contemporary one agree that, on a basic level, place on the Elizabethan stage issues from character and is a function of narrative. Turner adds: "The entrance of the actor onstage across the threshold had the performative power to create, instantaneously and in its movement, the very location that would give that entrance a fictional significance."[35] The locations where the action unfolds, the houses where the characters live, and the spaces through which they journey—are the function of dramatic narrative.[36] That is the territory that I am claiming for the present study. I propose to explore the complex, dynamic interplay between tragic character and emplacement of action, leading to an understanding of the place of home in the tragic experience.

The early modern theater represents the house as a special kind of place, the study of which requires textual and literary analysis and interdisciplinary research that cuts across the fields of anthropology, art and architectural history, social history, theater history, phenomenology, literary theory, and feminist and gender studies. Useful data also come from the scholarship about stage directions, and symbolic uses of properties. House, home, and domestic space have been studied from the perspectives of various disciplines, methodologies, and theoretical approaches in their "spatial and temporal dimensions," societal functions, and experiential forms.[37]

---

32 States 50; 56–7.

33 Bradley 21.

34 Henry S. Turner, *The English Renaissance Stage: Geometry, Poetics, and the Practical Spatial Arts 1580–1630* (Oxford: Oxford University Press, 2006) 168.

35 Turner 173.

36 Turner suggests that "the evidence of the stage 'plotts' indicates that the English writers composed plays in a series of scenes that were meant to be played continuously in the theatre, and not in five acts" (179).

37 For an overview of these approaches, see Roderick J. Lawrence, "Deciphering Home: An Integrative Historical Perspective," *The Home: Words, Interpretations, Meanings and Environments*, (eds) David N. Benjamin, David Stea, and Eje Arén (Aldershot; Brookfield, VT: Avebury, 1995) 53–68. I am grateful to Prof. David Saile, School of Architecture and Interior Design, University of Cincinnati, for drawing my attention to this and a wide range of literature on the concept of home, and sharing with me materials from his course, "House and Home."

An anthropology of home grapples with such topics as "the tribal house or an exotic domestic space," materiality of daily life, identity formation and expression, historical and temporary dimensions of inhabitation, and the "emotionalization of domestic space."[38] Research, which spans diverse time periods and geographical regions, makes apparent that the home remains "the focal point of most people's lives."[39] For example, Mary Thomas Crane contends that, in England, "*Home* had for several centuries been shifting its prototypical meaning from the household, village, or town of a person's origin to simultaneously larger and smaller units of nation and individual domestic household."[40] Yet in her influential book on housing and households in England in the early modern period, Lu Emily Pearson argues persuasively that, although housing conditions changed dramatically in the period, the home remained the center of life, and "From this center of life emerged whatever stability was present in political, social, or religious Elizabethan England."[41] As a powerful emblem of stability, continuity, and intimacy in everyday

---

38 Irene Cieraad, (ed.), *At Home: An Anthropology of Domestic Space* (Syracuse: Syracuse University Press, 1999) 1–11.

39 Cieraad 11.

40 Mary Thomas Crane, *Shakespeare's Brain: Reading with Cognitive Theory* (Princeton and Oxford: Princeton University Press, 2001), 45. Crane adds, "Although *home* had ceased to mean primarily 'village' or 'estate' in the Middle English period, it continued to narrow its emphasis from the full (economic) household to the nuclear family. Thus, as the role of kinship bonds and extended family decreased as a determinant of identity, *home* seems to have shifted from meaning primarily a village cluster of related families to meaning both smaller (individual household) and larger (national) units" (45). In *Shakespeare's Domestic Economies: Gender and Property in Early Modern England* (Philadelphia: University of Pennsylvania Press, 2002), Natasha Korda analyzes the "wife's emerging role as a keeper of household stuff" (112).

41 Lu Emily Pearson, *Elizabethans at Home* (Stanford: Stanford University, 1957), 4. I find her chapter VI, "Founding and Maintaining the Home" (363–453), to be particularly helpful; in this chapter, Pearson traces an increasing emphasis on home as a refuge from political, social, and religious upheaval. Most impressive is Lena Cowin Orlin's contribution to the scholarship in this area. Orlin has unearthed an array of archival evidence for the understanding of housing and domestic life in the period, including *Elizabethan Households: An Anthology* (Washington, DC: Folger Shakespeare Library, 1995), and *Locating Privacy in Tudor London* (Oxford: Oxford University Press, 2007), in addition to various articles and collections of essays that she has edited, *Material London, ca. 1600* (Philadelphia: University of Pennsylvania Press, 2000); and *Private Matters and Public Culture in Post-Reformation England* (Ithaca: Cornell University Press, 1994). Still unsurpassed is Orlin's essay, "Man's House as His Castle in *Arden of Feversham*," *Medieval & Renaissance Drama in England* 2 (1985): 57–89, in which she traces the effects of the dissolution of the monasteries, confiscation of individual real estates, and redistribution of property, and ensuing "economic, social, architectural, and ideological changes that impinged upon a Renaissance Englishman's estimation of his house" (67). Mary Thomas Crane, in *Shakespeare's Brain,* argues that "Between 1570 and 1640 the structure of English houses at all levels of society changed dramatically" (43). These changes affected the meaning of such key terms as householder and house. See also Crane, "Illicit Privacy and Outdoor Spaces in Early Modern England," *Journal for Early Modern Cultural Studies* 9.1 (2009): 4–22.

life, home "*holds us intimately*, from the inside": "We have our hearts set on such a world, a world of olfactory memory, memory of childhood places, of the body, of childhood gestures, of pleasures."[42] In the words of Michel de Certeau and Luce Giard, lived space offers an intimate "life narrative," and an exploration of these domestic spaces affords an "involuntary confession of a more intimate way of living and dreaming."[43]

As I will argue, in Shakespeare's tragedies, house and home remain a focal point of concern, especially as they intersect the public domain. Shakespeare makes use of what Michel Foucault refers to as "heterogeneous space": "In other words, we do not live in a kind of void, inside of which we could place individuals and things." Foucault states that we live "inside a set of relations" that delineates and defines our connection to geography and location.[44] No wonder Shakespeare represents domestic space as a web of tragic relations.[45]

The early modern house and home have been studied in relation to domestic economy, marriage, domestic violence, gender, subjectivity, interiority, inward struggle, habitual beliefs.[46] My analysis responds to and builds upon this vast

---

[42] Paul Leuilliot, "Preface," Guy Thuillier, *Pour une histoire du quotidian au XIXe siècle en Nivernais* (Paris and the Hague: Moulton, 1977) xi–xii, quoted in Michel de Certeau and Pierre Mayol, *The Practice of Everyday Life*, trans. Timothy J. Tomasik (Minneapolis: University of Minnesota Press, 1998) 3–4.

[43] Certeau, Giard, et al., 145–6.

[44] Michel Foucault, "Of Other Spaces," *Diacritics* 16.1 (1986): 23.

[45] Of interest here might be Rudolf Arnheim's *The Power of the Center: A Study of Composition in the Visual Arts*, revised edition (Berkeley: University of California Press, 1988) 2. In establishing what he calls "the power of the center" in the visual arts, Arnheim defines "centric" and "eccentric" forces as organizing principles of composition and the visual field.

[46] Fascinating recent studies of these matters include, among others, the following: Amy Louise Erickson, *Women and Property in Early Modern England* (London: Routledge, 1993); Charles Ross, *The Custom of the Castle: From Malory to Macbeth* (Berkeley: University of California Press, 1997), esp. chapter 6, "Hamlet's Ghost Fear," and chapter 7, "Macbeth's Future: 'A Thing of Custom'"; Laura Gowing, *Domestic Dangers: Women, Words, and Sex in Early Modern London* (Oxford: Clarendon Press, 1996); Heather Dubrow, *Shakespeare and Domestic Loss: Forms of Deprivation, Mourning, and Recuperation* (Cambridge: Cambridge University Press, 1999); *Material London, ca. 1600*, (ed.) Lena Cowen Orlin (Philadelphia: University of Pennsylvania Press, 2000), esp. Orlin's introduction, and Alice T. Friedman, "Inside/Out: Women, Domesticity, and the Pleasures of the City" (pp. 232–50); Naomi J. Miller and Naomi Yavneh, (eds), *Maternal Measures: Figuring Caregiving in the Early Modern Period* (Burlington: Ashgate, 2000); Michael Neill, "Servant Obedience and Master Sins: Shakespeare and the Bonds of Service," in *Putting History to the Question: Power, Politics, and Society in English Renaissance Drama* (New York: Columbia University Press, 2000), 13–48; Linda Woodbridge, *Vagrancy, Homelessness, and English Renaissance Literature* (Urbana: University of Illinois Press, 2001); Kari Boyd McBride, *Domestic Arrangements in Early Modern England* (Pittsburgh: Duquesne University Press, 2002);Wendy Wall's study of household guides in *Staging Domesticity: Household Work and English Identity in Early Modern Drama* (Cambridge: Cambridge University

body of scholarship, but will focus primarily on the tragic functions of home and domestic space. Therefore, my investigation concerns clusters of interrelated descriptions and phenomena, such as erasure, disappearance, juxtaposition and adjacency, and referential void. In these contexts, phenomena carry late sixteenth- and early seventeenth-century primary meanings of appearance and perception.[47] "Perception engages all the senses," and "enable[s] us to interact with objects in the world surrounding us."[48] Gail Kern Paster argues for the "unity of physical and psychological in early modern behavioral theory" in what she refers to as "a phenomenology" or "ecology" of the passions.[49] I am not, however, concerned with such a phenomenology or ecology, but rather Shakespeare's narrative and dramatic constructions of physical yet always virtual and *imagined* domestic surroundings in *King Lear*, *Othello*, *Hamlet* and *Macbeth*.[50]

Press, 2002), esp. 18–58; Corinne S. Abate, (ed.), *Privacy, Domesticity, and Women in Early Modern England* (Burlington: Ashgate, 2003); Michael Roberts, "Recovering a Lost Inheritance: The Marital Economy and Its Absence from the Prehistory of Economics in Britain," *The Marital Economy in Scandinavia and Britain 1400–1900*, (eds) Maria Ågren and Amy Louise Erickson (Burlington, VT: Ashgate, 2005) 239–56; Belinda Roberts Peters, *Marriage in Seventeenth-Century English Political Thought* (Basingstoke: Macmillan Palgrave, 2004); Catherine Richardson, *Domestic Life and Domestic Tragedy in Early Modern England: The Material Life of the Household* (Manchester: Manchester University Press, 2006); and Orlin, *Locating Privacy*.

47 "A thing which appears, or which is perceived or observed; a particular (kind of) fact, occurrence, or change as perceived through the senses or known intellectually; *esp.* a fact or occurrence, the cause or explanation of which is in question," *OED*, "Phenomenon."

48 Nicholas J. Wade, *Perception and Illusion: Historical Perspectives* (New York: Springer, 2005) 3. Particularly helpful is Wade's Chapter 4, "Perception in the Seventeenth and Eighteenth Centuries," 73–108. See also David Park, *The Fire Within the Eye* (Princeton: Princeton University Press, 1997); and Enrique García Santo-Tomás, "Fortunes of the *Occhiali Politici* in Early Modern Spain: Optics, Vision, Points of View," *PMLA* 124.1 (2009): 59–75, especially the discussion of the invention of eyeglasses and the glass industry in Venice in the late thirteenth century, which led to the baroque writers' reflection "on the way fantasy, movement, and manipulation accord with" the "material properties" of glass (61).

49 See especially, "Roasted in Wrath and Fire: The Ecology of the Passions in *Hamlet* and *Othello*," *Humoring the Body: Emotions and the Shakespearean Stage* (Chicago: University of Chicago Press, 2004) 25–76.

50 These are, of course, the "Bradley Four," plays that A.C. Bradley studied in his 1904 *Shakespearean Tragedy*. Bradley's book, which has remained in print for over a century, is arguably one of the most influential books on Shakespeare, especially as a study of character. Bradley studies the connections between character and action, which he considers to be the center of tragedy. A.C. Bradley, *Shakespearean Tragedy* (1904; Cleveland and New York: Meridian Books, 1963) 21. A very good overview of Bradley's life and assessment of his contribution to the field is Katherine Cooke, *A.C. Bradley and His Influence in Twentieth-Century Criticism* (Oxford: Clarendon Press, 1972); especially informative are Cooke's Chapter 3, "Critical Principles," and Chapter 8, "Bradley's Critics."

The first two chapters, building upon the foundation of earlier scholarship and readings of *King Lear* and *Othello*, explore representations and functions of the house in the tragic experience. Ideally, the house offers shelter and protection; as home and center of family life, it symbolizes security, continuity, and stability. In contrast, *King Lear* and *Othello* foreground the place of residence as a site of strife, disruption, and instability. Domestic space embodies tragic discontinuities that rip the fabric of everyday life apart. In *King Lear*, various types of discontinuities—emplacement and placelessness, and sequential discontinuities—produce vast expanses of space and voids that cannot be adequately filled. Responding to, and building upon, Heather Dubrow's thoughtful analysis of the role of "domestic loss" in *King Lear*,[51] I will argue that the *erasure* and *disappearance*, not loss, of Lear's castle and home become the central phenomena around which the experience of dwelling revolves. I will argue that Lear's castle vanishes from the characters' consciousness, leading to an exploration of architectural space, such as Lear's castle and the houses of Goneril, Regan and Gloucester. In this play, changes in early modern housing conditions intersect experiential discontinuity, habits of old age, a crisis of authority, and the disruption of patriarchal power.

By contrast, in *Othello* Shakespeare juxtaposes two ways of life: one European, sedentary, urban, home-centered, represented by Venice and centered on Brabantio's house; and the other, North African, nomadic, centered on mobile, non-permanent dwelling, and on what Othello himself refers to as his "unhousèd" condition of lifelong wandering. Therefore, one equates with European concepts of home life, household, hospitality; the other with ever-shifting, self-erasing images of exotic places, improbable experiences, and vague localities. The image of the dark, empty house looms large in *Othello*, as does the pervasive nature of darkness, which blurs boundaries, redefines the perception of architectural space, and reveals assumptions about racial attitudes. In this play, one is never very far from the edge of darkness. *Othello* calls for special lighting effects—scenes to be staged *a lume di notte* (by candlelight)—which unfold multiple layers of represented reality, blur the boundaries between actual and fictive space, and disclose a dynamic interplay of space, vision and the senses.[52] Lighting serves both to reveal and to conceal. On the one hand, the action occurs in the concrete here and now; on the other, it

---

[51] Dubrow, *Shakespeare and Domestic Loss*, 104–42.

[52] In "Caravaggio Reloaded: Neo-Baroque Poetics," Angela Ndalianis notes the ways in which "The neo-baroque articulates the spatial, the visual and the sensorial," especially "its delight in spectacles that playfully immerse the viewer in multiple layers of representational realities" (73). Her article appears in *Caravaggio & His World: Darkness & Light* (Sydney, N.S.W.: Art Gallery of New South Wales; Melbourne: National Gallery of Victoria, 2003) 72–7. Caravaggio, for her, represents "strategically orchestrated levels of reality." Caracci devises, in her words, an open and limitless two dimensional space. Likewise, Caravaggio wants to collapse "the frame that separates illusion from reality, fictive space from actual space." I think that these ideas are particularly helpful in trying to analyze Shakespeare's own experiments with lighting and special effects; therefore, I am adapting some of her terms for my own analysis of *Othell*o.

extends into the darkened, obscured mysterious background. The atmosphere of the poorly lit indoors extends into, folds upon a vast, limitless darkness.

The final chapters focus on embodied space, which is always oriented space; therefore, I will explore the concept of life as habit and the gaps, distortions, and voids associated with the concepts of home. Chapter 3, "At Home in *Hamlet*," explores the emplacement of the body as a focal point for the discussion of sensory experience. Hamlet's return to Elsinore for his father's funeral opens a vast chasm in his concept of home. To tragic ends, Hamlet deploys his own emotional history of pain in order to counter his uncle's powerful and seductive politics of pleasure. Pleasure and pain engender spectacles yet hide their referents, rendering them less real in a theatrical illusion.

Chapter 4, "Boundaries of Home," delves into the architecture and habits[53] of everyday living, whereby the house symbolizes adjacency, thereby exposing adjoining yet opposing ways of life, values and goals. Fernand Braudel writes: "A room for human habitation has always had four walls, a ceiling, a floor, one or more windows and one or more doors."[54] Architecture separates outside from inside, exterior from interior, above from below. In partitioning space, architecture not only envelops and encloses—walls, floors, and ceiling serve to set limits and define boundaries; architecture also connects: corridors, stairways, and doors bridge adjoining spaces; windows and doors allow passage to other spaces. In our experience of dwelling, architecture captures the essence of our being. In *Macbeth*, I am interested in how architecture intertwines with habits of living and everyday life, whereby the house becomes a central and powerful symbol for adjacency. The play, I submit, depends for its extraordinary dramatic effects upon an exploration of adjacency, juxtaposition, and contiguity. The house, household, and home life abut, border on, intermingle with a wild, fantastical domain.

Early modern commentators thought that tragedy had to depict a journey from prosperity to disaster. This was not a new idea. Dante, based on earlier authority, had already articulated this concept of tragedy; and Chaucer, in the Prologue to the *Monk's Tale* had written:

> Tragedie is to seyn a certeyn storie,
> As olde bookes maken us memorie,
> Of hym that stood in greet prosperitee,
> And is yfallen out of heigh degree
> Into myserie, and endeth wrecchedly.[55]

---

[53] The *OED* defines "habits" as our customary manners of acting, settled dispositions, and tendencies to act in certain ways, "especially those acquired by frequent repetition of the same act until it becomes almost or quite involuntary." It also means "The way in which a person is mentally or morally constituted; the sum of the mental and moral qualities; mental constitution, disposition, character" (*OED*).

[54] Fernand Braudel, *Capitalism and Material Life 1400–1800*, trans. Miriam Kochan (New York: Harper & Row, 1973) 212.

[55] Geoffrey Chaucer, *The Canterbury Tales*, (ed.) A.C. Cawley (London: J.M. Dent; New York: E.P. Dutton, 1958) 433.

Thomas Lodge in *Defense of Poetry* (1579) writes that the central themes of tragedy are "the sour fortunes of many exiles, the miserable fall of hapless princes, the ruinous decay of many countries."[56] For George Puttenham in *The Art of English Poesie* (1589), genre differentiation depends on the central characters' social status. For him, comedy deals with "the common behaviors and manner of life of private persons, and such as were the meaner sort of men"; whereas, tragedy "set[s] forth the doleful falls of unfortunate & afflicted Princes."[57] In *An Apology for Actors* (1612), Thomas Heywood, quoting *Donatus de octibus partibus orationis*, a well-known grammar named after the fourth-century Roman grammarian, Aelius Donatus, establishes the fundamental distinction between tragedy and comedy: "in comedies *turbulenta prima, tranquilla ultima*; in tragedyes, *tranquilla prima, turbulenta ultima*: comedies begin in trouble and end in peace; tragedies begin in calmes, and end in tempest."[58] But the question remains, how do early modern playwrights, especially Shakespeare in the tragedies in question, localize the characters' living places and ground the tragic experience in the material world?

Sir Philip Sidney, based on Aristotle's *Poetics*, argues that "the stage should alwaies represent but one place"; therefore, although he praises *Gorboduc*, which, in his opinion, manages to approximate Seneca's style, he finds great fault with contemporary plays, whose actions, in violation of "Aristotles precept and common reason," encompass "many dayes, and many places, inartificially imagined."[59] He writes:

> But if it be so in *Gorboduck*, how much more in al the rest? Where you shal haue *Asia* of the one side, and *Affrick* of the other, and so many other vnder-kingdoms, that the Player, when he commeth in, must euer begin with telling where he is, or els the tale wil not be conceiued.[60]

If according to ancient theatrical convention and precept the stage can represent only one location, then the staging problem here stems from imperfect composition rather than the technical limitations of the theater of his time. Tragedy, he adds, must follow the "lawes of poesie, and not of Historie." He concludes, "Againe, many things may be told which cannot be shewed, if they knowe the difference betwixt reporting and representing."[61] As Neil Carson points out, ancient and contemporary writers encouraged an emphasis on the verbal rather than the visual elements, which the non-illusionist nature of the Elizabethan platform stage, with

---

[56] Quoted in Karl J. Holzknecht, *The Backgrounds of Shakespeare's Plays* (New York: American Book Co., 1950) 322.

[57] Hardison 159.

[58] Hardison 224.

[59] Sidney 138.

[60] Sidney 138.

[61] Sidney 139.

a permanent façade and natural lighting, tended to reinforce.[62] Therefore, Carson adds, "Illusion on the open stage depended entirely upon the audience's willingness to participate imaginatively in the dramatic game."[63]

Reflecting on the audience's imaginative engagement in a theatrical production, Prospero announces the end of the "revels" of the masque for Miranda's betrothal in act four of *The Tempest*. He remarks that the theatrical spectacle resembles a "vision," the "baseless fabric," which melts into "thin air." The cloud-capped towers, the gorgeous palaces, solemn temples, and other places "shall dissolve, / And, like this insubstantial pageant faded, / Leave not a rack behind" (4.1.146–56). Prospero's towers, palaces, and temples are, of course, metaphors, a rhetorical tour de force, but the question remains as to the technical resources available to the Shakespearean theater to represent such architectural structures—houses, palaces, and castles. In his treatise on architecture, the first part of which appeared in English translation as *The First Booke of Architecture* (1611), the Italian architect Sebastian Serlio (1475–1554) proposes a solution: namely, building and painting in perspective fixed scenery. For comedy, he prescribes a stage set that contains "slight" houses for citizens, a "brawthell or bawdyhouse," a great inn, and a church; for "satirical" scenes, "rude and rusticall" things, such as trees, shrubbery, and country cottages. "Houses for Tragedies," he writes, "must bee made for great personages, for that actions of loue, strange aduentures, and cruell murthers, (as you reade in ancient and moderne Tragedies) happen always in the houses of great Lords, Dukes, Princes, and Kings. Therefore in such cases you must make none but stately houses, as you see here in this Figure."[64] The woodcut drawing alluded to in this passage depicts a tile-paved piazza located between two rows of stately buildings; an imposing, richly decorated connecting arch; an obelisk and statuary; and stairs, upstage and downstage.

---

[62] Neil Carson, "Shakespeare and the Dramatic Image," in *Mirror Up to Shakespeare: Essays in Honour of G.R. Hibbard*, (ed.) J.C. Gray (Toronto: University of Toronto Press, 1984) 35.

[63] Carson 37.

[64] Sebastian Serlio, *The First Booke of Architecture* (London, 1611), Fol. 25^{v}. In his Preface to Terence's *Andria* (1542), Charles Estienne seems to echo Serlio's ideas for scenic background. For comic scenes, he wants "*petites maisonnettes, ou bien bastimentz communs avec fenestraiges à la mode commune*"; but for tragedy, he writes: "*si la scene estoit pour une tragedie, l'on faisoit plus grand appareil et accoustrement qu'à la comique ou satyrique. Et y avoit columnes sumptueuses, richement accoustrées et aornées, avec maisons faictes en forme de chasteaulx et villes, force medales, statues et accoustrementz royaulx. La porte du meilleu, qu'ilz nommoient regia, estoit comme ung arc triumphal, de laquelle sortoient gens à cheval et grande compaignie de personnes*." See Bernard Weinberg, (ed.), *Critical Prefaces of the French Renaissance* (Evanston, IL: Northwestern University Press, 1950) 101.

In England, performance of masques at court did certainly incorporate especially constructed stage sets.[65] Inigo Jones, for example, designed a palace—or at least the interior of one—for a performance of Ben Jonson's *Oberon, The Fairy Prince*, at Whitehall in 1611.[66] Likewise, as David Bergeron has studied extensively, royal progresses and civic entertainments, such the 1604 royal entry of James in London, all contained elaborate scenic design. The city erected seven magnificent triumphal arches for the 1604 royal entry, including the Londinium arch at Fenchurch, which displayed a replica of the city of London, and the Dutch pageant at the Royal Exchange, which depicted an enthroned James in full royal regalia.[67] In 1605, students at Oxford University entertained King James with a theatrical production, for which they designed a special stage set:

> A false wall fair painted and adorned with stately pillars, which pillars could turn about; by reason whereof, with the aid of other painted cloths their stage did vary three times in the acting of one tragedy.[68]

As is widely known, performance at the London public playhouses, however, occurred under quite different theatrical conditions. These theater houses, with an essentially bare platform stage, did not make use of elaborate stage scenery.

The non-illusionistic staging naturally required the audience's inherent suspension of disbelief; it also underscored, as Neil Carson points out, "the discrepancy between the actor's ability to create a realistic illusion of psychological truth and the stage manager's failure to provide a similarly convincing stage environment."[69] Like Carson, Alan Dessen concludes: " ... given dialogue and skillful acting 'the scenery' on a permanent, non-localized stage can be said to materialize and then melt away in the imagination of the spectators."[70] Catherine Richardson memorably represents Dessen's position as follows: "For Dessen, seeing *less* almost always means perceiving *more*"; she concludes, however, that the staging of household and interior scenes would require, not a general sense of locale, but a keen sense of understanding of the "social, moral or political

---

65 See Stephen Orgel and Roy Strong, *Inigo Jones: The Theater of the Stuart Court*, 2 vols. (London: Southeby Parke Bernet; Berkeley: University of California Press, 1973).

66 See Figure 61 in Orgel and Strong 212–13.

67 For a discussion of the stage design of these entertainments, consult various works by David M. Bergeron, including *English Civic Pageantry 1558–1642*, revised edition (Tempe, AZ: Arizona State University Medieval and Renaissance Center, 2003); "Representation in Renaissance English Civic Pageants," *Theatre Journal* 40 (1988): 319–31; and "King James's Civic Pageant and Parliamentary Speech in March 1604," *Albion* 34 (2002): 213–31.

68 John Nichols, (ed.), *Progresses, Processions, and Festivities of James I* (London, 1828) 1: 538.

69 Carson, "Shakespeare and the Dramatic Image," 37.

70 Alan C. Dessen, *Elizabethan Stage Conventions and Modern Interpreters* (Cambridge, UK: Cambridge University Press, 1984) 62.

dynamics which pertain to the situations which actors conjure into being."[71] Obviously, as Stephen Orgel reminds us, "In *all* theater the imaginary is presented as, is taken for, the real."[72] As Richardson underscores, one should not, however, discount, for example, the complex dynamic of "the spatial and the interpersonal which characterizes domestic space" that a chamber represents;[73] nor should one underestimate the impact of visual and special effects that the Elizabethan and Jacobean playhouses could create.[74]

Andrew Gurr and Mariko Ichikawa put it best when they write about the much-debated bareness of the Elizabethan stage, which was in fact richly and elaborately decorated: "But it was bare in that it lacked any scenery or devices to fix a sense of location other than the standard portable props. It was simply a space for walking over, whether it was meant to depict an indoor scene or one out of door. With very few exceptions its scenes were fixed by word-painting rather than scene-painting."[75] Instead of scenery built in the style recommended by Serlio, the Shakespearean theater depended on other elements, including the public playhouse's own permanent physical features such as tiring house wall, inner stage, upper stage, trapdoors, columns, and doors; explicit verbal markers or subtle, implicit verbal references; character types, such as a shepherd or a fisherman to signal a pastoral or a seaside scene; costumes and sartorial conventions associated with specific locations, such as nightgowns for bedroom scenes and armor for battle scenes; furniture such as beds, thrones, and tables; props such as flower to evoke a garden and candles or torches to signal nighttime; and a repertoire of available special effects, such as music, clocks, cannons, bells, fireworks, and gunpowder.[76]

In *From Art to Theatre: Form and Convention in the Renaissance*, George Kernodle draws attention to the physical structure of the Elizabethan platform stage, with the acting space, enclosed by spectator galleries, and "a complex two-

---

[71] See a discussion of this matter in Richardson, *Domestic Life and Domestic Tragedy*, 8. Richardson's book focuses on the non-Shakespearean domestic tragedies, not on Shakespeare. A related work on domesticity and domestic tragedy is Viviana Comensoli, *'Household Business': Domestic Plays of Early Modern England* (Toronto: University of Toronto Press, 1999.) Comensoli refers in passing to Shakespeare, and does not deal with staging issues or representation of place.

[72] Orgel 557.

[73] Richardson 9. Of interest here is Catherine Richardson's essay, "Home, Household and Domesticity in Drama in Early Modern London," in *Imagined Interiors: Representing the Domestic Interior Since the Renaissance*, (eds) Jeremy Aynsley, Charlotte Grant, and Harriet McKay (London: V & A Publications, 2006) 50–63.

[74] G.K. Hunter, "Flatcaps and Bluecoats: Visual Signals on the Elizabethan Stage," *Essays and Studies* 33 (1980) 17.

[75] Gurr and Ichikawa, *Staging in Shakespeare's Theatres* (Oxford, UK: Oxford University Press, 2000) 62. See Glynne Wickham, *Early English Stages 1300 to 1600* (New York: Columbia University Press; London Routledge & Kegan Paul, 1963) 2; 1.208.

[76] John Bate's *The mysteryes of Nature, and Art*, first published in 1577, and reissued in another edition in 1634, served as a veritable guide to special effects and tricks available to the theater. See STC 1577.

story screen of arches and niches," which functioned as a formal, though malleable symbolic structure:

> The splendid façade at the back of the open platform presented at least six openings, either for entrances and exits or for small scenes to be disclosed in doorways behind curtains. At the stage level of the façade were two doorways and an inner stage, and on the upper level were balconies and windows.[77]

The architectural façade, as well as all the other architectural features of the playhouse, was readily available and could be easily incorporated in a production: "More than an arrangement of side doors and inner and upper stages, the façade was itself a symbol of castle, throne, triumphal arch, altar, tomb, and several other shows long familiar in art and pageantry."[78] Further, as Kernodle astutely observes, the built-in façade of the Elizabethan stage at the Globe, Fortune, and other public playhouses, had their origins in "the throne pavilion, the arches, and the inner and upper stages of street shows erected on civic occasions."[79] Even more significantly, Kernodle concludes: "An important way of using the Elizabethan stage was to suppose it a real place. If the scene were supposed outdoors in front of a house, there were the upper windows and upper-story gallery from which people could speak as from a real house."[80] In this sense, the façade clearly had a practical stage function similar to Serlio's fixed stage sets.

The Shakespearean platform stage was even more versatile, as it incorporated "the conventions of tableaux vivant of the street theatres"; it also functioned "as a theater machine, with quite different scenes presented at the same time, or next to each other, without any realistic tableaux conventions."[81] Glynne Wickham sees the Elizabethan stage caught up in and attempting to reconcile a medieval emblematic tradition with a Renaissance "scientific questing for the photographic image."[82] Robert Weimann, based on the work of Richard Hosley, concludes that the medieval theater had both "focused" and "dispersed" modes of production, observing a distinction between "'place' or platform-like acting area (the *platea*), and a scaffold, be it a *domus*, *sedes*, or throne (the *locus*)."[83] He adds: "In each

---

77 George R. Kernodle, *From Art to Theatre: Form and Convention in the Renaissance* (Chicago: University of Chicago Press, 1944) 130.

78 Kernodle, *From Art to Theatre* 130.

79 George R. Kernodle, *The Theater in History* (Fayetteville, AR: University of Arkansas Press, 1989) 318.

80 Kernodle, *Theater in History* 324–5.

81 Kernodle, *Theater in History* 325; 327.

82 Wickham 2; 1: 209.

83 Robert Weimann, *Shakespeare and the Popular Tradition in the Theater: Studies in the Social Dimension of Dramatic Form and Function*, (ed.) Robert Schwartz (Baltimore and London: Johns Hopkins University Press, 1978) 74. He adds: "Functionally, the *locus* corresponded to the scaffold in the circular theater and to the throne or hut on the pageant stage" (74).

case fixed, symbolic locations near and on the larger unlocalized acting area tend to define a more particular kind of action."[84] Weimann deduces that Shakespeare's platform stage in no way was "a homogeneous acting area" but relied, instead, on the traditional, dynamic "interplay between *platea* and *locus*, between neutral, undifferentiated 'place' and symbolic action." Therefore, he adds, it could accommodate, on the one hand, unlocalized, non-illusionistic action, and on the other, localized and illusionistic action: "Between these extremes lay the broad and very flexible range of dramatic possibilities so skillfully developed by the popular Renaissance dramatists."[85] Shakespeare made full use of this flexible approach to the staging of place: "The dramatic change from locality to neutral 'space' and back to locality again corresponds to a verbal change from dramatic illusion of conversation to a non-illusionistic, audience-directed generalizing monologue and back to dialogue. Such facility in alternating forms of speech is inconceivable without an equally flexible stage."[86]

Older methods of continuous staging allow Marston's characters in Act IV of *Sophonisba* to move "from a bedroom to a wood and back again without in each case leaving the stage."[87] Lucrezia Borgia, in *The Devil's Charter*, brings her own "locality" with her in the form of a chair that she plops down.[88] Muriel Bradbook remarks that the staging of place was so fluid and flexible that the audience did not even have to visualize a real or imaginary scenic background. Shakespeare, however, "nearly always suggests a background for his characters, but no other writer did it with such consistency."[89]

Editors' attempts to fix precise locations for most scenes in Shakespeare seem to ignore the fluidity of the Shakespearean stage and violate English Renaissance staging practice. Since the eighteenth century, however, various editors have done precisely that. Nicholas Rowe, in his 1709 edition of Shakespeare's works, introduced most scene locators we have become accustomed to. For various reasons, recent scholars, mindful of Renaissance stage traditions, deplore the use of scene locators. Barbara Mowat sensibly downplays the detrimental effect of Rowe's scene locators because they "have little effect on productions today, since largely unlocalized stage is once more the venue for Shakespeare."[90] She intimates, nonetheless, that scene locators, implying a naturalistic representation

---

84 Weimann 74.

85 Weimann 211–12.

86 Weimann 220.

87 Muriel C. Bradbrook, *Themes and Conventions of Elizabethan Tragedies* (Cambridge: Cambridge University Press, 1964) 8.

88 Bradbrook 9.

89 Bradbrook 8.

90 Barbara Mowat, "Nicholas Rowe and the Twentieth-Century Shakespeare Text," in *Shakespeare and the Cultural Traditions*, (eds) Tetsuo Kishi, Roger Pringle, and Stanley Wells (Newark, DE: University of Delaware Press; London: Associated University Presses, 1991) 318.

of place, "encourage readers of the plays to read them novelistically or to imagine them within a proscenium arch on a stage filled with backdrops and furniture."[91] Peter Holland, in his 1999 reprint of Rowe's edition of Shakespeare's works, notes that Rowe uses general definitions of place such as Rome or Vienna, particular ones such as a wood or prison, and precise ones as "*An Apartment* in Macbeth's *Castle*"; and he concludes that "such markers have no meaning in a theatre without scenery to define place."[92] In his Norton Critical Edition of *Othello*, Edward Pechter goes so far as to omit scene locations altogether, arguing that "scene locators, no matter how qualified or inconspicuous, do more harm than good."[93] Editors make decisions which best suit the uses to which their editions will be put. Mowat, Holland, and Pechter are correct in taking issue with Rowe's attempt to provide precise locations for each scene, as if the Shakespearean stage could render location in a realistic, cinematographic mode. But I would not go so far as to dismiss the identification of location, when internal textual evidence, if not stage direction, provides signposts to identify location.

E.K. Chambers, who surveyed approximately 600–700 extant English plays from the Elizabethan and Jacobean periods, classifies scene location into seven categories: unlocalized scenes; open-country scenes; battlefields; garden, orchard, and park; public spots in a city; and interiors, including tents, caves, bowers, tombs, shops, windows, halls, and chambers.[94] "Unlocalized scenes," according to Chambers, are those in which bits of conversation "might be carried on between the speakers wherever they happen to meet, and which give no indication where that meeting is supposed to be."[95] Chambers argues, however, that "these scenes are not so numerous as is sometimes suggested," and that they were nonetheless always located to the audience, who saw them against a background," although from certain vantage points from the stage, the "relation to the background would be minimized."[96] Chambers' monumental contribution in this regard rests in his emphasis on the representation of the material world, the concrete and real material, though imaginary and fictional, background for the action. For example, in the open-country scenes, "even where there is no evidence, in dialogue or stage-

---

91 Mowat 318.

92 Peter Holland, "Introduction" to *The Works of Mr William Shakespear, edited by Nicholas Rowe, 1709* (London: Pickering & Chatto, 1999) 1: xvi. For a study of eighteenth-century editing practices, consult Margreta de Grazia, *Shakespeare Verbatim: The Reproduction of Authenticity and The 1790 Apparatus* (Oxford: Clarendon Press; New York: Oxford University Press, 1991). De Grazia studies Edmond Malone's 1790 edition and the 1821 variorum, dealing with such topics as "construal of the past" and authenticity in the context of Enlightenment assumption and earlier textual practices. I find the first chapter, "The 1623 Folio and the Modern Standard Edition," to be particularly cogent.

93 Edward Pechter, "A Note on the Text," in *Othello*: *A Norton Critical Edition* (New York and London: W.W. Norton, 2004) xvi.

94 E.K. Chambers, *The Elizabethan Stage* (Oxford: Clarendon Press, 1951) 3: 50–68.

95 Chambers 3: 50.

96 Chambers 3: 51.

directions, for a dwelling, a table or a board may be suddenly forthcoming for a banquet."[97] Although the characters may allude to the landscape, Chambers does not think that the producers relied upon this literary device alone, for "in some cases practicable trees or rocks are certainly required by the action and must have been represented."[98] The play scripts do provide much, although often ambiguous information about staging requirements, as Alan C. Dessen in his trail-blazing studies of stage directions and the theatrical vocabulary of Elizabethan and Jacobean periods has demonstrated.[99] Likewise, there is no accurate way to reconstruct actual blocking used in early modern performances of these plays. Nonetheless, Dessen, Chambers, and others have made enormous strides in studying the "practical" problems, involving staging, blocking, and set requirements, which Elizabethan and Jacobean theater managers had to confront.

Although I do not attempt to deal with specific stage design per se, my argument has clear implications for the staging of these plays and the centrality of concepts of home to the tragic action. A.C. Bradley offers sage advice, when he remarks on the "absence of scenery" and editors' attempts to identify a scene's exact location: "as a rule, we know, broadly speaking, where the persons live and what their journeys are."[100] Where the characters live, where they have been, where they are going, and what experiences they associate with specific locations—all of these become quite clear, if they are important in their lives and in their stories, whether the English Renaissance theater producers had the technical capacity, resources, or inclination to render them in a realistic way or not.

Imagined places remain important, as the American poet Elizabethan Bishop reminds us in her poem, "Questions of Travel." She wonders why we travel far away, sometimes merely "to see the sun the other way around" or to view "the tiniest hummingbird in the world." She asks: "*Is it lack of imagination that makes us come / to imagined places, not just stay at home*?"[101] Throughout her poetry,

---

97 Chambers 3: 51.

98 Chambers 3: 52.

99 See especially Alan C. Dessen, *Elizabethan Stage Conventions*. Other seminal studies in this area include Linda McJannet, *The Voice of Elizabethan Stage Directions: The Evolution of a Theatrical Code* (Newark, NJ: University of Delaware Press; London: Associated University Presses, 1999); Frances Teague, *Shakespeare's Speaking Properties* (Lewisburg: Bucknell University Press; London; Cranbury, NJ: Associated University Presses, 1991); and Jonathan Gil Harris and Natasha Korda, (ed.), *Staged Properties in Early Modern English Drama* (Cambridge, UK; New York: Cambridge University Press, 2002). A fascinating new study of the symbolism of stage properties—crowns, bells, rings, wills—is Arthur F. Kinney, *Shakespeare and Cognition: Aristotle Legacy and Shakespearean Drama* (New York and London: Routledge, 2006), which builds upon his earlier *Shakespeare's Webs: Networks of Meaning in Renaissance Drama* (New York and London: Routledge, 2004).

100 Bradley 208.

101 Elizabeth Bishop, *The Complete Poems, 1927–1979* (New York: Farrar, Straus and Giroux, 1979) 74.

Bishop demonstrates the powerful and intimate ways in which our imaginations interweave our life experiences with geography, places, houses. As travelers in real life, Bishop suggests, we might pause and ask: "Is it right to be watching strangers in a play / in this strangest of theatres?" Peter Brook puts it in a similar way for playgoers: "One goes to the theatre to find life, but if there is no difference between life outside the theatre and inside, then theatre makes no sense."[102] Travel and theater may have a lot more in common than we think: they help us experience real or *imagined* places, observe real or *imagined* lives.

Throughout the study that follows, I will focus on the extent to which images of the house, home, and household become visually and emotionally vibrant, and thus reflect, define, and support a powerful tragic narrative. By examining such moments, we can understand early modern constructions of subjectivity. Shakespeare's characters serve as guides to the world around them.[103] Yet the representation of domestic space emerges only in fragmentary, unstable, contingent images. In large part because of the nature of phenomena of perception, domesticity and privacy encompass "overlapping spaces and habits" in "the nearly invisible background of patriarchal reality."[104] Such domestic sites revolve around patriarchal structures, overlapping spaces of reproduction and production; consequently, their boundaries are always provisional and unstable.[105]

---

[102] Peter Brook, *The Open Door: Thoughts on Acting and Theatre* (1993; rpt. New York: Theatre Communications Group, 1995) 11.

[103] In *The Visible and the Invisible*, (ed.) Claude Lefort, and trans. Alphonso Lingis (Evanston, IL: Northwestern University Press, 1968), Maurice Merleau-Ponty argues that vision " … envelops, palpates, espouses the visible things" (132).

[104] Mazzola and Abate, "Introduction: 'Indistinguished Place'," *Privacy, Domesticity, and Women* 3.

[105] In "'Players in your huswifery, and huswives in your beds': Conflicting Identities of Early Modern English Woman," Miller and Yavneh, (eds), *Maternal Matters*, Mary Thomas Crane, writing about domestic space, argues that women occupied the "unstable boundaries" between their potential as "'producers,' of income, goods, children" and their functions as "caretakers and preservers of money, goods, and offspring produced by the husband" (212). Likewise, in "Maternal Textualities," Miller and Yavneh, (eds), *Maternal Matters*, Susan Frye contends that "The female body" was marked as "maternal" in multiple household roles and household spaces because "its place in the world was determined by its interrelated capacities to reproduce and to produce the goods and services that nourished, clothed, taught, and otherwise managed the household" (229).

Chapter 1
The Vanishing Castle in *King Lear*

> An empty space makes it possible for a new phenomenon to come to life
>
> —Peter Brook, *The Open Door* (4).[1]

> The small worlds of direct experience are fringed with much broader fields known indirectly through symbolic means
>
> —Yi-Fu Tuan, *Space and Place* (88).[2]

In *Forest Fire* (c. 1505), a painting at the Ashmolean Museum in Oxford, the Florentine Piero di Cosimo (1462–1521) depicts a forest fire, which scatters domestic and wild animals. The flames consume trees and bushes, and smoke reaches up to the clouds. Flocks of birds fly overhead or seek safe trees to perch upon. Animals flee in different directions; whereas others stand as in a daze or seem unaware of danger. A shepherd guides farm animals back to a cottage, where excited human figures gesticulate. In his analysis, Richard Turner writes: "A freak of nature, a forest fire, governs activity in this world."[3] He suggests that a copse of trees blocks the view and directs one's eyes to the central area, where the fire "rages," and "From here, the line of vision is forced to shoot off towards the horizon on two different tangents."[4] Turner writes of a "paradox that permeates much of Piero's work," combining the sinister threat posed by the fire, and the "disarmingly naïve" presence of a man moving "about the landscape as King of the animals but little better than an animal himself. This world of flame, soot, and death is presented in clear and forceful imagery, so that the least thought of the nostalgic or delicate is throttled within us."[5] The great visual impact of the painting depends on creating both a sense of order, represented by the cottage, and images of turmoil, represented by the fire, the scattering of the animals, and the admixture of both docile livestock and wild fauna.

Indeed, fire, tornado, hurricane, earthquake, flood, military action, and other man-made or natural disasters may damage or destroy human habitations and cause much suffering and upheaval. In usage dating to 1509, such dreadful calamities

---

1 Brook, *The Open Door*, 4.

2 Yi-Fu Tuan, *Space and Place*, 88.

3 Richard Turner, *The Vision of Landscape in Renaissance Italy* (Princeton: Princeton University Press, 1966) 43. Throughout this paragraph, I am indebted to Turner's analysis of the painting.

4 Turner 44.

5 Turner 44. He explores Piero di Cosimo's connection to Paolo Uccello, as well.

and disasters have become synonymous with tragedy.[6] In everyday life, mortgages are foreclosed, and creditors repossess houses. In actual life, houses and castles also get damaged or destroyed, but they do not simply vanish into thin air. In folklore and literary creations, they do, as Andrew Marvell reminds us, " … when th' enchantment ends / The castle vanishes or rends."[7] In the story of the Grail, the Fisher King's deserted castle vanishes when Perceval on horseback jumps over the rising drawbridge and gallops away toward the forest, having failed to seek an explanation for the mysterious sights and events of the night before.[8] In *Buchedd Collen Sant* (c. 1536), Saint Collen is invited to visit the rich and marvelous castle of Gwyn, a mighty sovereign on a golden throne. All sorts of well-appointed courtiers, servitors, minstrels, musicians, and handsome youths riding priceless steeds give the saint a hearty welcome.[9] Suspecting that the king and courtiers are evil spirits, Saint Collen refuses a tempting invitation to an elegant banquet. Collen "sprinkles holy water" all around, and "the castle vanishes, leaving nothing but the green tussocks."[10] According to Roger Loomis, Annwn, the palace of the deities of the ancient Welsh, was believed to appear and then disappear in a familiar landscape; and the dwellers of Annwn were always "noted for their hospitality; the place abounded in treasure, particularly in costly vessels for the service of the table."[11] In Spenser's *The Faerie Queene*, Britomart binds Busirane and frees

---

[6] This first recorded usage in the *OED* is from Stephen Hawes, *The historie of graunde Amoure and la bell Pucel, called the Pastime of plesure* (London, 1509/1554). STC 12950. Fynes Moryson, in his Itinerary (1617) writes of war as initiator of "tragedy": "The warre of Hungarie made all those parts full of tragedies and miserie" (*OED*).

[7] Marvell, 1.1711.

[8] See Chrétien de Troyes, *The Complete Romances of Chrétien de Troyes*, trans. David Staines (Bloomington: Indiana University Press, 1990) 278–84.

[9] This summary is based on Roger Sherman Loomis, "The Spoils of Annwn: An Early Arthurian Poem," *PMLA* 56.4 (1941): 893–4. See *The Mabinogion, Mediaeval Welsh Romances*, Third Edition, trans. Charlotte Guest (London: D. Nutt, 1910). In *The Grail: From Celtic Myth to Christian Symbol* (Cardiff: University of Wales Press; New York: Columbia University Press, 1963), Loomis writes: " … we find in Celtic literature and Arthurian romance an atmosphere of wonder and supernatural paraphernalia such as are characteristic of mythology—revolving castles, sword-like bridges, springs haunted by fays, isles inhabited only by women, enchantresses who take the form of birds, hags changed by a kiss into damsels of peerless beauty, vessels of inexhaustible plenty, vessels moved by no visible agency, banqueters who preserve a youthful appearance in spite of their many years" (22).

[10] Loomis, "Spoils of Annwn," 893–4; and Loomis, The Grail, 21–2.

[11] Loomis, "Spoils of Annwn," 895. Philip Ariès refers to fantastical events recorded in the autobiography of Burkard Zink of Augusburg, who having followed two unknown horsemen into a Hungarian forest, finds himself pursued by wild boars before a gloomy castle. When Burkard prays to God for help, the castle suddenly vanishes. See Philip Ariès and Georges Duby, (eds), *A History of Private Life: Revelations of the Medieval World*, trans. Arthur Goldhammer (Cambridge, MA and London: Belknap Press of Harvard University Press, 1988), 2: 629. Burkard's account appears in Chronik des Burkard Zink, in Die Chroniken der deutschen Städte vom 14. bis ins 16. Jahrhundert, 5. Band (Leipzig 1866).

Amoret. As she exits the house of Busirane, the rooms and the rich furnishings of the house vanish behind her: "those goodly roomes, which erst / She saw so rich and royally arayd, / Now vanisht vtterly,and cleane subuerst / She found, and all their glory quite decayd."[12]

Likewise, in Shakespeare's *King Lear*, I submit, Lear's castle too vanishes, mysteriously and puzzlingly, to great dramatic and emotional consequences. I accept Linda Woodbridge's statement that "Lear's vanishing castle is more than a textual crux," but not her explanation: "that [Lear] never considers, when his daughters close up their houses, simply going back to the castle where the opening scenes took place suggests the text's commitment to homelessness as a theme."[13] I argue that Lear's castle vanishes in a way similar to the disappearance of the abodes of the Fisher King, Gwyn, Annwn, or Busirane, without any association with homelessness. Therefore, I propose that the *disappearance* or *erasure* of Lear's castle, home, and domestic sphere constitutes the central phenomenon around which the experience of dwelling revolves. I want to link the disappearing castle, a literary tour-de-force and the equivalent of a theatrical special effect, to a change in housing conditions, a crisis of patriarchal authority, and the disintegration of a way of life.

I am particularly interested in Lear's domestic space and the extent to which Shakespeare connects perception to tragedy's radical dislocation of habits of mind. When Lear divides his kingdom and casts out Cordelia, he also dismantles all the certainties that anchor his daily life. Lear presumably disposes of his abode, along with his throne, but in actuality the text remains silent on this issue. All that we

---

12 Edmund Spenser, *The Faerie Queene*, (ed.) Thomas P. Roche (London: Penguin, 1987), III.12.42. All quotations from Spenser, unless otherwise indicated, will be from this edition.

13 Linda Woodbridge, *Vagrancy, Homelessness, and English Renaissance Literature* (Urbana and Chicago: University of Illinois Press, 2001) 218. Woodbridge offers a brilliant analysis of the play; but, although she decries Universalist readings, she admits to one: "It is, then, with some chagrin that I now argue that on the issue of poverty and homelessness Shakespeare, in *King Lear* at least, stood head and shoulders above his culture and was centuries ahead of his time—and perhaps ahead of ours" (206). I am making no such claim. See also William C. Carroll, *Fat King, Lean Beggar: Representations of Poverty in the Age of Shakespeare* (Ithaca: Cornell University Press, 1996). To further contextualize and historicize assistance to the poor in England, consult Bronislaw Geremek, *Poverty: A History*, trans. Agnieszka Kolakowska (Oxford, UK and Malden, MA: Blackwell, 1997). Geremek argues that "In England new policies were implemented in stages, and even though reform sometimes seemed slow in comparison with the continent, by the end of the sixteenth century it had more than caught up, and seemed more successful than in France" (167). Particularly well developed were the administrative structures in place for distribution of assistance, although in the 1570s, English authorities came under "growing pressure root out public begging" (168). See also Paola Pugliati, *Beggary and Theatre in Early Modern England* (Burlington: Ashgate Publishing, 2003); John Pound, *Poverty and Vagrancy in Tudor England*, Second Edition. (London and New York: Longman, 1986); and J.F. Pound, "An Elizabethan Census of the Poor," *Historical Journal* 8 (1962): 135–61.

know for certain is that Lear's castle fades from the characters' consciousness, seemingly vanishing into thin air. Christian Norberg Schuz writes that home, being a primary site of "meaningful events of our existence," provides "points of departure from which we orient ourselves and take possession of the environment."[14] The disappearance of Lear's castle from the characters' consciousness signals a drastic disorienting effect that goes to the core of this tragedy: Shakespeare takes us to the shifting, unstable, idiosyncratic realm of perceptual space. Nothing can ever again be as it was.

In this play, a tragic nexus hinges on voids that the disappearance of Lear's domestic space and the fragmentation of Lear's affective domain create. To fill the voids, other places—the houses of Goneril, Gloucester, and Regan, and the hovel—become the focus of attention, revealing the sharp divide between inside and outside, indoors and outdoors. Awakened female sexual desire threatens to disrupt the household and subvert the integrity of the family. To a large extent, *King Lear* conforms to Jean Howard's characterization of Jacobean tragedy in general: "By contrast, tragedies, particularly those of the first Jacobean decades, narrativize the decline and fall of once dominant groups rather than the emergence of new ones."[15] In this play, the shift from Lear's castle to his daughters' houses embodies and symbolizes a reshuffling of the social order.

Historical Contexts

Home can be a castle, a sumptuous palace or country house, an urban townhouse, a cabin in the Flint Hills of Kansas, a black tent in the Maghreb, a mud hut in the Congo, or a shack in a Rio de Janeiro favela. These architectural structures provide shelter and protection from the elements; serve as center of family life; and, according to a Kirgiz proverb, become a sanctuary: "A man's tent is like a god's temple."[16] At times, it might be instructive to strip all human abodes down to elemental functions, as it might also to historicize major changes in housing conditions and availability in the early modern period. My discussion of *King Lear* emphasizes both.

As Arthur Fairchild, Lena Cowen Orlin, and others have argued, the dissolution of the monasteries and other policies introduced under Henry VIII precipitated

14 Christian Norberg-Schulz, *Meaning in Western Architecture* (New York: Rizzoli, 1980) 224.

15 Jean E. Howard, "Shakespeare, Geography, and the Work of Genre on the Early Modern Stage," *Modern Language Quarterly* 64.3 (2003): 314. By contrast, in *Dangerous Familiars: Representation of Domestic Crime in England, 1550–1700* (Ithaca: Cornell University Press, 1994), Frances Dolan defines the home "as a locus of conflict, an arena in which the most fundamental ideas about social order, identity, and intimacy were contested" (1).

16 Quoted in Torvald Faegre, *Tents: Architecture of the Nomads* (New York: Anchor Books, 1979) 1.

a major redistribution of lands and spurred a construction boom in England.[17] According to Fairchild, the erection of new churches had practically ceased and of public buildings had barely begun, with the exception of the Royal Exchange.[18] Architectural innovation, made possible by new wealth, reflected fundamental changes under way:

> The feudal castle or castellated mansion, with its moat, its fortified entrance, its high walls, and its narrow windows, all designed for protection against an enemy, was no longer felt to be necessary; and it rapidly gave way to the Elizabethan manor house or hall, an E or H open type of structure, which was designed to be a home. The castle, frigid, formidable, and forbidding in its external features, was replaced by a house which was hospitable, inviting, and attractive—a fit setting for a gentleman and an implied compliment to its occupant and its invited guest.[19]

The Tudor period witnessed "the decay of the old architectural form of the feudal lord's fortress,"[20] so much so that "castle" would become a proverbial metaphor for the early modern house, which was no longer a military fortress but rather a human habitation: "A man's house is his castle."[21] Social and economic changes, developments in warfare technology, and more effective defense strategies were making such medieval fortifications obsolete. "The new architecture was domestic. Mansions and great houses sprang up all over England."[22] Architectural innovations simultaneously derived from as well as ushered in new expectations and new degrees of comfort, privacy, individualism, and subjectivity.[23] This

---

[17] Arthur H.R. Fairchild, *Shakespeare and the Arts of Design*, University of Missouri Studies (Columbia, MO: University of Missouri, 1937); Lena Cowen Orlin, "Man's House as His Castle in Arden of Feversham," *Medieval and Renaissance Drama in England 2* (1985): 57–89; and Orlin, *Private Matters*.

[18] Fairchild 1.

[19] Fairchild 1.

[20] *Private Matters and Public Cultures in Post-Reformation England* (Ithaca: Cornell University Press, 1994), 2. In *The Custom of the Castle From Malory to Macbeth* (Berkeley: University of California Press, 1997), Charles Ross traces the representation of the castle as a symbol for "a flexible mode of thinking about tradition and convention" from Arthurian romance to the Renaissance, and contends that "As castles give way to rural estates, new images arise for the containment of social behavior" (140).

[21] Orlin argues that this statement had become proverbial in the Elizabethan period (2). See Orlin's discussion of this matter in her introduction (1–13). Throughout her book, Orlin is interested in locating "the private in property, both real and movable," domesticity, and household roles and relationships in domestic tragedy. Of interest here is also her article, "Man's House as His Castle," especially her summary of the major historical changes. See also, Crane, *Shakespeare's Brain*, 43.

[22] Fairchild 1.

[23] Fairchild 1. See the most helpful survey of the changes, including interior and exterior characteristics, of both the English country houses and of "houses of varied size, material and form," in H. Avray Tipping, *English Homes: Late Tudor and Early Stuart*

"architectural revolution," as Lena Orlin puts it, reflects "a higher standard of living, increased physical comfort, more individual privacy, and the segregation of laboring and domestic life, and more household spaces, each with specialized functions."[24] According to Mary Thomas Crane, the changes created "unstable boundaries," and also elicited considerable "anxiety" about the potential of women as "producers"—"of income, goods, children"—and their roles as "caretakers" and "preservers of money, goods, and offspring produced by the husband."[25] The word "housewife," adds Crane, epitomizes those unstable, contested boundaries, signifying simultaneously a woman "who manages her household with skill and thrift" and "a light, worthless, or pert woman or girl."[26]

Two definitions of home help contextualize the changes. In *The Elements of Architecture* (1624), a compilation of European architectural writings, such as those of Leon Batista Alberti, Sir Henry Wotton describes what the house represents in a person's life:

> Every Mans proper *Mansion* House and *Home*, being the *Theater* of his *Hospitality*, the *Seate of Selfe-fruition*, the *Comfortablest part* of his own Life, the *Noblest* of his Sonnes *Inheritance*, a kinde of priuate *Princedome*; Nay, to the *Possessors* thereof, an *Epitomie* of the whole *World*: may well deserue by these *Attributes*, according to the degree of the *Master*, to be *decently* and *delightfully* adorned.[27]

1558–1649 (London: Offices of Country Life and George Newnes; New York: Charles Scribner's Sons, 1922); and Olive Cook, *The English House Through Seven Centuries* (New York: Overlook Press, 1983), esp. Chapter 5, "Tudor Renaissance," and Chapter 6, "Elizabethan Baroque." For purposes of comparison, see Marta Ajmar-Wollheim and Flora Dennis, (eds), *At Home in Renaissance Italy* (London: V & A Publications; New York: Harry N. Abrams, 2006). Georges Duby argues that the castle was "an ambivalent symbol: it was both the seat of justice and the base of a potentially oppressive power, as sign of the lord's duty to protect his people and also of his right to command and, if necessary, punish them." See Georges Duby, *France in the Middle Ages* (1987; Oxford: Blackwell, 1991) 56, quoted in Ross, *Custom of the Castle*, 130. Ross discusses Lear only in passing (Appendix One, 141–2), but I agree with his concluding remark, which I think reinforces mine; namely, that Shakespeare sets the play in the distant past and therefore creates the illusion "that the social world of Lear is long established" (142).

24 Lena Cowin Orlin, (ed.), *Elizabethan Households: An Anthology* (Washington, DC: Folger Shakespeare Library, 1995) 3. Like Orlin, Natasha Korda, in *Shakespeare's Domestic Economies*, also focuses on a history of property and privacy, but seeks "to elucidate the matrices or interconnections between symbolic and material economies" (15).

25 Mary Thomas Crane, "'Players in your huswifery, and huswives in your beds': Conflicting Identities of Early Modern English Women," *Maternal Measures: Figuring Caregiving in the Early Modern Period*," (eds) by Naomi J. Miller and Naomi Yavneh (Burlington: Ashgate, 2000) 212.

26 Crane, "'Players in your huswifery'," 212.

27 Henry Wotton, *The Elements of Architecture, Collected by Henry Wotton Knight, from the best Authors and Examples* (London, 1624), sig. L^{v}. See the Folger Shakespeare Library facsimile reprint, (ed.) Frederick Hard (Charlottesville: University Press of Virginia,

In Wotton's formulation, the house embodies family life and household, hospitality, self-realization and security, comfort, a financial investment and legacy, a "private princedom," and a microcosm. Reflecting deeply-ingrained contemporary notions of privacy and domesticity, which had been evolving since the Renaissance, Gaston Bachelard, however, writes: "our house is our corner of the world," and the house is "our first universe, a real cosmos in every sense of the word."[28] The early modern house embodies both the death of the medieval castle and the birth of the modern home. In the Tudor and early Stuart periods, "England began to house itself."[29] In this context, Lear fails to negotiate the shift from the medieval castle to the early modern house, being unprepared to make the transition from an unflinchingly patriarchal household to an emerging wider diversity of households, which, though still functioning within patriarchal systems, might be headed by women, and new domestic arrangements in which husband and wife might—increasingly—share domestic responsibilities.

Lear's Castle and Household

In Act I, Lear refers to his "court," where both France and Burgundy have made their long amorous sojourn, although the seventeenth-century editions of the play do not specify the location of the scene. Modern editions locate the first scene in the throne or audience room in Lear's palace. Kenneth Muir in his 1952 Arden edition of the play gives the location of the scene in a stage direction: "A State Room in King Lear's Palace."[30] R.A. Foakes, in his 1997 new Arden Shakespeare edition, does not give a stage direction to identify location, but writes in a footnote: "Presumably a throne or chair of state was placed on stage to signal a ceremonial scene, and prepare for the entry of the King. … Although the play takes place nominally in the mythical reign of a king who ruled in antiquity, the characters may well have worn contemporary costume."[31] Stephen Orgel in the new Pelican Shakespeare gives the location in a footnote as "Lear's Palace." Quite logically, we should assume that the first scene of the play takes place where Lear dwells and holds his court, presumably his own castle or palace.

However, by the end of the first scene of the play, Lear's dwelling place and seat of government mysteriously and inexplicably seem to vanish into thin air,

---

1968) 82. A very handy anthology, which contains excerpts from Wotton and other writers on architecture, the house, household, rooms, goods, and social order is Lena Cowen Orlin, *Elizabethan Households: An Anthology* (Washington, DC: The Folger Shakespeare Library, 1995). Orlin reprints the passage from Wotton on p. 15.

[28] Bachelard 4.

[29] Fairchild 1.

[30] *King Lear*, (ed.) Kenneth Muir, Arden Shakespeare (New York: Random House, 1952) 3.

[31] King Lear, (ed.) R.A. Foakes, *Arden Shakespeare, Third Series* (London: Thomas Nelson and Sons, 1997) 157.

not to be seen again. From that moment on, the action takes place in various other locations such as Gloucester's house, Goneril and Albany's castle, a hovel, and the outdoors. Presumably, Lear loses ownership of and by extension access to his properties, but my point is that Lear's castle fades from the characters' consciousness. Symbolically, Lear's castle ceases to exist. As Peter Brook memorably puts it, "An empty space makes it possible for a new phenomenon to come to life."[32] He adds, "no fresh and new experience is possible if there isn't a pure, virgin space ready to receive it."[33] I contend that Lear's former abode becomes one such "empty space."

Lear has ruled as an absolute monarch in his kingdom and managed his household as an all-powerful patriarch. In *Moralia*, Plutarch defines "character" as "habit long continued"; Lear's abdication would therefore signal a fundamental break in the accustomed rhythms of life.[34] *King Lear* explores a radical and fundamental change of routine and rhythm in the central character's life. Lear intends to step down from the daily business of the state and from the active supervision and management of his castle, household, and estate.

In the first scene, Lear attempts to deal with personal, familial, and public affairs: division of property and distribution of his daughters' inheritance, making provisions for his future living arrangements, negotiating Cordelia's marriage contract and his separation from her, and settling the succession to the throne. Lear's announcement and subsequent miscarried plans bring to an end what his subjects, friends, and family must have seen as a sense of continuity, if not stability, associated with the monarch's extremely long life—"fourscore and upward" (4.7.63)—and very long reign. Later in the play, at Lear's death, Kent remarks on how unusually old Lear was: "The wonder is he hath endured so long; / He but usurped his life" (5.3.323–4). Even as Edgar in the Folio text or Albany in the Quarto searches for words to "Speak what we feel, not what we ought to say" (5.3.331), he cannot express anything more profound than amazement at what one can see and experience in a very long life: "The oldest hath borne most; we that are young / Shall never see so much, nor live so long" (332–3). Lear's longevity also implies that things have remained the same for a long time, although nature is obviously running its unimpeded course.

Predictability, one infers, characterized the past experience of the characters. Kent offers an ever-fixèd mark of constancy and loyalty: "Royal Lear, / Whom I

---

[32] Brook, *The Open Door*, 4.

[33] Brook, *The Open Door*, 4.

[34] See *OED*, "ethos", Gr. ἦθος ("character")—"a person's nature or disposition"—and "ethic." "Aristotle's statement that Polygnotus excelled all other painters in the representation of 'ethos' app. meant simply that his pictures expressed 'character'; but as Aristotle elsewhere says that this painter portrayed men as nobler than they really are, some mod. writers have taken ethos to mean 'ideal excellence.' The opposition of ethos and pathos ('character' and 'emotion'), often wrongly ascribed to Aristotle's theory of art as expounded in the Poetics, really belongs only to Greek rhetoric" (*OED*).

have ever honored as my king, / Loved as my father, as my master followed, / As my great patron thought on in my prayers—" (1.1.14043). Even when sent into exile, he says he will "shape his old course in a country new" (1.1.192). When Cornwall wants to teach him a lesson by putting him in the stocks, Kent remarks, "Sir, I am too old to learn" (2.2.125), suggesting long friendship as well as habits of mind grounded in the highest sense of virtue. As Frederick Kiefer points out, Shakespeare's audience would have read Kent iconographically as an emblem of loyal friendship and as virtue under siege: "For in the moral interludes that precede Shakespeare's play, as well as in sixteenth-century prints, representations of virtue are confined in stocks by their evil adversaries."[35] Even in his wrath, Lear confirms his constancy in keeping his "vows" (1.1.174); and Burgundy attests to the contract he thought Lear had agreed to: "I crave no more than hath your highness offered" (1.1.199), and "Give me that portion which yourself proposed" (1.1.247). Words such as "long," "always," and "ever" occur at key moments throughout the play to indicate duration of past events, unbroken continuity, and sameness. Throughout his long reign, Lear has fostered in his court what Plutarch, in *Life of Dion*, calls "habits of submission," and was surrounded by those "accustomed to a life … of servility and intimidation."[36] In other words, the court knew where they stood with and what to expect from Lear, as long as they did not rock the boat, and always deferred to Lear's judgment.

The need to find a husband for Cordelia, Lear's advancing age, and the question of succession require urgent decisions. Lear states that the King of France and the Duke of Burgundy, rivals for Cordelia's hand, "*long* in our court have made their amorous sojourn" (1.1.47; emphasis mine), but he does not explain why one of the two suitors has not yet been chosen. Shakespeare does not explain the reason for the long "sojourn" of Burgundy and France, or for Lear's delay in finalizing Cordelia's marriage contract. As the action progresses, however, it becomes clear that Lear grants Burgundy the right of first refusal of Cordelia's hand, despite the expected order of precedence due to the King of France's seniority as a reigning monarch. Perhaps whimsically, but more likely in an attempt to circumscribe the sphere of influence and balance the power of his three sons-in-law, Lear prefers a duke rather than a reigning monarch for his youngest daughter.

Burgundy's right of first refusal may throw light on Lear's original plan for the succession to the throne: the breakup of the kingdom into three more or less

---

35 Frederick Kiefer, *Shakespeare's Visual Theatre: Staging the Personified Characters* (Cambridge, UK; Cambridge University Press, 2003) 12.

36 Plutarch, "Life of Dion," http://classics.mit.edu/Plutarch/dion.html, August 23, 2009. See also *The Lives of the Noble Grecians and Romans*, trans. Thomas North (1579; New York: The Heritage Press, 1941), 2: 1778. North translates this passage as follows: "For Dion having from a child been brought up with humble conditions under a tyrant, and acquainted with a servile, timorous life, with a proud and insolent reign, with all vanity and curiosity, as placing felicity in covetousness; nevertheless, after he had felt the sweet reasons of philosophy, teaching the broad way to virtue, his heart was inflamed straight with earnest desire to follow the same" (1778).

equal dominions or dukedoms, with Lear functioning as ceremonial head of state. Upon the death of the sovereign, the kingdom would cease to exist as a national entity, power having been devolved to regional states. Each daughter, married to a duke, would govern her dominion. As a duke himself, Burgundy seems perfectly contented to have his share of Lear's kingdom, without the right to kingship. If he and Cordelia were required by contract to reside in Britain, at least during Lear's lifetime, the aging sovereign could journey from one daughter's house to the next, without having to travel abroad. Lear seems to have no contingency plan, however, should Cordelia marry the King of France and move to Paris, or should she marry Burgundy but move to his duchy in Europe. Lear intends for Cordelia to have a "more opulent" third of the kingdom. Again, what makes Cordelia's share "more opulent"—richer, wealthier, more affluent—is unclear, unless it includes Lear's own royal castle, seat of government, and principal place of residence. This opulence might serve as sufficient enticement for Cordelia and Burgundy to reside in Britain rather than in his estate in Burgundy. Lear could continue to live with Cordelia and Burgundy, but would feel free to travel to the houses of Albany and Cornwall, whenever he felt inclined to do so. His home base unchanged, he would turn over the daily running of his own house to Burgundy and Cordelia and only occasionally discharge his ceremonial role of monarch, as his age and state of health permitted. This arrangement would resemble the development, in late medieval and Tudor England, of an "abiding household," a permanent residence, and a "riding household," satellite hunting lodges or other country residences: "This arrangement of a greater house and satellites not only allowed the King to set up at one house and continue with short hunting trips to the lesser houses around, but enabled him to make day trips with somewhere to rest and eat."[37]

This plausible, conjectural scenario suggests phased or gradual "retirement," which in usage traced to Shakespeare's *Henry V* (1599), means "withdrawing into seclusion or privacy," and, to a letter written by Oliver Cromwell (c. 1648), in which it means, "Withdrawal from occupation, office, or business activity."[38] The *OED* also records a more modern sense of the verb "to retire" (1667): "to withdraw from office or an official position; to give up one's business or occupation in order to enjoy more leisure or freedom (esp. after having made a competence or earned a pension)." According to the *OED*, the word "pension," meaning "A regular payment made to a person of rank or a royal favourite to enable him or her to live to an expected standard," can be dated to 1548. In fact, "pension," "large allowance," and "portion" are used interchangeably in referring to the financial support that King Leir, Shakespeare's prototype king, receives in the anonymous

---

[37] Simon Thurley, *The Royal Palaces of Tudor England: Architecture and Court Life 1460–1547* (New Haven and London: Yale University Press, 1993) 69. See Thurley's discussion of the logistics involved in royal perambulations and of an itinerant court (67–84).

[38] *OED*.

True Chronicle Historie of King Leir.[39] Shakespeare's Lear, however, lacks Leir's foresight and fails to stipulate such a pension. His large retinue not only adds a considerable burden to the daily expenses but also compounds the disruption and inconvenience caused by the presence of this retinue in his daughters' households. This fact neither exonerates Goneril and Regan of their crimes nor excuses their heartlessness, cruelty, and lack of filial affection. It shows, however, that Lear has unrealistic expectations of his daughters'—or anyone's—goodwill, love, and patience.

As the play begins, the king's emotional state seems to be unstable, fluctuating, and unpredictable. Kent introduces the point: "I thought the king had more affected the Duke of Albany than Cornwall" (1.1.1–2). In fact, throughout the play, Kent senses change and often remarks on things to come.[40] Gloucester's response explains the change: "It did always seem so to us; but now, in the division of the kingdom, it appears not which of the dukes he values most, for equalities are so weighed that curiosity in neither can make choice of either's moiety" (1.1.3–6).[41] Both agree that, as a matter of course, Lear favors one son-in-law over the other. Now, for this *new* Lear, the two sons-in-law have become each other's true "moiety," halves of each other, and therefore entitled to equal shares of the divided kingdom. Despite having played favorites before, he now treats his daughters and sons-in-law more equally, perhaps more justly, by more evenly apportioning his affection and favor. The king has turned over a new leaf in his relationship with his family.

In his abdication, Lear surrenders his "power, / Preeminence, and all the large effects / That troop with majesty" (1.1.131–3), although he retains the title and "all th'addition to a king" (137). He plans to reside alternately in his daughters' houses: "Ourself, by monthly course, / With reservation of an hundred knights, / By you to be sustained, shall our abode / Make with you by due turn" (133–6). "All th' addition" may include a royal crown, royal robes, and other appendages appropriate to the comfort, pomp, and privilege of a monarch, but it does not include a house of his own, nor does it include any source of income. Before long, his own Fool points out the obvious: "If I gave them [his daughters] all my living,

39 Geoffrey Bullough, (ed.), *Narrative and Dramatic Sources of Shakespeare* (London: Routledge and Kegan Paul; New York: Columbia University Press, 1973) 7:337–402, lines 763, 799, and 807.

40 Some examples of this include: his exile parallels and anticipates Cordelia's, as does his return to serve Lear; the mistreatment he receives from Regan and Cornwall anticipates their rejection of Lear and the blinding of Gloucester. See, for example, Act III, scene 1, where Kent refers to the imminent civil war between the houses of Cornwall and Albany. In a powerful, yet ironic reversal of this pattern, Kent enters in Act 5, scene 3, "To bid my king and master aye good night" (240), arriving just in time for Lear's entrance with the dead Cordelia in his arms and then for Lear's own death.

41 The *OED* dates the first usage of "moiety" to 1444: "a half; esp. in legal or quasi-legal use"; another meaning, which emerged in 1596 also pertains to the passage from Lear: "One or two [or more] parts into which something is divided; one's share" (1596).

I'd keep my coxcombs myself" (1.4.105–6). In other words, the Fool would keep the means by which he could earn income. Lear envisions his remaining life as a permanent royal progress, which David M. Bergeron defines as the sovereign's "summer provincial tour" to "the private estates of noblemen," where elaborate "progress pageants" or especially-designed, highly allegorical and emblematic theatrical entertainments would be performed for the visitor.[42] One should add that the prestige and privilege of hosting such visitors and their retinues came at considerable expense and perhaps inconvenience to owners of country estates. In his plan, Lear gives no thought to the expenses involved, the difficulties that travel poses for an elderly person, and the ever-increasing likelihood of his failing health. Simply put, he counts on his daughters footing his bills.

Emotion clashes with reason; rage trumps common sense. Cordelia's refusal to play along with the seemingly ceremonial expression of affection for her father arouses Lear's uncontrollable wrath and rash nature, and leads to Kent's banishment and her own disowning. Everything now is up for grabs.[43] Lear compounds the problem when he divides Cordelia's share between Regan and Goneril. By the end of the first scene, the kingdom has been turned upside down. As I will discuss, the text makes clear that Lear has not only thrown his family, court, and kingdom into turmoil, but his home has also vanished.

In the realm of perception and artistic license, the disappearance of Lear's palace will leave an empty space. Empty spaces are certainly put to fascinating uses both in this play and in art. In his seminal *Meaning in the Visual Arts: Papers in and on Art History*, Erwin Panofsky contrasts uses of empty spaces in the anonymous *Christ Resurrecting the Youth of Nain* (c. 1000), and in the later, more realistic *Middelburg Altarpiece of the Three Magi*, by Rogier Van der Weyden (1400–64) in order to teach the importance of historical context in iconographical

[42] David M. Bergeron, *English Civic Pageantry*, 1558–1642, Second edition (Tempe: Medieval and Renaissance Texts and Studies, Arizona Center for Medieval and Renaissance Studies, Arizona State University, 2003) 2. Bergeron writes that these royal visits and the accompanying entertainment for these progresses "typically spread out over several days and different locations. Demands of hospitality often governed how the noblemen shaped these estate entertainments. Regularly pageants of various kinds made use of the materials at hand, making place serve dramatic purpose. Or, as in the case of the Earl of Hertford at Elvetham in 1591, one might create a new place: here, a specially constructed crescent-shaped pond for the battle between the wood gods and sea gods. In these places audiences gathered, made up of multiple social and economic classes" (4). See also Bergeron's "Symbolic Landscape in English Civic Pageantry," *Renaissance Quarterly* 22. 1 (1969): 32–7.

[43] This development parallels Gloucester's own attempt to weigh Edgar, his legitimate son, and Edmund, his illegitimate son who has been away for nine years. Although Gloucester confesses that he has "so often blushed to acknowledge" Edmund, he now is "brazed" to do so: "But I have a son, sir, by order of law, some year elder than this who yet is no dearer in my account: though this knave came something saucily to the world, before he was sent for, yet was his mother fair, there was good sport at his making, and the whoreson must be acknowledged" (1.1.18–23).

description.[44] The infant Jesus of the altarpiece floats in midair, seemingly suspended in "space with no means of support," as a supernatural apparition to the three Magi, who are kneeling down in a worshipful posture. The miniature from the Ottonian period (c. 900–1050), known for its exquisite manuscript illuminations, depicts the resurrection of the youth of Nain (Luke 7:11–17), along with the city of Nain, where the miracle occurred, suspended in midair.[45] Panofsky points out that the first image represents a supernatural apparition, whereas the second does not. Panofsky writes: "In the miniature of around 1000 'empty space' does not count as a real three-dimensional medium, as it does in a more realistic period, but serves as an abstract, unreal background."[46] He adds:

> The curious semicircular shape of what should be the base line of the towers bears witness to the fact that, in the more realistic prototype of our miniature, the town had been situated on a hilly terrain, but was taken over into a representation in which space has ceased to be thought of in terms of perspective realism.[47]

I suggest that, as in the Ottonian miniature, Shakespeare makes use of nonrealistic space in order to create and then imaginatively fill empty spaces.

In *King Lear*, if something vanishes, something else makes an appearance in its place. Take, for example, Cordelia's departure for France at the end of Act I, scene 1; the appearance of the Fool in Act I, scene 4; his disappearance in Act III, scene 6, with his memorable last line, "And I'll go to bed at noon" (83); Cordelia's reappearance in Act IV, scene 4; and then the two of them are fused in Lear's desperate lament: "And my poor fool is hanged: no, no, no life?" (5.3.312).[48] Similarly, when Burgundy rejects the impoverished Cordelia, France decides to "take up what's cast away," commenting on the mysterious forces that have moved him: "'Tis strange that from their cold'st neglect / My love should kindle to inflamed respect" (1.1.260–61). The "nothing" of Cordelia's response and the "nothing" of Edmund's forged letter leave voids that must be filled with

---

44 Erwin Panofsky, *Meaning in the Visual Arts: Papers in and on Art History* (Garden City, NY: Doubleday Anchor Books, 1955) 33–4. See Rogier van der Weyden, Middelburg Altarpiece, Three Magi, detail, ca.1445–1448, oil on panel, Gemaldegalerie, Berlin.

45 See John Beckwith, *Early Medieval Art* (New York: Praeger, 1964), and V.D. van Aalst and Krijna Nelly Ciggaar, *Byzantium and the Low Countries in the Tenth Century: Aspects of Art and History in the Ottonian Era* (Hernen: A. A. Brediusstichting, 1985), and especially the following catalogue of an exhibition on Bernward, bishop of Hildesheim (ca. 960–1022) and manuscript and book illumination: Michael Brandt and Arne Eggebrecht, *Bernward von Hildesheim und das Zeitalter der Ottonen: Katalog der Ausstellung, Hildesheim 1993*, 2 vol. (Hildesheim: Bernward Verlag; Mainz am Rhein: von Zabern, 1993).

46 Panofsky 34.

47 Panofsky 34.

48 Scholars believe that this is evidence of doubling of the roles.

such things as Lear's wrath and madness or Gloucester's anger and blindness, unfettered ambition, banishment, persecution, violence, and much else.

Space thus functions as an "abstract, unreal background" that can be filled, as the action requires. Strange though effective juxtapositions become a hallmark of this text. Other competing spaces loom large in place of Lear's castle: Albany and Goneril's house, Cornwall and Regan's house, Gloucester's house, a hovel, open country near Dover, battlefields, and the outdoors. As Yi-Fu Tuan argues in *Space and Place*, "Man-made space can refine human feeling and perception. … Architectural space—even a simple hut surrounded by cleared ground—can define such sensations and render them vivid. Another influence is this: the built environment clarifies social roles and relations."[49] As Lear's palace vanishes, social relations and social rules are thrust into turmoil and chaos. In Goneril's and Gloucester's houses, the characters redefine and reconfigure their social relations and rules, discard old alliances, form new partnerships, and assert their newly-acquired power and authority. To render these phenomena, Shakespeare, accustomed to the Elizabethan theater's continuous staging of place, envisions a dynamic interplay between unlocalized, nonillusionistic action and localized and illusionistic action, with linguistic markers, props, costumes, or other staging techniques to provide sufficient directional signposts.

Goneril's House and the Space of Woman's Will

Mazzola and Abate argue that in this play, "the household is attacked from within and from without," and that "the reach of female interests and their fierce opposition to both the home and the state" seem "most horrifying, most inexplicable."[50] Woodbridge proposes that the absence of "domestic coziness … fits perfectly a play where 'home' is a myth to be exploded."[51] Heather Dubrow, focusing on domestic loss, contends that in the play " … physical edifices variously facilitate and threaten social bonds."[52] I want to frame the issue in a different way. Goneril's house emerges as the first rival architectural space to replace Lear's vanishing palace, and within this architectural space, a fierce battle of wills over household management occurs. This does not, however, mean that women oppose home and state alike. In the play, home is no more of a myth to be exploded than it is in the self-destructive royal household of Sophocles's *Oedipus* trilogy. Rather, Goneril and Regan, in their own different ways, try to modify, redefine, or bring to an end the tyrannical patriarchal regime associated with their father and centered in his now vanished castle. The troubles of Sir Francis Willoughby's household at Wollaton Hall offer a historical parallel to Lear's household, conditions from

---

[49] Yi-Fu Tuan, *Space and Place: The Perspective of Experience* (Minneapolis: University of Minnesota Press, 1977) 101.

[50] Mazzola and Abate, *Introduction to Privacy, Domesticity, and Women,* 1.

[51] Woodbridge 206.

[52] Dubrow, *Shakespeare and Domestic Loss*, 116.

which Goneril and Regan seek an escape. These troubles continued even after Sir Francis' death in 1596:

> While the stated reasons for the difficulties between Sir Francis, his wife, and the members of their household varied from incident to incident, it is clear that the underlying cause was a frenzied cutthroat competition for his personal favor and, through him, for the rights to his property.[53]

Like Lear, Sir Francis apparently fostered this atmosphere of competition and in fact "fanned the flames of discord raging in his household even as he protested this behavior in others."[54]

No wonder, then, that within their homes, both Goneril and Regan work towards an alternative worldview, which is dramatized as a fight over control of domestic space. Lear's abdication becomes, for Goneril, "this last surrender of his will" (1.1.310), and she proposes immediate action: "We must do something, and i' th'heat" (312). Lear's palace empties out: Cordelia leaves for France; Goneril and Regan return with their husbands to their estates in Albany and Cornwall; Kent gets ready for his journey into exile; and Lear commences his journey to Goneril's house, with whom he intends to live for a while. At the end of Act I, scene 1 remarking on the implications of the recent events at court, Goneril ominously predicts: "if our father carry authority with such disposition as he bear, this last surrender of his will but offend us" (302–4). Therefore, I contend that Goneril's house, the first space that I will discuss, serves not only to "refine human feeling and perception" but also emerges as the pivotal feminine-gendered place of Goneril's will in counterpoise to Lear's masculine-gendered royal palace of the first scene.

Later, Edgar, after killing Oswald, discovers Goneril's letters in her dead servant's pockets in which she reminds Edmund of their "reciprocal vows," and encourages her lover to kill Albany, and claim her hand. If Albany is allowed to "return the conqueror," she adds, "Then am I the prisoner, and his bed my jail; from the loathed warmth whereof deliver me, and supply the place for your labor" (4.6.262–8). In astonishment at her brazenly adulterous, murderous plot, Edgar describes hers as the "indistinguished place of woman's will" (270). According to Edgar, the "indefinable"[55] place of a woman's will escapes reason and the bounds of morality. His definition echoes Hamlet's response to the ghost's description of Gertrude's impudence: "O most pernicious woman!" (1.5.105).

In "Untitled: The Housing of Gender," Mark Wigley explores the "relationships between the role of gender in the discourse of space and the role of space in the

---

[53] Alice T. Friedman, *House and Household in Elizabethan England: Wollaton Hall and the Willoughby Family* (Chicago and London: University of Chicago Press, 1989) 53.

[54] Frideman, *House and Household,* 53.

[55] C.T. Onions and Robert D. Eagleson, *A Shakespeare Glossary* (Oxford: Clarendon Press, 1986) 298.

discourse of gender."[56] He is particularly interested in the "familiar sense of the patriarchal construction of the place of woman as the house," and the systems of patriarchal surveillance. Goneril offers a clear example of resistance to attempts at her domestication, whereby a woman internalizes "the very spatial order that confines her."[57] Wigley writes of Xenophon's Socratic discourse *Oeconomicus*,[58] Leon Battista Alberti's fifteenth-century treatise, *On the Art of Building in Ten Books* [*De re aedificatoria*], published in 1485, and even the modern university as "a mechanism that sustains a system of spaces, an architecture, by masking the particular constructions of sexuality that make those spaces possible," but he does not discuss *King Lear*; nonetheless, I think his ideas can prove most pertinent to the housing of gender in Shakespeare's play.[59] Goneril's house, the place to which she retires after the partition of the kingdom and to which Lear first turns in his new status of king in name only, becomes a highly contested space.

Goneril vies with Lear, and to an extent with Albany, for control of this contested space. Lear's stay with Goneril has quickly soured, and relations have palpably deteriorated. Goneril remarks that Lear "flashes into one gross crime or another / That set us all at odds," and that she will "not endure it" (4–5). She is determined to confront him, when he returns from hunting. In the Quarto text she makes an even harsher assessment of her father:

> Idle old man,
> That still would manage those authorities
> That he hath given away. Now, by my life,
> Old fools are babes again, and must be used
> With checks as flatteries, when they are seen abused. (16–20)

In this speech, she seems to be laying the groundwork for a legal case against her father, who seems to be usurping her and her husband's rightful management of their own house. This speech also provides further context for her intentions and what she sees as her rightful authority. She must grab the bull by the horns, if Lear's willful and outrageous nature, like that of a child, is to be broken and brought under control.

An overbearing, ebullient Lear returns from the hunt, amidst the blaring sounds of horns (1.4). Feeling re-invigorated and very sure of himself, Lear thinks that he can run the house and make whatever demands. In his treatise on hunting,

---

[56] Mark Wigley, "Untitled: The Housing of Gender," in *Sexuality & Space*, (ed.) Beatriz Colomina (Princeton: Princeton Papers on Architecture, 1992) 325.

[57] Wigley 340.

[58] The first English translation of *Oeconomicus*, by G. Hervet, appeared in 1532 as Xenophons treatise of householde (STC 26073). See Leo Strauss, *Xenophon's Socratic Discourse: An Interpretation of the Oeconomicus*, with translation of *Oeconomicus* by Carnes Lord (Ithaca: Cornell University Press, 1970; South Bend, IN: St. Augustine's Press, 2004).

[59] Wigley 328.

Xenophon writes of the beneficial effects of hunting, although the activity is recommended for a much younger man than Lear: "With the practical side of hunting I have finished. But the advantages that those who have been attracted by this pursuit will gain are many. For it makes the body healthy, improves the sight and hearing, and keeps men from growing old; and it affords the best training for war."[60] In the commendatory verses to his 1576 *The Noble Arte of Venerie or Hunting*, George Gascoigne concurs that hunting helps exercise the minds of "Men of Noble kinde," makes for better soldiers, and contributes to bodily and mental health: "Since by the same, mens bodies be, in health mainteyned well, / It exercyseth strength, it exerciseth wit, / And all the poars and sprites of Man, are exercised by it."[61] Xenophon, however, addresses common objections to hunting—"Some say that it is not right to love hunting, because it may lead to neglect of one's domestic affairs"; "therefore," he adds, "if keen sportsmen fit themselves to be useful to their country in matters of vital moment, neither will they be remiss in their private affairs: for the state is necessarily concerned both in the safety and in the ruin of the individual's domestic fortunes."[62]

When we first observe Lear at Goneril's house, then, Lear is hungry from the hunt and energized by the chase. However, he comes across as imposing and overbearing when he orders an attendant, "Let me not stay a jot for dinner; go get it ready" (8). He loses his temper with Oswald, whom he calls a blockhead, and soon the alleged riotous knights in Lear's retinue speak of Goneril's insolent servants and the perceived "great abatement of kindness," not only on the part of servants but—more alarmingly—on the part of Goneril and Albany. In his own cryptic way, the Fool tries to point out the obvious; namely: Lear should realize that he no longer has much leverage, now that he has "given away [his] land" (138), failed to take a "monopoly out" on some profitable enterprise (150), and showed lack of wisdom, having disposed of his throne. Lear confronts Goneril, when she enters at line 183, with complaints that she is "too much of late i'th' frown" (185). He is still in the mood for sport; she is determined to put him in his place as a guest. If hunting has not made him remiss in his private affairs, he at least appears to be out of sync with and unaccustomed to the daily routines and rules of his daughter's house. Various witnesses and the audience's own observation suggest that there is little doubt, that he appears to be behaving abominably. Lear behaves as if he were master of the house; Goneril takes him for an insolent houseguest who is overstepping the acceptable boundaries of hospitality.

---

60 Xenophon, "On Hunting," in *Xenophon in Seven Volumes*, 7 (Cambridge, MA: Harvard University Press; London: William Heinemann, Ltd., 1984), translated by Sir John Sandys; revisions by T.K. Hubbard, http://www.perseus.tufts.edu/cgi-bin/ptext?lookup=Xen.+Hunt.+12.1, August 23, 2009. The most authoritative and popular English treatise on the subject in the period is George Gascoigne's *Noble Arte of Venerie or Hunting* (London, 1576), STC 24328, which was reissued in 1611 (STC 24329).

61 Gascoigne, *Noble Arte of Venerie*, sig. A3v.

62 Xenophon, "On Hunting."

In this scene, Goneril carefully builds a case against Lear, first to Oswald and then to both Lear and Albany. Her argument centers on orderly household governance. To Oswald, she complains of Lear's "all-licensed fool," and the "insolent retinue" of knights who "hourly carp and quarrel, breaking forth / In rank and not-to-be-endured riots" (1.4.195–8). In what she calls his "new pranks," she says that Lear condones insubordination; therefore, she warns him: "As you are old and reverend, [you] should be wise" (1.4.232, 234). To provoke him further, she blames him for corrupting her house, interfering with household management, and setting an altogether bad example:

> Here do you keep a hundred knights and squires,
> Men so disordered, so debauched and bold
> That this our court, infected with their manners,
> Shows like a riotous inn. Epicurism and lust
> Makes it more like a tavern or a brothel
> Than a graced palace. The shame itself doth speak
> For constant remedy. (1.4.235–41).

She accuses him of striking her "people" and his "disordered rabble" of making "servants of their betters" (250–51). Goneril thus clearly draws the line in the sand and roundly puts Lear in his place, as a guest not master of the house.

When Albany appears, he finds Lear in a rage; and for the rest of the scene, Goneril wants her husband to observe and judge Lear's outrageous behavior. Affronted by Goneril's remarks, Lear retaliates by attacking her womanhood, and cursing her womb with sterility. He invokes Nature's curse to "Dry up in her the organs of increase" and "Turn all her mother's pains and benefits / To laughter and contempt" (1.4.282–3). So strongly offensive are these words, that mild-mannered Albany wonders: "Now, gods that we adore, whereof comes this?" (286). Goneril retorts: "Never afflict yourself to know more of it, / But let his disposition have that scope / As dotage gives it" (287–9). In other words, given scope to show his prevailing tendency, compounded by an age-induced state of feeblemindedness, Lear will show his true rash and enraged nature and be deemed unfit to manage his affairs. In his *Life of Lysander*, Plutarch writes that "Moral habits, induced by public practices, are far quicker in making their way into men's private lives, than the failings and faults of individuals are in infecting the city at large."[63] Ironically, Goneril seems to agree with Plutarch's philosophy of life, the foundation of which consists of good habits coupled with obedience to virtue; hence her seeming condemnation of luxuriousness, loss of self-discipline, and habits contrary to a life of virtue.

When Lear exits, Goneril turns to Albany, expecting agreement: "Do you mark that?" (307). She insists that Lear's knights may pose a threat to her and

[63] Plutarch, http://classics.mit.edu/Plutarch/lysander.html, August 23, 2009. See Thomas North's translation of this passage in Vol. I, p. 709: "But we are rather to think that private men's manners are conformed according to the common uses and customs of cities, than that the faults and vices of private men do fill cities and commonweals with ill qualities."

Albany's safety: "He may enguard his dotage with their pow'rs / And hold our lives in mercy" (1.4.323–4). When Albany insinuates that she may be overreacting ("Well, you may fear too far," I.4.325), Goneril retorts, "Safer than trust too far," and she claims she knows Lear's heart and has proven his "unfitness." When she realizes that Albany remains skeptical, she refers to his "milky gentleness," and the conversation ends in an impasse:

> ALBANY. How far your eyes may pierce I cannot tell;
> Striving to better, oft we mar what's well.
> GONERIL. Nay then—
> ALBANY. Well, well; th' event. (1.4.342–6)

Albany obviously does not agree with Goneril. The exchange reveals their emerging political, let alone conjugal conflict and marks the beginning of events that will lead to the breakup of their marriage. At this point, Goneril still pays lip service to Albany's role as her husband and master of the house, perhaps mindful of prevailing notions of the duties of a wife and good household governance, such as the ones presented in Leon Battista Alberti's *Della Famiglia*: "The woman, as she remains locked up at home, should watch over things by staying at her post, by diligent care and watchfulness. The man should guard the woman, the house, and his family and country, but not by sitting still."[64] Mark Wigley suggests that Alberti opposes "male mobility in the exterior to female stasis in the interior," a belief in consonance with Xenophon's ideas in *Oeconomicus*. According to the ancient writer, architecture shapes and maintains established gender roles.[65] As housewife, Goneril relies on expected roles to assert her authority, first in the management of her house; in the process, however, she extrapolates that role as she rebels against her father and then her husband. Familial relationships fall apart and, as Diane Elizabeth Dreher writes, these failed relationships demonstrate "the savagery to which human life would descend without essential bonds of love and respect."[66]

---

64 Leon Battista Alberti, Della Famiglia, trans. Renée Neu Watkins, *The Family in Renaissance Florence* (Columbia: University of South Carolina Press, 1969), 3.207; quoted in Wigley 334.

65 Wigley 334. In his *A Priest to the Temple* or, *The Country Parson His Character, &c.* (1632), George Herbert prescribes fixed roles in a religious household of a generation later. He argues that a parson must be "very exact in the governing of his house, making it a copy and model for his Parish," whose wife must be religious and she has clear responsibilities in the religious education of the children, in being a nurse capable of "curing, and healing of all wounds and sores with her own hands," and finally, in "providing for her family in such sort, as that neither they want a competent sustentation, nor her husband is brought in debt" (p. 238). See *The Works of George Herbert*, (ed.) F.E. Hutchinson (Oxford: Clarendon Press, 1959) 238.

66 Diane Elizabeth Dreher, *Domination & Defiance: Fathers and Daughters in Shakespeare* (Lexington: University Press of Kentucky, 1986) 104.

Regan's House

No scenes in *King Lear* are set in or near Regan and Cornwall's castle. The action in Act II and parts of Act III moves away from Goneril's to Gloucester's house and to other spaces, such as the outdoors and the hovel. Before I discuss Gloucester's house, however, I would like to focus on Regan's house, which although not represented, serves an important symbolic function in the play. Lear's intention to go to Regan and Cornwall's house and Edgar's apparent plot against his father bring about a double crisis. Therefore, most of the characters convene under Gloucester's roof. The house of Gloucester and the castle of Regan and Cornwall are symbolically, politically, and after a while even sexually connected, when the widowed Regan decides to marry her lover Edmund; it is, therefore, difficult to talk about one without mentioning the other. Gloucester makes clear the nature of his alliance to the Duke of Cornwall, when he announces the visit of his "worthy arch and patron" (2.1.59) and indicates that he will launch a search for Edgar by his patron's ducal authority. Cornwall refers to Gloucester as his "noble friend" (86), suggesting some degree of intimacy. Likewise, Regan speaks of Gloucester as an intimate in her father's house, with Lear serving as Edgar's godfather (91–2). Their arrival follows shortly at the heels of Edgar's apparent conspiracy and sudden escape; as friends, Cornwall and Regan can give the support that Gloucester needs.

Cornwall and Regan's journey from their house to Gloucester's comes out of the blue. It also acquires important meaning. At the beginning of Act II, scene 1, Edmund learns from Curan of the imminent visit and possible war between Cornwall and Albany. To Edgar, Edmund suggests that Cornwall and Regan may suspect Edgar of conspiring with Albany; hence the sudden visit. Cornwall and Regan leave behind a locked empty house, an image with which they become increasingly associated. After Lear's, theirs is the second house that is emptied out and kept out of sight. Regan suggests that, having heard of Goneril's troubles with Lear, she and Cornwall decided to abandon their house, so that if Lear and his retinue "come to sojourn at my house, / I'll not be there" (2.1.103–4). To Gloucester, she explains that they have decided to visit him, "Thus out of season, threading dark-eyed night," with a double purpose—to comfort Gloucester in his hour of need and to seek his advice on her father's troublesome behavior: "Our good old friend, / Lay comforts to your bosom, and bestow / Your needful counsel to our businesses, / Which craves the instant use" (2.1.126–9).

Two other accounts reconstruct unrepresented events at Regan and Cornwall's house. Lear remarks, "'tis strange that they [Regan and Cornwall] should so depart from home, / And not send back my messenger" (2.4.1–2); to which the Gentleman adds that the night before there was no indication that the duke and the duchess intended to travel. Kent, disguised as Caius, tells Lear that something even stranger occurred when he, arriving at their "home," delivered Lear's letters to Regan, only to be rudely interrupted by Oswald bearing letters from Goneril. Cornwall and Regan, he adds, promptly read these letters, and "on whose contents / They summoned up their meiny, straight took horse" (2.4.33–4), and left Kent waiting for an answer. The *OED* defines the archaic "meinie" (OF. *Meyné*, *mesnie*, from L. *mansionata*, *mansionem* [whence French *maison*]) as follows: a family; household; a body of retainers and dependents; a retinue; a multitude of persons; a herd, drove, or flock of animals. Like the herd of animals displaced by a forest fire in Piero di Cosimo's painting that I discussed earlier, the entire household has picked up and left, clearing the whole estate. After the initial discussion of Regan's abode and the evasive action that Regan and Cornwall took to avoid receiving Lear, the castle or house in Cornwall, like Lear's dwelling place, fades from the characters' consciousness. Thus, Regan's confrontation with Lear and the conflict between Kent and Oswald over the insolent interruption remains to be resolved somewhere else; namely in Gloucester's house, which becomes the site of decisive events in the play. In the meantime, like Lear's castle, Regan's house has been abandoned—at least temporarily—by its occupants. Once again, disrupted and uprooted, another group has to abandon their house and seek refuge somewhere else.

Gloucester's House

As a symbolic substitute for Lear's, Gloucester's house is the stage upon which various conflicts play out. Architecture mingles with familial and political conflicts. The house becomes a symbol for the radical reshuffling of the social order in the play. Gaston Bachelard writes, "A house constitutes a body of images that give mankind proofs or illusions of stability. We are constantly re-imagining its reality."[67] In Gloucester's house, various characters re-imagine fundamental social and cultural relations; it is the location, where "Outside and inside form a dialectic of division."[68] In this dialectic, as in *King Lear*, the door plays an important role in the symbolic realm that envelops our sense of physical space, or in Bachelard's formulation, one of the primal images: "If one were to give an account of all the doors one has closed and opened, of all the doors one would like to re-open, one would have to tell the story of one's entire life."[69]

Here, other characters discard their former selves and reinvent themselves in a new world order based on notions of an upside-down world, which reverses customary relations. As I have written elsewhere of *A Midsummer Night's Dream*, "Symbolic inversion projects alternatives to the patriarchal order. Through images of inversion, Shakespeare depicts a world that seems uncertain about is boundaries."[70] In Lear's dominion, as in Theseus's, the focus of cultural, political, and gender relations oscillates between the cultural center, represented by Lear's patriarchal authority, and a marginal world, embodied by upside-down images

---

67 Bachelard 17.

68 Bachelard 211.

69 Bachelard 224.

70 Sousa, *Cross-cultural Encounters*, 21.

and situations.[71] Again, as I have discussed elsewhere, Balthasar Gracian of the Society of Jesus argues in *El Criticon* (1651): "the things of this world can be truly perceived only by looking at them backwards."[72] Sixteenth-century woodcuts, such as the Venetian *Il Mondo Alla Riversa* (c. 1560s) and a Dutch one by Ewout Muller, depict images of a cart going before a horse, women going to war while the men stay home and spin, ships traveling on land, and a client telling the fortune of a gypsy fortune-teller.[73] Consequently, "Images of the world turned upside down, where nothing is as it seems, present an oppositional view of culture, invert and subvert power relations, and permit the artist to reconfigure the imaginary cultural map."[74] Barbara A. Babcock defines "symbolic inversion" as "any act of expressive behavior which inverts, contradicts, abrogates, or in some fashion presents an alternative to commonly held cultural codes, values, and norms, be they linguistic, literary or artistic, religious, or social and political."[75] I suggest that symbolic inversion, at first centered in Gloucester's house, spreads and scatters outward to other areas of experience. In Gloucester's house, the legitimate and illegitimate sons trade positions; and hospitable practices stand on their head when Regan and Albany arrive as Gloucester's guest, but take over the house.

An outsider in his own father's house, Edmund re-imagines the reality of this house; and he sets out to displace Edgar and thereby take possession of the lands and of Gloucester's love:

> Well, then,
> Legitimate Edgar, I must have your land,
> Our father's love is to the bastard Edmund
> As to th' legitimate. Fine word, "legitimate,"
> Well, my legitimate, if this letter speed,
> And my intention thrive, Edmund the base
> Shall top th' legitimate. I grow, I prosper,
> Now, gods, stand up for bastards. (1.2.15–22)

Edmund finds an opening brought about by an apparent change in Gloucester's affective domain. To Kent, Gloucester admits: "I have so often blushed to acknowledge him that now I am brazed to't" (1.1.9–10), although he has of course sent Edmund away for nine years. The change may be rooted in a new sense of equality that the two sons seem to have achieved in Gloucester's heart:

---

71 This sentence is recast almost verbatim from Sousa, *Cross-cultural Encounters*, 21.

72 See Sousa, *Cross-cultural Encounters*, 11.

73 See Sousa, *Cross-cultural Encounters*, 11.

74 Sousa, *Cross-cultural Encounters*, 11.

75 Barbara A. Babcock, (ed.), *The Reversible World: Symbolic Inversion in Art and Society* (Ithaca, NY: Cornell University Press, 1991), p. 13. Of interest here also is Peter Stallybrass, "The World Turned Upside Down: Inversion, Gender and the State," in Valerie Wayne edition, *The Matter of Difference: Materialist Feminist Criticism of Shakespeare* (Ithaca, NY: Cornell University Press, 1991) 201–20.

> But I have a son, sir, by order of law, some year elder than this who yet is no dearer in my account: though this knave came something saucily to the world before he was sent for, yet was his mother fair, there was good sport at his making, and the whoreson must be acknowledged. (18–23)

Despite the intention to acknowledge his illegitimate son and the expression of equality in love, Gloucester seems still of two minds, referring to Edmund as "whoreson" and suggesting that Edmund must soon depart again. Edmund speaks of his "lodging" (1.2.168) rather than perhaps more permanent quarters at or near his father's house.

As an outsider and social outcast, he seeks to undo "the plague of custom" that defines legitimate and illegitimate, noble and base, although "in the lusty stealth of nature," both legitimate and illegitimate children are equally conceived "within a dull, stale, tired bed" (12; 13).

In his closet, the private chambers, Edmund explains to his gullible father that Edgar has rebelled against "the oppression of aged tyranny" and seeks to undermine the "policy and reverence of age": "But I have heard him oft maintain it to be fit that, sons at perfect age, and fathers declined, the father should be as ward to the son, and the son manage his revenue" (73–7). Liberated from moral constraints, Edmund reveals a new approach to life: "Let me, if not by birth, have lands by wit; / All with me's meet that I can fashion fit" (181–2). Thus, he seeks to reverse the roles of insider and outsider with Edgar. He opens a door for himself to Gloucester's house, and closes another to Edgar. He succeeds so thoroughly that Gloucester, incensed at Edgar's presumed betrayal, says, "All ports I'll bar" (2.1.80) to his legitimate son; in other words, he will shut seaports and town gates, so that Edgar cannot escape and will be brought to justice. When Edgar reemerges disguised as a homeless madman in II.3, he confronts a new reality of overwhelming patriarchal surveillance: "No port is free, no place / That guard and most unusual vigilance / Does not attend my taking" (3–5). To escape, he must become "nothing," the markers of his identity having been utterly removed, freeing himself from the architecture of his father's house. Gloucester's house becomes a veritable upside-down world, which also reverses the roles of outsider and insider in other ways. Regan and Cornwall enter the house as friends, patrons, and guests of Gloucester; however, they take over the house, reshaping its function and reconfiguring familial and social relations.

William Vaughn, in *The Golden-grove, moralized in three books* (1600), defines hospitality as "the chiefest point of humanity, which an household can show, not only unto his friends, but also unto strangers & wayfaring men."[76] Later in the seventeenth century, George Wheler, in *The Protestant Monastery* (1698), refers to hospitality as "a liberal entertainment of all sorts of men, at one's house,

---

[76] William Vaughn, in *The Golden-grove, moralized in three books* (London, 1600), sig. P6r, quoted in Daryl W. Palmer, *Hospitable Performances: Dramatic Genre and Cultural Practices in Early Modern England* (West Lafayette, IN: Purdue University Press, 1992) 1.

whether neighbors or strangers, with kindness, especially with meat, drink, and lodgings."[77] In *Hospitable Performances*, Daryl Palmer explains the profound and intricate relations centered on hospitable practices in the early modern period: "hospitality existed as a code of exchange between competing, often conflicting, orders of society: between the poor and the rich, noble and plebeian, noble and noble, male and female, patriarch and family, family and society, English and non-English, Anglican and Puritan."[78] In this context then, Shakespeare dramatizes the breakdown of hospitality in Gloucester's house as a measure of the large array of inversion that the characters in this tragedy experience.

Regan and Cornwall arrive at Gloucester's house as guests, friends, and patrons; before long, however, they take over the management of the house and become Gloucester's hosts, enemies, jailors, and torturers. As Woodbridge writes, "Hospitality violations abound. The Cornwalls are both poor guests and poor hosts."[79] Their transformation from guest to host and from host to guest occurs quickly and decisively in three events: the punishment of Kent, the barring of the door to Lear, and the blinding of Gloucester and barring the door of Gloucester's house to Gloucester himself. All three episodes center on the reversal of the function of the house.

Oswald's arrival at Gloucester's house in 2.2 and the exchange between Oswald and Kent start out as customary hospitable practices only to deteriorate quickly into insults and a row:

> OSWALD. Good dawning to thee, friend. Art of this house?
> KENT. Ay.
> OSWALD. Where may we set out horses?
> KENT. I' th' mire.
> OSWALD. Pritee, if thou lov'st me, tell me.
> KENT. I love thee not.
> OSWALD. Why then, I care not for thee. (1–7)

Having traveled all night to deliver Goneril's letters, Oswald seeks accommodation for himself and his horses. Oswald's question, "Art of this house?" underscores the extent to which Gloucester's house defines the boundaries of who belongs and who doesn't. Kent assumes that he is of this house and that those in the house will endorse his verbal and physical assault on the villainous Oswald. The brawl between Kent and Oswald rouses the house. Edmund parts the combatants (2.2.41); and Gloucester tries to take charge: "Weapons? Arms? What's the matter here?" (44). Instead, Cornwall, as the highest-ranking member of the nobility present, orders: "Keep peace, upon your lives. He dies that strikes again" (2.2.45–6). As Oswald indicates, Kent's earlier assault on him "got praises of the king" (118). Cornwall orders punishment for Kent: "Fetch forth the stocks! / You stubborn

---

77 George Wheler, in *The Protestant Monastery* (1698) 173, quoted in Palmer 1.

78 Palmer 4.

79 Woodbridge, *Vagrancy, Homelessness, and English Renaissance Literature*, 207.

ancient knave, you reverent braggart, / We'll teach you" (2.2.123–5). Gloucester finds the punishment unbecoming for a follower of the king, since it is a form of "low correction" for "the most common trespasses" committed by the "basest and contemnèd'st wretches" (2.2.139–47). Regan brushes aside his concerns, and Gloucester himself looks to appease Cornwall with entreaties on Kent's behalf. In his humiliating punishment, Kent hopes that Lear may never see this "shameful lodging" (172).

Later on, inside Gloucester's house, Cornwall nurses his "fiery quality," unmoved and fixed in his course. He and Regan refuse to come out. Outside the house, Lear notes with dismay and anger the shameful punishment of his servant and threatens to disturb the peace: "Bid them come forth and hear me, / Or at their chamber door I'll beat the drum / Till it cry sleep to death" (2.4.116–17). When Regan and Cornwall do come out from inside Gloucester's house and Goneril arrives, the two sisters present a united front against Lear. For the first time, Lear seems to grasp his dire situation. Addressing Regan, he begs for the bare necessities of life: "On my knees I beg / That you'll vouchsafe me raiment, bed, and food" (153–4). Regan, however, promptly dismisses his gesture as "unsightly tricks" (155). Regan points out that, being away from her own home, she is "out of that provision / Which shall be needful for your entertainment" (204–5), and encourages him to seek help from Goneril. Lear objects (206–8). In turn, Regan sides with Goneril, warning that a household cannot properly function under "two commands" (241). Cornwall and Regan agree to go back into the house, leaving Lear to meet his fate outdoors (2.4.288–9). Regan orders the doors closed (307–9) to her father and throws him into the storm. Once again, the barring of the door to Lear epitomizes the struggle for control over and access to a house.

In Act III, Gloucester tries to provide a bridge between insider and outsider. In scene 3, he laments the "unnatural dealing" of Cornwall and Regan, as he explains to Edmund: "When I desired their leave that I might pity him [Lear], they took from me the use of mine own house, charged me on pain of perpetual displeasure neither to speak to him, entreat for him, or any way sustain him" (3.3.1–6). Edmund characterizes the behavior of the usurpers of the house as "most savage and unnatural" (7), only to confess his true belief as soon as Gloucester exits: "The younger rises when the old doth fall" (24). In the next scene, against the express command of Cornwall and Regan, Gloucester seeks Lear out and entreats Lear to "go in with me" (146). He knows that he is risking his life, in helping Lear both by being in communication with Cordelia and by offering to assist Lear:

> My duty cannot suffer
> I obey in all your daughters' hard commands.
> Though their injunction be to bar my doors
> And let this tyrannous night take hold upon you,
> Yet have I ventured to come seek you out
> And bring you where both fire and food is ready. (3.4.146–51).

If not in Gloucester's house, then perhaps they can find shelter in a hovel and weather the storm. The battle lines harden; they center on control of Gloucester's house, with Cornwall vouching revenge on Gloucester ere he departs from this house (3.5.1–2). In fact, the revenge will come in scene 7, when Regan and Cornwall arrest, interrogate, torture, and mutilate their host. Gloucester reminds them of their special status in his house: "Good my friends, consider / You are my guests" (30–31). Not without irony, Gloucester learns, a bit too late, that Edmund has betrayed him: "O my follies! Then Edgar was abused" (92). Regan and Cornwall thrust Gloucester out of his own house, and bar the door to him, as they had done to Lear. Thus Kent, Cordelia, Edgar, Lear, and finally Gloucester—one by one—experience the loss of their house, face exile or abandonment, and must seek refuge wherever they can find it. The repeated barring of doors becomes a powerful symbol for the fierce battle for control of domestic space.

In her review of Richard Eyre's 1998 film adaptation of the play, starring Ian Holm in the title role, Ariel Swartley writes: "Indeed, to think of Lear is, almost universally, to think of a man outdoors and dwarfed by nature."[80] But the play juxtaposes indoors and outdoors, inside and outside, house and homelessness. For the Elizabethans, the household was a prototype for and should function as a perfect commonwealth. In *A Preparative to Marriage* (1591), Henry Smith advises his readers: "As a kingdom cannot stand if it be divided, so a house cannot stand if it be divided, for strife is like fire which leaves nothing but dust and smoke and ashes behind it."[81] As Catherine Richardson remarks, writers of the period often use images of the house to embody and describe human relationships, and bodily images to describe the house, "merging the categories of 'body' and 'house' in peculiar ways."[82] The collapse of the old order associated with Lear's or Gloucester's house makes room for new visions of the house and household relations, especially as conceived by Goneril and Regan; it also lays bare the vast expanses of Lear's kingdom.

"Let copulation thrive": Women and the Management of the House

The scenes in Goneril's and later in Gloucester's house suggest that both Goneril and Regan feel empowered by their father's abdication of his authority, distribution of his wealth, and erratic behavior. Each, however, follows a different path in her marriage. As we have seen, Goneril makes at first tactful but eventually forceful attempts to control her husband and to assert her own authority over her house and household. Regan forges a partnership with her husband first against her father and eventually against Gloucester. Like Macbeth and Lady Macbeth, Regan and Cornwall have a cruel, criminal mind, and act together in several ways: they abandon their house, travel to Gloucester's, put Kent in the stocks, take over

80 Ariel Swartley, "Shakespeare, and the Wilds Found Indoors," *The New York Times*, 4 October, 1998, 45.

81 Henry Smith, A Preparative to Marriage (London, 1590); rpt. in Orlin, Elizabethan Households, 40. See also discussion of this matter in Comensoli 16–24.

82 Richardson 45.

Gloucester's house, band together against Gloucester, and support and advance Edmund and his cause. They join forces to gouge out Gloucester's eyes and throw their old ally out into the cold. Unlike Goneril and Albany, Regan and Cornwall work together, not at cross purposes. Cornwall, gouging Gloucester's second eye, receives a fatal wound from a servant. His death creates a rift between Goneril and Regan. Empowered by her new widowed state, Regan quickly moves to claim Edmund for herself. Goneril, however, has already given up on her mild-tempered, "milk-livered" husband, and expects to develop an adulterous relationship with Edmund. The two sisters vie for Edmund's love and become deadly enemies. They embody quite different approaches to household management, marital relations, and sexual freedom.

In the anonymous *King Leir*, Gonorill and Ragan never emerge as sexual beings. Upon their military defeat at the end of the play, they retreat to their home territories with their husbands, Cambria and Cornwall, respectively, as Cornwall summarizes the situation: "The day is lost, our friends do all revolt, / And joyne against us with the adverse part: / There is no meanes of safety but by flight, / And therefore ile to Cornwall with my Queene" (Sc. 31). Likewise, Cambria, Gonorill's husband, concludes, referring to Mumford: "I thinke, there is a devil in the Campe hath haunted me to day: he hath so tyred me, that in a maner I can fight no more," and takes to flight.[83] In Shakespeare's play, however, Edmund's presence poisons not only the relationship between the two sisters, Regan and Goneril, but also Goneril and Albany's marriage. Further, Shakespeare depicts the awakening of Regan and Goneril as sexual beings. A specific moment encapsulates the two daughters' blossoming sexual desire. In Act V, scene 1, Regan sounds Edmund on his feelings for Goneril: "Do you love my sister?" (9). When he prevaricates in his answer—"In honored love"—Regan cuts to the chase and asks point blank: "But have you never found my brother's way / To the forfended place?" (10–11). "Forfended place," like the word "nothing" in its slang usage in Shakespeare's time, becomes a euphemism for female genitalia and in *King Lear* for the force that fills the void left by the dismantling of Lear's patriarchal hold on his family and on his country. Female sexuality becomes a strong distinctive force rivaling patriarchal power.

Goneril's sexual desire awakens relatively early. Goneril takes a dislike to her "mild husband" and disdains "the cowish terror of his spirit," and also develops an admiration for Edmund's daring conduct. At home, she knows that she must defer to the master of the house: "I must change names at home, and give the distaff / Into my husband's hands" (4.2.17–18). She notes "the difference of man and man"; to Edmund, she pledges her "woman's service," while Albany, "my fool usurps my body" (4.2.26–8).

The Quarto text contains the announcement of the death of the Duke of Cornwall: "[he was] slain by his servant, going to put out / The other eye of Gloucester" (4.2.71–3). As a widow, now Regan can marry Edmund, which adds

83 Bullough 7: 401.

to the rivalry between Goneril and Regan. Goneril goes so far as to write a letter to Edmund, encouraging him to kill Albany, because if Albany returns home alive: "Then am I the prisoner, and his bed my jail; from the loathed warmth whereof deliver me, and supply the place for your labor" (4.6.265–7). Having sworn his love to Goneril and Regan, Edmund faces a dilemma as to whether he should have only one of the sisters or enjoy both (5.1.56–70). Finally, each sister claims Edmund for herself. As a widow, Regan asserts her sovereignty over her destiny: "In my rights / By me invested, he compeers the best" (5.3.70–71), and attempts to create him her "lord and master" (79). When confronted with evidence of treason and murder conspiracy, Goneril defies her husband and the law: "the laws are mine, not thine, / Who can arraign me for't" (5.3.160–61). This suggests that with her poisoning of Regan and the defeat of the forces of Cordelia and Lear, she is hoping to gain control not only as master of her own house but also to claim sovereignty as queen in her own right.

Thus the dismantling of Lear's home, Edmund's ascendancy, and a collapse of patriarchal control create a power vacuum, which Goneril and Regan try to fill. As Gloucester feels his way to Dover and Lear crosses over to a state of homelessness and insanity, the two sisters discover a new sense of sexual liberation and of freedom from patriarchal mores. Lear will never again see the inside of a house, wandering through the heath, seeking refuge in a hovel, recovering in a tent on the battlefield, and finally, defeated on the battlefield, being sent to jail. Away from the castles, palaces, and country houses, he journeys into the realm of poverty. Homelessness looms large in the consciousness of the characters, as they struggle for survival. Shakespeare takes the loss of the house to its logical consequence: a state of "houseless poverty" and a struggle for survival, which become central concerns in Act II and parts of IV, before war breaks out and differences are to be settled on the battlefield.

The Hovel and Survival Situations

In survival situations, contemporary survival guides instruct, one should look for shelter or build a makeshift shelter at least two hours before sunset. In a harsh, hostile environment, warns one of such guides, "your need for shelter may take precedence over your need for food, possibly even your need for water."[84] Prolonged exposure to cold temperatures leads to fatigue, exhaustion, and a passive attitude. The guide adds:

> A shelter can protect you from the sun, insects, wind, rain, snow, hot or cold temperatures, and enemy observation. It can give you a feeling of well being; it can help you maintain your will to survive.[85]

---

[84] United States Department of the Army, *U. S. Army Survival Manual* (New York: Dorset Press, 1991) 8–1.

[85] *U.S. Army Survival Manual* 8–1.

Types of improvised shelters include a poncho tent; parachute tepee; a "lean-to" built out of branches, palm leaves, and rope or vine; a so-called swamp bed; a hammock; a tree-pit or beach-shade; and a cave.[86] The *SAS Survival Handbook* adds an encouraging note, if the survival situation derives from the destruction of one's house: "In a domestic situation there is likely to be shelter, unless it has been totally destroyed, or the area has become a danger zone and evacuation is imperative."[87] Such guides provide an analogy for the survival conditions that the characters in *King Lear* face, as they, wandering in the wilds, seek shelter in a hovel or wherever they find it.

The word "hovel" occurs four times as a noun and once as a verb in Shakespeare, all in *King Lear*. A "hovel" means, of course, an open shed used as a storage place for grain or tools or as a shed for cattle (*OED*). It also means a miserable dwelling-place or a shed used as a human habitation (*OED*). In the Quarto text, Cordelia employs it as a verb to express her dismay at Lear's makeshift accommodation in the stormy night: "was thou fain, poor father, / To hovel thee with swine and rogues forlorn / In short and musty straw?" (4.7.39–41). The distinctively Brazilian Portuguese word *tapera*, somewhat synonymous with hovel but without the connotation of shed, derives from Tupi-Guarani *ta 'pera* (*tawa*, "pueblo"; *pwera,* "that which has been").[88] The Portuguese word refers to the ruins of an abandoned abode, previously used exclusively for human habitation but now reclaimed by vegetation and wildlife. *Tapera* bears the intense spectral markers of its mysterious late occupants and the *ubi sunt* of their disappearance. It embodies a human narrative; it tells a human story. In *King Lear*, the hovel will serve as a temporary, intermediary habitation before Lear and others are thrust into the vast empty countryside; but it is also *pwera*, an emblem of that which is no more.

In Act II, scene 4, blinded by rage, Lear storms out of Gloucester's house into the desolate countryside in the dark, stormy night. Cornwall seconds Regan's order to Gloucester that the doors to the house be shut close: "Shut up your doors, my lord; 'tis a wild night. / My Regan counsels well. Come out o' th' storm" (308–9). Act III juxtaposes and contrasts Gloucester's sturdy, comfortable house and the precarious, fragile, miserable hovel where Kent, the Fool, Lear, and Edgar seek refuge from the storm. Bachelard underscores the extent to which we depend on the house for our sense of security, safety, and protection: "The house does not tremble, however, when thunder rolls … In our houses set close one up against the other, we are less afraid."[89] Even a hut still embodies "the house's powers of protection

---

86 For an explanation of these terms and precise instructions on how to construct these improvised shelters, see *U.S. Army Survival Manual* 8–1. For most of these, instructions assume that you have at least a good knife with you.

87 *SAS Survival Handbook 560.*

88 Antônio Houaiss, Mauro de Salles Villar, and Francisco Manoel de Mello Franco, *Dicionário Houaiss da Língua Portuguesa* (Rio de Janeiro: Editora Objetiva Ltda., 2001).

89 Bachelard, *Poetics of Space*, 27.

against the forces that besiege it."[90] But in Act III, house and hovel trade and invert functions. The house, transformed by the cruel and harsh guests who take it over, becomes, in Kent's description, the "hard house," in fact "harder than the stones whereof 'tis raised" (3.1.63–4). Displaying "scanted," deficient courtesy, the house has denied Kent entrance (66–7). The hovel enters the characters' consciousness when Kent promises bareheaded Lear, nursing "heart-struck injuries" (3.1.17): "Gracious my lord, hard by here is a hovel; / Some friendship will it lend you gainst the tempest" (3.2.61–2). The house, despite its stone walls and heavy doors and gates, offers no security; whereas the hovel, lacking proper doors and walls, feels safe and welcoming. One represents the dangers of human cruelty; the other, warmth, safety, and protection from the "the tyranny of the open night" (3.4.2).

The refugees from the house are in a survival situation. Shakespeare carefully establishes the unusually inclement spell of weather. The storm resembles the hurricanes or tropical storms that form off the coast of Africa, course toward the Caribbean, develop a rotation pattern, wreak havoc in North America or in Bermuda, and then, moving in a northeasterly-easterly direction and being recharged by the warm waters of the Gulf Stream, still retain gale force winds when they make landfall in England. The first sounds of the storm appear in a stage direction, "*Storm and tempest*" (2.4.283), just before Lear, the Fool, Kent, and Gloucester go off into the darkness of the night. Cornwall calls attention to the storm, "Let us withdraw; 'twill be a storm," and Regan rationalizes her own cruelty, "This house is little: the old man and's people / Cannot be well bestowed" (187–9). In III.1, Kent and the Gentleman connect "foul weather" to Lear's mind—"One minded like the weather, most unquietly"(1–2); they also speculate about "division," still covered by "mutual cunning" and not yet open warfare, between Albany and Cornwall.

An urgent survival situation becomes apparent in Act III, scene 2. Fuming with rage, Lear wanders about with the Fool and, like a mad conjurer or magician,[91] commands the storm to rip the world apart: "Blow, winds, and crack your cheeks! Rage, blow! / You cataracts and harricanoes, spout / Till you have drenched our steeples, drowned the cocks" (1–3). The rest of the speech refers to "sulph'rous and thought-executing fires," "oak-cleaving thunderbolts," "all-shaking thunder"—all strong enough to "crack nature's molds," and spill "all germens," all seeds, that generate "ingrateful man." Shakespeare describes thunder and lightning as "heaven's artillery" (*Shrew*, 1.2.205), reflecting contemporary meteorological theories and punning on the usual method, which used canon balls, gunpowder, and fireworks to produce special theatrical effects in the "heavens" of the public playhouses.[92] The title page of *Looke Up and See Wonders* (1628) depicts

[90] Bachelard, *Poetics of Space*, 37.

[91] Philip Butterworth, *Magic on the Early English Stage* (Cambridge: Cambridge University Press, 2005), offers a fascinating study of magic tricks on the early stage.

[92] See Philip Butterworth, *Theatre of Fire: Special Effects in Early English and Scottish Theatre* (London: Society for Theatre Research, 1998).

heavenly artillery and drums and armies battling in the sky.[93] Meteorologists and laypersons were, of course, familiar with various theories of the origins of these meteorological phenomena and the destructive power of lightning, which burnt the steeples of St Paul's Cathedral in 1561 and 1563.[94] Pierre de La Primaudaye, in *The French Academie* (1601), describes the effects of lightning on the human body and on the bodies of animals: "Those which are stroken therewith, be they men or beasts, remain all consumed within, as if their flesh, sinewes, and bones were altogither molten within their skin, if remayning sound & whole, as if they had no harme."[95] In ancient Greece, Zeus was believed to use, as instruments of his wrath, thunderbolts and lightning, which the Cyclops manufactured in Vulcan's underground forges.[96] In *King Lear*, the storm, acquiring an anthropomorphic dimension, blends the tumultuous elements and Lear's wrath. The storm in the mind and the meteorological phenomenon resonate in each other's domains—rumbling, spitting, and spouting their "horrible pleasure" (19).

In such a night, the need for shelter takes precedence, despite Lear's earlier furious resolution, "No, rather I abjure all roofs, and choose / To wage against the enmity o' th' air" (2.4.207–8). The Gentleman intuits that the cub-drawn bear chooses to "couch," go hungry, and the lion and the "belly-pinchèd wolf" to keep their furs dry rather than venture forth in the cold rain (3.1.12–14). Kent, later, comments that "Things that love night, / Love not such nights as these. The wrathful skies / Gallow the very wanderers of the dark / And make them keep their caves" (3.2.42–3). As even Lear seems aware, "this contentious storm / Invades us to the skin" (3.4.8–9). Chilled to the bone, Kent, Lear, the Fool, and Gloucester stand at the entrance of the hovel, where Tom o'Bedlam has already taken refuge, and try to figure out what to do next. Gloucester grumbles about his guests having taken "the use" of his own house (3.3.3).

Later, returning from his house, where he had gone to fetch fire, Gloucester approaches the hovel. The Fool takes him from a distance as "a little fire in a wild field," as if he were "a walking fire," a terrifying apparition (3.4.111–13). He still hopes to persuade Lear to return to the house, "where both fire and food is ready" (151). The word "enter," used several times in this scene, suggests their trepidation in entering such a miserable abode. Only when Edgar as Tom o'Bedlam complains, "Tom's acold," does Gloucester respond—"In fellow, there, into th'hovel; keep thee warm" (3.4.174). The hovel is good enough for a beggar but of course not for a king. Lear, however, sensibly orders: "Come, let's in all" (175). The English mineralogist, John Mawe (1766–1829), in poor health, while traveling on horseback to the Diamond District in the Brazilian highlands in the early nineteenth-century, stayed in many a makeshift shelter and *taperas*.

93 S.K. Heninger, Jr. *A Handbook of Renaissance Meteorology* (Durham, NC: Duke University Press, 1960; rpt. New York: Greenwood Press, 1968) 77.

94 Heninger, 81n.

95 Qtd. in Heninger, 79.

96 Heninger, 86.

Upon arrival at a particularly dismal abode, and after an arduous day's journey, he concludes: "These were miserable accommodations; but sleep knows little distinction between the hovel and the palace, and a man thoroughly disposed may enjoy it as soundly in one as in the other."[97] Lear, momentarily practical-minded, would concur: "The art of our necessities is strange, / And can make vile things precious" (3.3.71–2). In Scene 6, inside the hovel, Gloucester also agrees that "here it is better than the open air," and promises to smuggle out of his usurped house whatever additional "comfort[s]" he can (1–2).

Scenes 6 and 7 juxtapose and compare inside the hovel and inside Gloucester's house. In the hovel, Edgar imagines Nero angling in the lake of darkness. Lear sees red burning spits and hears hissing. At one time, he sees and hears his three little dogs, Tray, Blanch, and Sweetheart, bark. At another, Edgar imagines packs of chasing, barking, biting mastiffs, greyhounds, mongrels, spaniels, and hounds. In his house, not far away, Gloucester confronts Regan and Cornwall, and imagines Regan and Goneril, as hellhounds, using their "cruel nails" to pluck out Lear's eyes and their "boarish fangs" to bite into their father's flesh (3.7.57–9). He seems to anticipate, perhaps he even unwittingly inspires, the torture, mutilation, and cruelty his guests intend for him; for Cornwall and Regan blind Gloucester, leaving him "all dark and comfortless" (86), and eject him from his own house, so that, like a dog, he has to "smell / His way to Dover" (3.7.94–5). In the Folio text, the scene ends when Cornwall asks Regan to "turn out that eyeless villain" and wants her help for he has received "a hurt," in fact a mortal wound, from an anonymous First Servant who fought and sacrificed his own life to save Gloucester's eye. Gloucester receives no comfort. In the Quarto text, however, two anonymous servants apply flax and whites of eggs to Gloucester's wounds, the prescribed medical treatment for injuries to the eye,[98] and will seek a Bedlam beggar to guide the old earl about. In contrast, the hovel affords Lear enough comfort in an imaginary bed: "Make no noise, make no noise; draw the curtains. / So, so. We'll go to supper i' th' morning" (3.6.82–3). Also, in the quarto text, Edgar takes comfort that his misery has found company: "Who alone suffers suffers most i' th' mind" (3.6.103). He does not know, of course, that his father, in the Folio text, suffers utterly alone in body and mind.

Linda Woodbridge aptly underscores that the scenes set near or in the hovel draw attention to the plight of the poor, homelessness and questions of social justice.[99] In the process, the play sheds light on endemic poverty, abject homelessness, and pervasive neglect in Lear's kingdom. I want, however, to place these issues in the

---

[97] John Mawe, *Travels in the Interior of Brazil; particularly in The Gold and Diamond Districts of That Country* (London, 1816) 165. See also H.S. Torrens, 'Mawe, John (1766–1829)', *Oxford Dictionary of National Biography* (Oxford: Oxford University Press, 2004).

[98] David M. Bergeron, "King Lear and John Hall's Casebook," *Shakespeare Quarterly* 23 (1972): 206–7.

[99] Woodbridge, *Vagrancy, Homelessness, and English Renaissance Literature*, 212–27.

context of survival situations. What had begun in Lear's palace continues under Gloucester's roof. In this house, extraordinary upheaval, dislocation, and uprooting occur and take shape, as one by one Kent, Cordelia, the Fool, Lear, Edgar, and Gloucester leave their houses and, with the exception of Cordelia, have no place to go. Animals instinctively seek shelter; human beings need a roof over their heads, whether in a hovel, a hut, a cave, a lean-to, or a tree-pit. They need shelter from the "extremity of the skies," as Lear states at the sight of the "uncovered," begrimed, mortified body of Tom o'Bedlam:

> Is man no more than this? Consider him well. Thou ow'st the worm no silk, the beast no hide, the sheep no wool, the cat no perfume. Ha! Here's three on's are sophisticated. Thou art the thing itself: unaccommodated man is no more but a poor, bare, forked animal as thou art. (3.4.103–8)

The Gospel writer refers to the great divide Christians face: "And beside all this, between us and you there is a great gulf fixed: so that they which would pass from hence to you cannot; neither can they pass to us, that would come from thence" (Luke 16:26).[100] In the pre-Christian world of this play, where Christian imagery crops up with startling frequency, the dismantling of Lear's patriarchal hegemony lays bare the great gulf between *potens* and *pauper*, rich and poor, powerful and powerless, young and old, male and female. The presence of the house as a symbol of shelter, security, stability, and continuity recedes from view; in its place, the play offers vast expanses of landscape, often without houses, and a struggle for survival.

Shakespeare explores the centrality of the house to how the characters define and see themselves; naturally, this also reveals the extent to which pervasive poverty and homelessness intertwine with the lives of the more privileged. In his book, *Poverty: A History*, Bronislaw Geremek traces coexisting different value systems that shaped attitudes toward poverty in Western Europe: the Gospels and early patristic literature exalt poverty as a virtue and "as a spiritual value, accessible to rich and poor alike" (19). In early theological history, poverty represented "the Christian model of the ideal life," and therefore many gave away their possessions and chose a life of poverty as a Christian ideal. Actual poverty, brought on by disadvantages of birth or by the circumstances of life, gave the economically better-off Christians an opportunity to perform charity to the genuinely poor. In practice, the Christian ethic regarding poverty depended on economic status and social setting. For the elites, if they chose to renounce their material possessions, poverty was a privilege; but "For the working masses [poverty] meant accepting one's lot with humility; for them, abandoning their social role by renouncing work would be an act not of humility but of pride" (201). Therefore, "The Christian

[100] I am quoting from The Authorized King James Version (Iowa Falls: World Bible Publishers, n.d.). The Geneva Bible (1560) reads: "Besides all this, between you and us there is a great gulf set, so that they which would go from hence to you, can not; neither can they come from thence to us."

doctrine of poverty had little to do with social reality; [poverty] was treated as a purely spiritual value" (201).

A new ethos of poverty emerges in the late middle ages and early modern period, with the appearance of charitable institutions and a new emphasis on institutionalized charitable activity and centralized aid to the poor.[101] Geremek suggests that begging becomes a recognizable profession, whereby real beggars were to be set apart from impostors. Beggars, therefore, had to conform to specific cultural expectations of what a beggar was supposed to look like and how he was supposed to behave. Poverty developed its own iconography, as for example the representations of St Martin and the work of Hieronymus Bosch, to depict human affliction:

> A beggar's external appearance was not only a reflection of his genuine need but a part of his professional technique. Clothes were the main thing. Medieval iconography portrays beggars barefoot and in rags; often, in many images of St Martin offering his clothes to a beggar, they are also naked … The common accessories of the wandering beggars, such as the staff and the sack, were both functional and symbolic … Equally important in the beggar's appearance is his body: it, too, crippled and racked with illness, old age or poverty, is part of his professional technique, and must be exposed to public view in the right way. … Singing belongs to what one might call the 'artistic production' side of the beggar's craft.[102]

Begging becomes a spectacle, and a public performance of "ostentatious misery," so that it was often difficult to discern the genuinely poor from impostors.[103] Shakespeare's Edgar, for example, although he becomes unexpectedly and suddenly dispossessed of his properties, family, and station in society, knows

---

[101] Geremek summarizes the situation in England: "the historian E.M. Leonard distinguishes three stages in the development of social aid in England in the sixteenth century: the years from 1514 to 1568, when reforms were initiated mainly by individual cities; those from 1569 to 1597, when legislation began to play a larger role; and finally, the period after 1597, when the problem was dealt with by the Privy Council, whose decisions were handed down to local courts. … Most of these took the form of laws against vagrancy, involving punishments much more cruel and severe than those on the continent" (163–4). In Portugal, for example, lay brotherhoods (Misericórdias) were especially set up to provide aid to the poor. For a study of these brotherhoods and specific situation in Braga, Portugal, see Maria Marta Lobo de Araújo, "The Archbishops of Braga and their Assistance to the Poor in Early Modern Portugal," *Mediterranean Studies: Journal of the Mediterranean Studies Association* 17 (2008): 97–117. For purposes of comparison to these administrative structures in Portugal, see Brian S. Pullan's study of the Catholic institutions in Venice: *Rich and Poor in Renaissance Venice: The Social Institutions of a Catholic State, to 1620* (Cambridge: Harvard University Press, 1971).

[102] Geremek 48–50.

[103] Geremek 51.

exactly how to impersonate a Bedlam beggar. Lear neglected the poor all his life, and now must share their plight.

In *King Lear*, Shakespeare offers representations of poverty, both voluntary and forced, exploring such topics as the house as the material foundation of his characters' lives, the stripping away of material possessions, need and the necessities of life, and the equitable redistribution of material possessions. Lear, Edgar, and Gloucester, stripped of clothes, house, and material possessions, embody what Lear himself terms "houseless poverty," but in the hovel or the heath, or on the way to the White Cliffs of Dover, they discover a new sense of communion with others and with the world.[104]

Ironically, perhaps unwittingly, Lear, like Timon of Athens, chooses poverty, when he announces his abdication and redistribution of his wealth and power. In the process, he also strips Cordelia of her material possessions—her dowry—as well as of paternal care, "propinquity, and property of blood." In his anger, he mocks her about what she now "owes"—"infirmities" (207), since she is now without friends, hated, dowerless, estranged with a curse, deprived of "grace and favor," and cast away, were it not for France's charity. By scene 4, Lear tells the disguised banished Kent that "If thou be'st as poor for a subject as he's for a king, thou art poor enough" (1.4.21–2), and later he reminds Regan and Goneril that he chose poverty: "I gave you all" (2.4.250). Questions of survival loom large, as the play focuses on the essential necessities of life—food, clothing, shelter (2.4.153–4), asking, in Lear's words, if the bare necessities suffice (2.4.264–70).

Lear offers a distinction between "houseless poverty," which affects those who are born poor or become poor and those, like himself, who renounce their riches in pursuit of a spiritual ideal:

> Poor naked wretches, wheresoe'er you are,
> That bide the pelting of this pitiless storm,
> How shall your houseless heads and unfed sides,
> Your hoped and windowed raggedness, defend you
> From seasons such as these? (3.4.30–8).

Although the houseless poor seem invisible, Lear senses their presence, and recognizes that his own government bears the responsibility for doing too little to alleviate their suffering: "O, I have ta'en / Too little care of this!" Ironically, he has discovered that no one can truly experience the suffering of the abject poor, unless one gives up voluntarily all one possesses; only then can one truly commune with the less fortunate and "show the heavens more just" (3.4.5–8).

As Edgar's plight proves, the poor fall through the cracks of the social fabric, have no identity, and are anonymous, helpless, and invisible. As his brother

---

[104] In *The Making of Jacobean Culture: James I and the Renegotiation of Elizabethan Literary Practice* (Cambridge: Cambridge University Press, 1997), Curtis Perry argues that *King Lear* and *Macbeth* "take up the newly topical rhetoric of royal bounty" and deploy "gendered language" to symbolically "deconstruct" concepts of "patriarchal kingship" (148).

Edmund makes his move to force Gloucester to disown Edgar and reapportion the family wealth and favor, we catch a glimpse of a world turned upside down. Without the support of family, love, and charity, this social experiment turns into the "image and horror." Edgar must seek refuge in the interstices of the social fabric, embodying the opposite of a life of privilege and power. To escape, he tells us, he must assume "the basest and most poorest shape" of penury—a word whose roots derive from Latin *penuria*, need, and Greek *pema*, "suffering, capable of enduring, patient" (*OED*). He grimes his face with "filth," wraps a "blanket" around his loins, and creates what he calls a "presented nakedness"—a representation, an iconography of a beggar. This involves a recognizable performance (2.3.1–21) and ironically becomes "nothing." The language of the passage suggests that "nothing" signifies suffering, endurance, and pain. A beggar must get used to being pelted with a succession of blows or having objects hurled at him; to hearing "bans"—malediction, curses—and facing hostile laws and ordinances; and to seeing his wounds become "mortified"—necrotic and gangrenous. The *OED* suggests that "nothing," in usage dating from late Middle English, signifies "a thing (or person) not worth reckoning, considering, or mentioning," "insignificant, worthless." Indeed, as the Fool comments, "Fortune, that arrant whore, / Ne'er turns the key to th' poor" (2.4.51–2); in other words, the rich and powerful never open the door to the poor. After his eyes have been gouged out, stumbling in utter darkness, Gloucester journeys to Dover as if to Damascus, now imbued with new vision: "So distribution should undo excess / And each man have enough" (4.1.73–4). Like Gloucester, Lear must discard his habitual indifference to suffering and suffer himself; like Phillip of Macedonia, he must be reminded of his mortality.

In "Of Repentance," Montaigne speaks of the difficulty in overcoming certain long-ingrained habits: "One may disown and retract the vices that surprise us, and to which we are hurried by passions; but those which by a long habit are rooted in a strong and vigorous will are not subject to contradiction."[105] Shakespeare suggests, however, that the tragic journey requires that Lear and Gloucester learn to modulate their wrong-headed wills, mollify their hardened hearts, and venture forth into the voids of Lear's kingdom.

Spectral Places

After Act III, references to permanent dwellings are few and far between. Unlocalized scenes predominate. The exceptions are Act IV, scene 2, and Act IV, scene 5, which editors generally identify as being set before Albany's castle and in Gloucester's house, respectively. The other scenes are in the "open country" or somewhere "near Dover," or in the British or French army camps.[106] Signposts

[105] Michel de Montaigne, "Of Repentance," in *Essays*, trans. Charles Cotton, http://oregonstate.edu/instruct/phl302/texts/montaigne/montaigne-essays--2.html, August 23, 2009.

[106] See, for example, Stephen Orgel's New Pelican edition of *King Lear* (New York and London: Penguin, 1999).

Fig. 1.1 "King Philip of Macedon in His Bedchamber." M. de La Serre, *The mirrour which flatters not*, trans. T. Cary (London, 1639). STC 20490. By courtesy of the Folger Shakespeare Library.

of precise location become rare, except for a general convergence of all the characters toward the battlefields near and around Dover. Goneril and Edmund, for example, exit in 3.7.22, just before the blinding of Gloucester, and arrive together presumably at Albany's castle in 4.2. Goneril wonders why her "mild husband" has not come out to greet them, as Oswald has obviously done. She asks her steward, "Now, where's your master?" (1); and he replies: "Madam, within" (2). We have not seen Albany since 1.4, and the only other reference to him is in 3.7, when Cornwall writes him a letter, informing him that "the army of France is landed" (2–3). According to Oswald, Albany has radically changed, obviously quite distressed about Gloucester's supposed treachery and Edmund's ascendancy. As Albany enters (4.2.29), he hurls insults at his wife, both in the Quarto and in the Folio texts: "O Goneril, / You are not worth the dust which the rude wind / Blows in your face" (31–3), although the Quarto text expands the fight in additional lines. He learns of Cornwall's death and the shocking news of the blinding of Gloucester. His last words in this scene contain his pledge to "revenge" Gloucester's eyes.

Act IV, scene 5, presumably set in Gloucester's house, revolves around Regan and involves her discovery that Goneril has written a letter to Edmund, which Oswald has come to deliver but discovers that Edmund has departed in search of Gloucester in order to dispatch his "nighted life" (15). It has no markers of location, except that the text contains no information to suggest that she has gone anywhere since we saw her last in Gloucester's house in Act III, scene 7. Regan also reveals that she and Edmund have talked, presumably since we last saw him with Goneril, and have decided that he is "more convenient" for her than for her sister. Regan announces that "Our troops set forth tomorrow" (18). These two scenes, which in actuality could be set anywhere, serve as transitional, intermediary stations in the general movement of all the characters towards the vicinity of Dover.

In a sense, Gloucester, guided by Tom o'Bedlam, and Lear serve as the audience's guides, as the action dislocates to the battlefields around Dover. The audience ironically depends on the blind and the madmen to get its bearings. The landscape becomes more diffuse, locations less precise, although the characters and the audience know the general direction in which the action is moving. At the beginning of Act IV, Gloucester enters, led by an elderly man, who identifies himself as a tenant in Gloucester's estate for some "fourscore years" (4.1.14). Gloucester himself feels totally disoriented. He reveals that he does not need eyes to see because he has "no way" (18), no particular place to go. In fact, he concludes that his eyes had been worthless, "I stumbled when I saw" (19). Recognizing the voice of Tom o'Bedlam, however, he asks for directions to the Cliffs of Dover, "Know'st thou the way to Dover?" (15), which will become his final resting place: "From that place / I shall no leading need" (79–80).

Edgar, still disguised as a Bedlam beggar, leads Gloucester in Act IV, scene 6. Gloucester assumes they are headed for Dover, but he cannot rely on his senses to tell him if they have reached the top of the cliff, or even if they are actually climbing a hill, for the "ground is even." He cannot even hear the sea, but Edgar explains: "Why, then, your other senses grow imperfect / By your eyes' anguish" (5–6). Ambroise Paré (1510–90) first recorded and studied "phantom limbs," the illusions or sensations of pain that come from an amputated limb. Unlike such phantom sensations, dependent on the sense of touch, "damage or loss of other senses results in the absence of experiences formerly associated with their function," such as in the case of blindness and deafness.[107] As Wade points out, we generally grasp the material, visible world globally through the "principles of perception grouping," which were first described by Gestalt psychology (1923).[108] Vision serves "to determine the location of objects"[109]; in the absence of vision, as is the case of Gloucester, one has to depend on touch and hearing, to get one's bearings and to interact with the outside world. Likewise, at night or in dim lighting conditions, the red-orange-yellow-green-blue-indigo-violet spectrum of visible light narrows to blue-green, "the range of wavelengths to which the human eye is best adapted at night."[110]

Edgar further confuses Gloucester when he announces, "Here's the place" (11) and creates through language the illusion of dizzying heights where they presumably stand. This may be an odd dramatization of medieval concepts of tragedy, associated with the wheel of fortune. One rises to the top of the wheel, and then comes tumbling down from the dizzying heights. According to Edgar, "crows and choughs," like the Andean condors and the American eagles, glide in the air, riding on the rising warm air. Perched on the white cliffs, someone harvests samphire, a coastal plant with culinary uses; fishermen walk on the beach; and a boat lies anchored off shore. He also explains the absence of the "murmuring surge" on account of the great height where they stand. The scene, however puzzling it might seem to us or to Shakespeare's original audience, advances Edgar's plan to dislodge Gloucester's suicidal feelings, and to give him a new purpose in life. When Gloucester, having fallen forward in a swoon, wakes up, Edgar tell him: "Thy life's a miracle." Edgar adds: "Think that the clearest gods, who make them honor / Of men's impossibilities, have preservèd thee" (4.6.73–4). This scene resembles wondrous moments of rebirth in Shakespeare's romances, such as Hermione's restoration in *The Winter's Tale*, or Cymbeline's reunion with his long-lost sons, Guiderius and Arviragus, and his daughter Imogen, which by their very miraculous nature defy human understanding. Gloucester and Lear come together one more time; yet there is no sense of location. Bedecked with flowers, Lear raves mad, lost in a fiendish world, where "copulation thrives," his daughters are centaurs from the waist down, and a "farmer's dog" barks at a beggar. Yet, he has moments of lucidity to tell Gloucester that "a man may see how this world goes with no eyes" (150–51); to know that "We came crying hither" (178); and momentarily to be on the verge of recognizing Gloucester. After Lear exits, Edgar promises to lead his father to "some biding" (224), some unknown

[107] Nicholas J. Wade, *Perception and Illusion: Historical Perspective* (New York: Springer Science+Business Media, Inc., 2005) 40.

[108] Wade 7.

[109] Wade 3.

[110] C. Claiborne Ray, "Little Blue Lights," *New York Times*, August 7, 2007, D2.

dwelling. Later, he reveals that he had to leave Gloucester in "the shadow of this tree" (5.2.1), where Gloucester peacefully passed away.

Likewise, Lear, carried in a chair, wakes up in Act IV, scene 7. He is now under the care of Cordelia, but, like Gloucester, he too is disoriented. He does not know where he is, "Where have I been? Where am I?" (53). He adds, "Nor I know not / Where I did lodge last night" (690–70), but Cordelia assures him that he is in his own kingdom (121). The audience also does not know where Lear and Cordelia are, although we assume that they must be in a field tent, preparing for the battle. The play has two other references to tents. In the Quarto text, Edmund refers to Albany's tent (5.1.34); and later, when Regan, having been poisoned by Goneril, says that she is sick, Albany orders an attendant: "She is not well. Convey her to my tent" (107). Defeated in battle, Cordelia and Lear become Edmund's prisoners, and Lear attempts to console Cordelia in saying that they will be like birds in a cage. However, the prison must be in some nearby castle, for Edmund refers to "a castle" (250). The proximity of the castle becomes apparent when Lear enters carrying in his arms the dead body of Cordelia, who was hanged, presumably in her prison cell.

King Lear is the most rural of the tragedies. In Act IV, scene 3, a scene that occurs only in the Quarto text, Kent tells the Gentleman that "the poor distressèd Lear's i' th' town" (39), but there are no other references to any towns or to the great cities of England, such as London and York. In his prophecy, a speech that occurs only in the Folio text, the Fool indicates that the realm of Albion is yet to come to great confusion, when everything will become upside down, even where, as in Spenser's Giant of the Scales' vision, "every case in law is right" (3.3.86). Lear's kingdom consists of a barren landscape and sparsely populated countryside, punctuated with occasional dwelling places, such as Lear's castle, the abodes of Gloucester, Regan, and Goneril, the hovel, a tree under which Gloucester dies, Albany's tent, and an unidentified castle, where Lear and Cordelia are held in prison. These locations materialize momentarily, but then recede into the vast, dark expanses of Lear's kingdom. Ironically, references to Dover help us at least visualize the general direction of the characters' journey. Precise locations become less distinct. *King Lear* truly illustrates Yi-Fu Tuan's point about our perception of place: "The small worlds of direct experience are fringed with much broader fields known indirectly through symbolic means."[111]

In the play, Shakespeare gives us the "life" of a king who, by discarding kingly trappings, discovers a perceptual gap. Lear must see the everydayness of his and other characters' lives. But the tragedy suggests that house and kingdom are intimately interconnected, and that the house intertwines with who the characters are and how they see themselves. At the very end of the play, the three survivors—Kent, Albany, and Edgar—are each associated with one of the three houses represented in the play: Lear's, Albany and Goneril's, and Gloucester's.

[111] Yi-Fu Tuan, *Space and Place: The Perspective of Experience* (Minneapolis: University of Minnesota Press, 1977) 88.

Kent, closest in age to Lear, represents the old generation; Edgar represents the young generation, victimized by the older generation; and Albany offers a bridge between the two generations. Unmarried or widowed and childless, they face the bleak prospects that the future holds for them. Kent has no place to go. Empty, lonely houses await Edgar and Albany.

In *King Lear*, the house, as an imagined place, takes center stage through direct experience and through symbolic means. The play explores different types of dwelling—a castle, cave, someone else's house, a hovel. It also explores different modes and concepts of dwelling, and unsettles notions of "inside"—entering, belonging, being accepted—and "outside"—leaving, closing of doors, exile, not belonging. When disaster occurs, the *SAS Survival Handbook* cautions, we may be left to manage for ourselves, completely cut off from "the usual services and food supplies."[112] In such a situation, we might be contented with any shelter we can find, as Kent wishes for banished Cordelia: "The gods to their dear shelter take thee, maid" (1.1.187). But when the castle vanishes or rends, however, it leaves behind an open space and emptiness. There is no turning back. With the technological resources of the modern theater, stage producers could make Lear's castle vanish before our eyes through spectacular special effects. The vanishing castle represents not only a perceptual phenomenon; it also helps localize and dramatize pivotal historical changes in housing conditions, family expectations, and gender roles in the early modern period.

[112] John 'Lofty' Wiseman, *The SAS Survival Handbook: How to Survive in the Wild, in any Climate, on Land or at Sea* (London: Harper Collins, 1999) 557.

Chapter 2
Unhoused in *Othello*: Roots, Routes and the Edge of Darkness

> At vero Desdemona illa apud nos a marito occisa, quanquam optime semper causam egit, interfecta tamen magis; cum in lecto decumbens spectantium misericordiam ipso vultu imploraret.—spectator account of production at Oxford University in 1610.[1]
>
> [But truly that Desdemona was killed among us by her husband, although she always pleaded her case well, for all the more she was slain; when resting on her bed, she called with her very countenance the pity of those watching.]

In "Traveling Cultures," James Clifford proposes a view of culture based on opposing yet interconnected concepts of dwelling and traveling, "roots" and "routes"; he argues for "a comparative cultural studies approach to specific histories, tactics, everyday practices of dwelling, and traveling: traveling-in-dwelling, dwelling-in-traveling."[2] This chapter explores these interconnected concepts of roots and routes in Othello's tragic journey. The experience of dwelling in *Othello* hinges on a contrast between European and non-European housing conditions and on the recovery of racially and culturally-charged attitudes associated with darkness, blackness, and shadows.

In *Othello*, Shakespeare juxtaposes two ways of life: one European, sedentary, urban, home-centered, represented by Venice and centered on Brabantio's house; and the other revolves around a space elsewhere, reflecting mobile, non-permanent forms of dwelling—what Othello calls an "unhousèd" condition of lifelong wandering. Shakespeare compares characters who dwell in houses, and those who inhabit mobile, non-permanent, or temporary places. Therefore, one underscores European concepts of home life, household, hospitality; the other relates to ever-shifting, self-erasing images of exotic travel and improbable experiences in far away places.

---

[1] In Vol. 10 of his papers (folios 83–4), William Fulman (1632–1688) transcribes excerpts from Henry Jackson's Latin correspondence written some 50 years earlier. In these excerpts, Jackson records a performance of *Othello*, along with Ben Jonson's *The Alchemist*, at Oxford in September 1610. See Geoffrey Tillotson, "*Othello* and *The Alchemist* at Oxford in 1610," *TLS*, July 20, 1933: 494, translation mine.

[2] James Clifford, "Traveling Cultures," *Routes: Travel and Translation in the Late Twentieth Century* (Cambridge: Cambridge University Press, 1997) 36. See Susan Stanford Friedman's discussion of these concepts in her essay, "Spatial Poetics and Arundhati Roy's *The God of Small Things*," *A Companion to Narrative Theory*, (eds) James Phelan and Peter J. Rabinowitz (Oxford: Blackwell, 2005) 194.

The image of the dark, empty house looms large in *Othello*, as does the pervasive nature of darkness, which blurs domestic boundaries, redefines the perception of architectural space, and exposes assumptions about race relations. Therefore, the first part of this chapter will focus on the concept of home; in particular, I will argue that "home" engages three different living arrangements centered on ill-defined vast ancestral African landscapes of Othello's childhood and youth, Brabantio's palazzo in Venice, and Othello and Desdemona's state apartments at the mighty fortress of Cyprus. The second part of the chapter will explore a cluster of images associated with blackness, darkness, and shadows. Throughout the play, Shakespeare weaves narratives connecting and contrasting home spaces and alien spaces elsewhere.

Roots and Routes

According to Susan Stanford Friedman, Walter Benjamin suggests that the history of narrative situates the storyteller in relation to the spatial "archaic types" of the seaman "who has come from afar" with a story to tell, and the "man who has stayed at home … and knows the local tales and traditions."[3] Friedman concludes: "Home and elsewhere—both spatial locations—are for Benjamin the coconstituents of story, not incidental to it, as narrative tradition has evolved through time and across many societies."[4] Friedman distrusts a narrative poetics that sees space as "'the description' that interrupts the flow of temporality or as the 'setting' that functions as static background for plot, or as the 'scene' in which the narrative events unfold in time."[5] Affirming the centrality of space, she proposes that "Such borders, frontiers, are not the background of narrative, mere description where time unfolds its plot. They are, instead, the generative energy of narrative, the space that contains time."[6] Clifford, Benjamin, and Friedman invite us to rethink our cultural experiences in terms of narratives oscillating between "sites of dwelling *and* travel."[7] This is precisely where I situate the experience of dwelling and the representation of home in Shakespeare's *Othello*.

The power of narrative in *Othello* has long been recognized. Stephen Greenblatt analyzed the extent to which Iago "construct[s] a narrative into which he inscribes ('by this hand') those around him": "[Iago] does not need a profound or even reasonably accurate understanding of his victims; he would rather deal in probable impossibilities than improbable possibilities."[8] Othello himself fits Benjamin's

[3] Walter Benjamin, "The Storyteller," *Illuminations: Essays and Reflections*, (ed.) H. Arendt, trans. H. Zohn (New York: Schocken Books, 1969) 84, as quoted in Friedman, 195.

[4] Friedman 195.

[5] Friedman 192–3.

[6] Friedman 203.

[7] Clifford 31.

[8] Stephen Greenblatt, *Renaissance Self-Fashioning: From More to Shakespeare* (Chicago: University of Chicago Press, 1980) 234.

paradigm of the storyteller who comes from afar and tells a powerful story. Indeed, he wins Desdemona's heart, as he puts it, by telling Brabantio and Desdemona "the story of my life / From year to year—the battles, sieges, fortunes / That I have passed" (1.3.129–31). I am not, however, primarily interested in analyzing the functions of these storytellers; rather, like James Clifford, I will focus on roots and routes; and like Friedman, I will argue for space as providing "the generative energy" of the dramatic narrative.

Desdemona entreated Othello to "dilate"[9] the "pilgrimage" of his life, which consists of a series of adventures and disasters, which he describes as "disastrous chances," "accidents by flood and field," "hairbreadth scapes," "slavery," and "remission" [freedom] from slavery (1.3.134–38). From his childhood, Othello has been on the go, never anchored in a home and never supported by family life. Desdemona's empathy creates an emotional bond that binds them together:

> My story being done,
> She gave me for my pains a world of kisses,
> She swore in faith 'twas strange, 'twas passing strange;
> 'Twas pitiful, 'twas passing pitiful. (1.3.158–61).

Othello concludes that "She loved me for the dangers I had passed, / And I loved her that she did pity them" (1.3.167–8). However, in the Venetian Senate Chamber, Othello sketches only in the most general way that story; it is nothing more than "the story of his telling Desdemona the stories of his life."[10] His story, however, is a marker of his alien status; his blackness, as Virginia Vaughan notes, is "the visual signifier of his Otherness."[11]

Nowhere else does Othello volunteer more specific details about his life. The importance of the story becomes apparent, but Shakespeare leaves the characters, alongside the play's audience, with unanswered questions about Othello's roots, let alone the routes of Othello's journey. Perhaps, Claude Lévi-Strauss puts it best when he describes a particularly clumsy, unfriendly building—"a tube of cement" of a hotel in Goiania, Brazil, which he visited in 1937—as "a place of transit not of residence."[12] That is precisely my point: Othello has encountered many places of transit, but has not found a place of residence.

---

9 See Patricia Parker, "Shakespeare and Rhetoric: 'Dilation' and 'Delation' in *Othello*," in *Shakespeare & the Question of Theory*, Patricia Parker and Geoffrey Hartman, (eds). (New York and London: Methuen, 1985) 54–74. Parker argues that "Rhetoric in the Renaissance is inextricably embedded in other discourses—of logic and politics, of theology and the ideology of sexual difference" (70).

10 Russ McDonald, "Introduction," *Othello*, *Complete Pelican Shakespeare*, 1395.

11 Virginia Mason Vaughan, Othello: *A Contextual History* (Cambridge: Cambridge University Press, 1994) 51.

12 Claude Lévi-Strauss, *Tristes Tropiques*, trans. John and Doreen Weightman (New York and London: Penguin, 1973) 126. Clifford cites and discusses this example in *Routes* 17.

African Landscapes

Throughout the play, Shakespeare obscures rather than clarifies Othello's birthplace. Nothing in the play connects Othello to a precise place, but rather to a large geographical and cultural region. In referring to his origins, Othello relies upon a storehouse of widespread popular images and beliefs about Africa, rather than recollections of identifiable locations. In Shakespeare's time, a "Moor" was a generic term that did not necessarily identify a specific homeland.[13] It could mean a "tawny" or "white" Moor, such as the Prince of Morocco, or the Moorish woman, to whom Lorenzo refers as the "Negro" Lancelot got "with child" (3.5.34–5) in *The Merchant of Venice*, as well as Muly Mahamet, also from Morocco, and the character, Zareo, "a Moor of Argier," in George Peele's *The Battle of Alcazar* (1594?).[14] Oftentimes, the word Blackamoor[15] appears to label a sub-Saharan African, such as Aaron, who is also simply called "the Moor," in *Titus Andronicus*, and who appears as a defiant black man in Henry Peacham's drawing of a composite scene from Shakespeare's tragedy.[16] "Moor" was also applied to a Moslem from Ethiopia, the Sudan, and even the Indian subcontinent (*OED*). George Abbot makes a racial distinction between "Moors" and sub-Saharan Africans: "All the people in general to the South, lying within the *Zona torrida*, are not only blackish like the Moores: but are exceedingly black."[17] Peter Heylyn (1652) describes the Moors as "of a duskish colour, comely of body, stately of gait, implacable in hatred, constant in affection, laborious and treacherous."[18]

In Act IV, Iago refers to what we could take as Othello's homeland, "Mauritania" (4.2.224–5); but even here "Mauritania" refers to a large area spreading across the

[13] *OED* defines the term as follows: "Originally: a native or inhabitant of ancient Mauretania, a region of North Africa corresponding to parts of present-day Morocco and Algeria. Later usually: a member of a Muslim people of mixed Berber and Arab descent inhabiting north-western Africa (now mainly present-day Mauritania), who in the eighth century conquered Spain." In his edition, Russ McDonald discusses the vagueness and complexity of the term (*Complete Pelican Shakespeare*, 1393–4).

[14] See also the anonymous *The Famous History of the A Life and Death of Captain Thomas Stukeley* in *The Stukeley Plays*, (ed.) Charles Edelman (Manchester and New York: Manchester University Press, 2005).

[15] "A black-skinned African, an Ethiopian, a Negro; any very dark-skinned person" (*OED*).

[16] In *Performing Blackness on English Stages, 1500–1800* (Cambridge: Cambridge University Press, 2005), Virginia Mason Vaughan discusses the representation of blackness from the Middle Ages to the end of the eighteenth century. See especially her discussion of Peacham's drawing (48–9).

[17] Abbot, sig. C7.

[18] Peter Heylyn, *Cosmographie in four bookes (*London, 1652), in Edward H. Sugden, *A Topographical Dictionary* (Manchester: Manchester University Press, 1925) 351.

Sahara, the Sahel, and the Sudan.[19] Even Aleppo, where Othello once cut the throat of "a turbaned Turk" who spoke ill of Venice (5.352–4), implies not a homeland for Othello but a well-known trade emporium on the route for such commodities as frankincense and myrrh, along with gum arabic, Othello's "medicinable gum," at first harvested in the Middle East but later in West Africa.[20] Two major trade routes branched off at Aleppo, the northern land route ultimately leading to central Asia, China and India through the Black Sea and Asia Minor; the southern sea route communicating with the East by the Red Sea. Aleppo gained renewed prominence after 1507, when the Portuguese enforced a blockade of the Red Sea and the Persian Gulf, therefore diverting the trade to the Northern route.[21] Venice, which had competed with Genoa for control of these trade routes, saw its commercial interests curtailed, although it continued to find supplies of spices for sale in Alexandria.[22] Another reference in *Macbeth* (1.2.07) shows Shakespeare's awareness of the commercial importance of Aleppo, to where, for example, the English ship, the *Tiger*, owned by Sir Edward Michelbourne, set sail for the East on December 5, 1604; possibly the same ship had "made a voyage to Aleppo in 1583."[23] Therefore, "The indiscriminate mixing of black and Moorish impressions serves to endow Othello with an unstable quality that adds to and may be at the heart of his terrifying strangeness."[24]

The Arabian trees Othello refers to were reputed to yield "no gumme but in the darke night."[25] Gum arabic, still used as a thickener and colloidal stabilizer in the pharmaceutical industry and in the manufacture of candy, appears in medieval

---

[19] See George Abbot, *A brief description of the whole worlde* (London, 1599), sig. C6–C7.

[20] Gus W. Van Beek, "Frankincense and Myrrh," *The Biblical Archaeologist* 23.3 (1960): 70–95; and "The Trade in Gum Arabic," in James L. Webb, Jr., *Desert Frontier: Ecological and Economic Change along the Western Sahen, 1600–1850* (Madison: University of Wisconsin Press, 1995) 97–131. See also Peter Stallybrass, "Marginal England: The View from Aleppo," in *Center or Margin: Revisions of the English Renaissance in Honor of Leeds Barroll*, (ed.) Lena Cowen Orlin (Selingsgrove: Susquehanna University Press, 2006) 27–39.

[21] A.H. Lybyer, "The Ottoman Turks and the Routes of Oriental Trade," *The English Historical Review* 30.120 (1915): 577, 584, 588.

[22] Lybyer 584. For a fascinating study of the rivalry between Genoa and Venice, see George L. Gorse, "Christopher Columbus and Andrea Doria: The Two Worlds of Renaissance Genoa," *Mediterranean Studies* 16 (2007): 120–42. Venice set its sight on the Eastern Mediterranean; whereas Genoa, through Andrea Doria and Christopher Columbus, looked beyond the Mediterranean basin, across the Atlantic.

[23] Edward Alleyn Loomis, "Master of the *Tiger*," *Shakespeare Quarterly* 7.4 (1956): 457; and Henry Neill Paul, *The Royal Play of Macbeth* (London: Macmillan, 1950) 302–3.

[24] Edward Pechter, *Othello and Interpretive Traditions* (Iowa City, IA:: University of Iowa Press, 1999) 35; also quoted in Virginia Mason Vaughan, *Performing Blackness*, 94.

[25] Robert Greene, *Greenes Mourning Garment: Given Him by Repentance at the Funerals of Love* (London, 1616), sig. C2.

Arabic toxicology as a powerful antidote.[26] As James Webb writes, the trade in gum arabic, originally centered in Arabia and the Nilotic Sudan, shifted by the sixteenth century to the southwestern corner of the Sahara, so much so that by the eighteenth century, it "was the single most important product traded by Europeans who stopped along the 'gum coast' of southern Mauritania or traded at the Senegal river."[27] In the play, references to specific locations or commodities—Mauritania, Aleppo, and medicinable gum from Arabian trees—tend to blur the distinction between Africa and the Middle East and emphasize routes, not roots; travcling, not dwelling. As Jerry Brotton contends, Shakespeare combines "ocularity and historiography … to create the fluid geographical movement and exotic topography of *Othello*."[28]

In the literature of the period, Africa conjures up a complex, confused cluster of images associated with landmarks, geographical characteristics, climate, distinctive fauna and flora, and ethnic, linguistic, or cultural diversity, which was in fact poorly understood. Edward Sugden remarks: "The interior of Africa was almost a *terra incognita*. It was believed to be mainly a huge desert, fertile in uncouth monsters, and rich in gold and gems and spices."[29] A few examples will suffice to illustrate my point. In his *Diuersarū nationum habitus* (1594), a picture book of typical national costumes, Pietro Bertelli has two images presumably representing typical African dress, but in the process he also represents imaginary African landscapes.[30]

The first image, "Mulier in Africa," depicts a barefoot attractive young woman, wearing knee-length flowing robes, a headscarf, anklets, and bracelets. Nothing extraordinary appears in this female figure; but around her, the landscape consists

---

[26] Martin Levey, "Medieval Arabic Toxicology: The Book on Poisons of ibn Wahshīya and Its Relation to Early Indian and Greek Texts," *Transactions of the American Philosophical Society*, New Series, 56.7 (1966): 1–130. Gum arabic had and still has multiple uses in the candy and pharmaceutical industries, the manufacture of dentures, and as a thickener and colloidal stabilizer (*OED*). The anonymous *A very proper treatise, wherein is breefely set forth the art of limming* (London, 1583) contains a recipe for making "gum water to temper colours withal" (Fol. 4).

[27] James L.A. Webb, Jr., "The Trade in Gum Arabic: Prelude to French Conquest in Senegal," *The Journal of African History* 26.2–3 (1985): 149. For a discussion of sixteenth- and seventeenth-century trade routes in West Africa, see Boubacar Barry, *Senegambia and the Atlantic Slave Trade* (Cambridge: Cambridge University Press, 1998) 5–54.

[28] Jerry Brotton, "Tragedy and Geography," in *A Companion to Shakespeare's Works: The Tragedies*, vol. 1, (eds) Richard Dutton and Jean E. Howard (Oxford: Blackwell, 2003) 232.

[29] Sugden 5.

[30] These images are available in the British Library copy (Shelfmark 810.c.2) of Pietro Bertelli, *Diuersarū nationum habitus, centum, et quattuor iconibus in œre incisis diligenter expressi, item ordines duo processionum ... opera P. Bertellii* (Patauij, 1594, 96). A similar book does not contain these illustrations: Cesare Vecellio, *De gli habiti antichi, et moderni di diuerse parti del mondo libri dve, fatti da Cesare Vecellio, & con discorsi da lui dichiarati* (Venice, 1590).

Fig. 2.1 "Mulier in Africa" (African Woman). Pietro Bertelli, *Diuersarū nationum habitus* (Patauij, 1594, 96). © British Library Board. Shelfmark 810.c.2. By permission of the British Library.

of sand dunes and scraggy desiccated vegetation. In the background, to her left and right, two monsters share the viewer's attention, one of which is a naked man with a dog's head; the other is what Pliny called "Umbrella-footed, because when the weather is hot they lie on their backs stretched out on the ground and protect themselves by the shade of their feet."[31]

The other image, "Nobilis fœmina in Africa," portrays an elegantly dressed noblewoman, who wears proper shoes, although a landscape similar to the first one surrounds her. In the background, to the right, stands what seems to be a Plinian "satyr" with "no human characteristic except their shape"; and to the left, a giant specimen of the Blemmyae, who according to Pliny, "are reported as being without heads, their mouths and eyes are attached to their chest."[32] George Abbot, in *A briefe description of the whole worlde* (1599) remarks that Africa has all sorts of wildlife, "oftentimes new and strange shapes of beasts." He explains that since the country is "hot and full of wildernesses" and has little water, "the beasts of all sorts are inforced to meete at those few watering places that be, where oftentimes contrarie kinds have conjunction the one with the other: so that ariseth newe kinds of species, which taketh part of both."[33]

Likewise, John Lok, who undertook a voyage to Africa in 1554, summarizes widespread misconceptions: the Libyan Garamentes, whose women the males share promiscuously among themselves; the Blemines, who have "their eyes and mouth in their breasts," the Anthropophagi, who "eat mans' flesh."[34] A Jesuit priest reports that the African Chibadi "are men attired like women, and behave themselves womanly, ashamed to be called men; are also married to men, and esteeeme that unnatural damnation an honor."[35] Africa displayed a strange ecology marked by heat of the sun, deserts, and strange animals; as a cultural region, Africa contained monstrous creatures, deviant sexual behavior, and gender inversion. Therefore, as Virginia Vaughan demonstrates, "blackness and forbidden sex, blackness and heathenism, blackness and slavery—all were linked in the English mind from the earliest descriptions of African people."[36]

Three early modern maps illustrate the confusion about African geography. A Portuguese map, known as the Cantino Planisphere (1502), depicts major

---

[31] For convenience, I am quoting from Pliny, the Elder, *Natural History: A Selection*, trans. John F. Healy (Harmondsworth, UK, and New York: Penguin, 1991) 78, but a 1601 translation, by Philemon Holland, was available to Shakespeare: *The historie of the world* (London, 1601), STC 20029.

[32] Pliny 57–8.

[33] Abbot, sig. C8^{r-v}.

[34] Richard Hakluyt, *The principal navigations, voyages, traffiques & discoveries of the English nation* (Glasgow, J. MacLehose and sons, 1903–05), 6: 168–70.

[35] Samuel Purchas, *Hakluytus posthumus, or, Purchas his Pilgrimes: contayning a history of the world in sea voyages and lande travells by Englishmen and others* (Glasgow: J. MacLehose and Sons, 1905–07) 9: 260.

[36] Vaughan, *Othello: A Contextual History*, 54.

2.2 "Nobilis Foemina in Africa" (African Noblewoman). Pietro Bertelli, *Diuersarū nationum habitus* (Patauij, 1594, 96). © British Library Board. Shelfmark 810.c.2. By permission of the British Library.

geographical landmarks such as the Atlas Mountains in the North, "Serra Lioa" [Sierra Leone], Mountains of the Moon, and the Cape Promontory, as well as Portuguese constructions, such as the Fort of São Jorge da Mina on the Gold Coast. Most of Africa consists of open spaces, including deserts or areas full of wildlife and vegetation.[37] Leo Africanus says that on Mount Centopozzi, there is a "hole or drie pit of so great a depth that the bottom thereof can in no wise be seen."[38] This cave apparently becomes Othello's "anters vast" (Latin *antrum*, cave).[39] Some of these landmarks connect with specific myths. A nation of women warriors supposedly inhabited the Mountains of the Moon. The Portuguese Duarte Barbosa, in 1518, describes a nation of African Amazons.[40] The Atlas Mountains were reputed to be extremely high, as George Abbot observes: "This hill is so high that unto those who stoode on the bottome of it, it seemed to touch heaven with his top."[41] In his translation of John Leo Africanus's *A Geographical History of Africa* (1600), a possible source for *Othello*, John Pory includes a map of Africa depicting a continent dotted with place names and landmarks; yet, upon closer inspection, except for place names along the coast, we find nothing but vague references to "Amazones," "Troglodite," "Nubia," "Libia," "Nigritarum," and so forth.[42] A *Chart of the Coasts of Europe* (1562) at the British Library shows the interior of Africa as a vast open space, "decorated with elaborate tents."[43]

---

[37] The map is named after Alberto Cantino, a spy for the Duke of Ferrara, who smuggled the map out of Portugal, and it is now at the Biblioteca Estense in Modena, Italy. Digital copies of the map are readily available on the Internet. See R.A. Skelton, *Explorers' Maps: Chapter in the Cartographic Record of Geographical Discovery* (London: Routledge and Kegan Paul, 1958), esp. Chapter 2; and, for a discussion of other caricatures of Africans, consult Jean Michel Massing, "The Image of Africa and the Iconography of Lip-plated Africans in Pierre Desceliers's World Map of 1550," in *Black Africans in Renaissance Europe*, (eds) T.F. Earle and K.J.P. Lowe (Cambridge: Cambridge University Press, 2005) 48–69.

[38] John Leo Africanus, *A Geographical Historie of Africa*, trans. By John Pory (London, 1600); rpt. *The History and Description of Africa*, 3 vols., (ed.) Robert Brown (London: Hakluyt Society, 1896), 2: 555.

[39] Etymology is from the *OED*.

[40] Duarte Barbosa, *The Book of Duarte Barbosa: An Account of the Countries Bordering the Indian Ocean and Their Inhabitants*, trans. Mansel Longworth Dames (London: Hakluyt Society, 1918) 1: 12. See my discussion of this matter in *Shakespeare's Cross-Cultural Encounters*, 13–14.

[41] Abbot, sig. C6^{v}.

[42] See Lois Whitney, "Did Shakespeare know Leo Africanus?," *PMLA* 37 (1922): 470–88; and Edward Berry, "Othello's Alienation," *SEL* 30.2 (1990): 315–33.

[43] British Library MS Add. 9810, *Chart of the Coasts of Europe,* dated October 10, 1562, by Giacopo Veschonte. The interior of Africa would remain largely unexplored well into the nineteenth century, as Jean Michel Massing points out in "The Image of Africa," in Earle and Lowe, (eds), *Black Africans*, 55.

In his address to the reader, John Pory describes Leo Africanus in terms reminiscent of Othello's life. He marvels at how Leo Africanus could have escaped "so manie thousands of imminent danger," posing a series of rhetorical questions:

> For how many desolate cold mountains, and huge, drie, and barren deserts passed he? How often was he in hazard to haue beene captiued, or to haue had his throte cut by the prouling Arabians, and wilde Mores? And how hardly manie times escaped he the Lyons greedie mouth, and the deuouring iawes of the Crocodile?[44]

Indeed, Leo Africanus describes the "sandie seas" and the "dangerous heapes of sande," which are "subiect to the extreme heate of the sunne" (14), snow-capped mountains (16), large swaths of deserts, where travelers have "no other places then tents and wide fields to repose themseues in" (131). He also notes that when the Moslems go to war, "each man carries his wife with him, to the end that she may cheere vp her good man, and giue him encouragement" (159). From his account, Othello would no doubt have recognized these images of Africa, as he might the multi-purpose housing compound in Cape Mesurado, Liberia.

European fantasies about Africa abound in contemporary texts, maps, and art. As Jyotsna Singh writes, "[Othello] is simply a 'character' in an imaginary landscape which viewers, then and now, recognize as a semi-fictional creation of colonialist travel narratives—from antiquity through the nineteenth century."[45] Shakespeare makes Desdemona and Othello complicit in these fantasies. When Desdemona tries to counter Emilia's remark about the extreme nature of Othello's jealousy, she cannot name Othello's homeland: "I think the sun where he was born / Drew all such humors from him" (3.4.30–31). The handkerchief, apparently the

44 Pory, "To the Reader," in Leo Africanus, I: 6.

45 Jyotsna Singh, "Othello's Identity, Postcolonial Theory and Contemporary African Rewritings of *Othello*," *Othello: Contemporary Critical Essays*, (ed.) Lena Cowen Orlin (Houndsmills; New York: Palgrave, 2004) 172. See also Philip D. Collington, "Othello the Liar," in *The Mysterious and the Foreign in Early Modern England*, (eds) Helen Ostovich, Mary V. Silcox, and Graham Roebuck (Newark: University of Delaware Press, 2008) 197. Collington argues that Othello often "lapses into boundless rhetorical flights" (197). Of particular interest here is Ania Loomba's discussion of contemporary beliefs about Blacks and Muslims in "*Othello* and the Racial Question," Chapter 4 of her book, *Shakespeare, Race, and Colonialism* (Oxford: Oxford University Press, 2002) 91–111. Other important studies of race in the period include Kim F. Hall, *Things of Darkness: Economies of Race and Gender in Early Modern England* (Ithaca: Cornell University Press, 1995); Ania Loomba, *Gender, Race, Renaissance Drama* (Manchester: Manchester University Press, 1989); and Dympna Callaghan, *Shakespeare Without Women: Representing Gender and Race on the Renaissance Stage* (London and New York: Routledge, 2000). In *Moorings: Portuguese Expansion and the Writing of Africa* (Minneapolis: University of Minnesota Press, 2009), Josiah Blackmore offers a fascinating overview of the Portuguese experience in and with Africa. His chapter on "Africa and the Imagination" is of particular interest.

Fig. 2.3 Housing Compound in Cape Mesurado, Liberia. John Green, *A new general collection of voyages and travels*. London,1745–47. © British Library Board. Shelfmark V 9733. By permission of the British Library.

only artifact connecting Othello to his home, appears in contradictory stories: it is, as he says, a fantastical talisman that "an Egyptian" gave his mother, and "an antique token / My father gave my mother" (5.2.216–17). If "Egyptian," as I have argued elsewhere, means Gypsy, then the rootlessness lies at the origin of the cloth.[46] In the first version, a 200-year-old "sibyl" sewed her "prophetic fury" into the web of the silk spun by hallowed worms, "dyed in mummy" and "conserved of maidens' hearts" (3.4.69–75). Momentarily incredulous, Desdemona asks, "I'faith? Is't true?"; to which Othello responds with "Most veritable" (3.4.75; 76), perhaps illustrating a proverb William Camden quotes: "A traueller may lye by authoritie."[47] The Moor in *The Merchant of Venice* is the "prince" from a known kingdom; and although *Titus Andronicus* does not explicitly identify Aaron's homeland, at least he has a "countryman," whose white son is exchanged with Aaron and Tamora's child. In comparison to Shakespeare's other Moors, Othello stands apart, if not starkly alone.

For Othello, life is a journey, which has taken him along a network of routes leading to "anters vast," "deserts idle," "rough quarries, rocks, and hills whose heads touch heaven" (1.3.140–41), and to the lands of "cannibals" and of Blemmyae, "whose heads / Do grow beneath their shoulders" (143–4).[48] Like Othello, Leo Africanus too states that he traveled in a strange geography; but unlike Othello, Africanus makes a bona fide effort to offer a credible travel account, which describes well-known landmarks and retains the flavor of an eyewitness report, as for example when he writes that the Africans from Barbary are "somewhat needie and couetous, being proud and high-minded, and wonderfully addicted to wrath," for they "will deeply engraue in marble any iniurie be it neuer so small, & will in no wise blot it out of remembrance." He adds that they are so credulous "that they will beleue matters impossible, which are told them."[49] Othello's mountains that seem to touch heaven could refer to the proverbially tall Atlas Mountains. Othello seems to rely on hearsay and fantastical myths, and perhaps proves Africanus's assessment that Moors tend to "beleue matters impossible." Instead of telling a story about his roots, Othello spins narratives about the fantastical routes along which he has traveled. One wonders if Shakespeare offers ironic commentary on Desdemona's or any young Venetian woman's credulity, when the Duke remarks: "I think this tale would win my daughter too" (171).

Even references to Othello's more recent military record in the service of Venice simply reinforce attention to routes, not roots. Iago, for example, bears witness to the fact that he fought alongside Othello "At Rhodes, at Cyprus, and on other grounds / Christened and heathen" (1.1.28–9). Othello relies on his well-

---

46 Sousa, Shakespeare's *Cross-Cultural Encounters*, 140–46.

47 William Camden, *Remaines concerning Brittaine* (London, 1629) 261. Desdemona seems to become gradually more credulous about whatever Othello says.

48 See William Shakespeare, *Othello*, (ed.) Michael Neill, Oxford Shakespeare (Oxford: Oxford University Press, 2006) 223n.

49 Africanus, I: 85.

established record of "services" to the Venetian state to "out-tongue" Brabantio's complaints (19). So clear and so obvious is that record that the Duke does not hesitate to side with Othello, and dismisses Brabantio's complaints. Later overcome with fear of losing Desdemona, and losing confidence in his own military abilities, Othello offers an *ubi sunt* speech, a farewell to arms, revealing the importance of the military profession to his personal identity. With the loss of the "tranquil mind" also vanish "the plumed troops," "the big wars, / That makes ambition virtue," "the neighing steed," the trumpets, the drums, "the fife," "the royal banner," the "mortal engines"—all that pertains to "Pride, pomp, and circumstance of glorious war" (3.3.355).

Othello's travels and military history feed into and reinforce each other, underscoring Othello's restlessness, mobility, wandering, and displacement; consequently, as Patricia Parker remarks, they direct the audience's eyes to "exotic worlds beyond the direct reach of vision" and help "chart the crossing in this play of domestic and exotic, 'civil' and 'barbarian.'"[50] Roderigo, unkindly, describes Othello as "an extravagant and wheeling stranger / Of here and everywhere" (1.1.134–5), punning on Othello's foreign status, lack of a permanent place of residence, and shifty nature.[51] Othello describes his own "unhousèd free condition" (1.2.26), which he says he gave up when he married Desdemona. That former "unhousèd" condition as an exile, slave, traveler, and soldier contrasts with "circumscription and confine" that his new married status requires. Throughout his life, Othello had many places of nonpermanent residence: lodgings, caves, huts, and tents and common makeshift shelters, as Richard Eden describes in his account of West Africa: "certayne lowe cottages made of boughs of trees, plastered with chauke, and covered with straw."[52]

Othello's remembrance of the "tented field" (1.3.85) most immediately evokes his military life, but it brings to mind the tent of nomads and of those "who rely on movement to survive."[53] "Black tents," the traditional dwellings of nomads, consist of a tent cover, made of animal hair, such as goat hair, poles, and cord. Over the centuries, "black tents," so called from the blackness of the goat hair used, have served as the primary form of shelter for a variety of ethnic groups

---

[50] Patricia Parker, "Fantasies of 'Race' and 'Gender': Africa, *Othello* and Bringing to Light," in Margo Hendricks and Patricia Parker, (eds), *Women, 'Race', and Writing in the Early Modern Period* (London and New York: Routledge, 1994) 94.

[51] I have addressed this matter in a pedagogical essay on *Othello*, in "Unhoused in *Othello*," *Approaches to Teaching Shakespeare's Othello*, (eds) Peter Erickson and Maurice Hunt (New York: The Modern Language Association of America, 2005) 133–40, revised and adapted for this chapter, and republished by permission of MLA.

[52] Richard Eden and Richard Willes, (eds), *The History of Travayle in the West and East Indies* (London, 1577), Fol. 337[r-v], qtd. in Alden T. Vaughan and Virginia Mason Vaughan, "Before Othello: Elizabethan Representation of Sub-Saharan Africans," *The William and Mary Quarterly*, 3rd series, 54.1 (1997): 19–44.

[53] Robert L. Freeden, et al., *Nomads of the World* (New York: National Geographic Society, 1971) 10.

extending from the western coast of North Africa to Tibet.[54] Faegre notes that "Black-tent dwellers are weavers," weaving "not only the roofs, walls, and floors of their homes," but also furnishings such as "wall cloths, spindle bags, carpet bags, and the carpets."[55] In English usage dating from 1297, a "tent" can be defined as "A portable shelter or dwelling of canvas (formerly of skins or cloth), supported by means of a pole or poles, and usually extended and secured by ropes fastened to pegs which are driven into the ground; used by travelers, soldiers, nomads, and others" (*OED*).[56] Faegre points out that nomads and desert dwellers actually spend much time outdoors, shepherding herds, rather than in tents. Further, he writes: "The tent does not erect a clear boundary between inside and outside much as we are used to in our own housing";[57] rather, the tent allows wind, rain, and snow to come in. Nomads, however, prefer these conditions and "are so accustomed to the feel of a flexible cloth roof over their heads that a solid roof constitutes a threat."[58] He adds: "There are many stories of how these nomads cannot at first sleep in a solid house for fear that the roof will fall and crush them."[59]

In iconography, tents stand for the impermanent, fleeting nature of life on earth. An emblem, titled "*Super terram peregrinans*," in Henry Peacham's *Minerva Britanna*, depicts a large tent and explains its symbolism:

> Nor house, nor home, hath wretched man on earth,
> Ne ought he claimeth iustly as his owne:
> But as a Pilgrim wandring from his birth
> In Countries straunge, and Deserts wild vnknowne.[60]

The emblem shows that earthly house and home are transitory; therefore we should "supply / Our inward wantes" and seek refuge in heavenly things, which "neither Moth, nor Canker shall decaie." Richard III, in Bosworth Field, seems to have such meaning in mind, when he instructs his followers: "Up with my tent! Here will I lie tonight. / But where tomorrow?" (5.3.7).[61]

Shakespeare relegates crucial information about Othello's background and identity to a space elsewhere, a place that Hanna Scolnicov refers to as "theatrical

---

[54] Torvald Faegre, *Tents: Architecture of the Nomads* (New York: Anchor Books, 1977) 10. Faegre writes: "The Bedouin tent is the most widespread of black-tent designs and the most refined for desert use" (18).

[55] Faegre 10.

[56] The most comprehensive study of the black tent, so called from the color associated with goat hair used in its manufacture, is C.G. Feilberg, *La Tente Noire* (Copenhagen: Nationalmuseets Skrifter, 1994).

[57] Faegre 7.

[58] Faegre 7.

[59] Faegre 7.

[60] Henry Peacham, *Minerva Britanna* (London, 1612), fol. 196.

[61] The *OED* cites an example from Fynes Moryson (*Itinerary*, II.82): "The weather grew so extreme, as it blew downe all our Tents, and tore them in pieces."

Super terram peregrinans. 196

NOR houſe, nor home, hath wretched man on earth,
Ne ought he claimeth iuſtly as his owne:
But as a * Pilgrim wandring from his birth
In Countries ſtraunge, and Deſerts wild vnknowne,
Like * *RECHABITE*, or thoſe Tartarian * *HORDES*,
Whoſe vaſteſt Region but a Tent affordes.

Betime hence learne we wiſely to ſupplie
Our inward wantes, ere hence we flit away:
And hide in Heauen, that treaſure carefully,
Which neither Moth, nor Canker ſhall decaie:
In * following ſtate, eke not to ſpend our ſtock,
Where oft for merit, we but gaine a mock.

* 1 Pet: *Cap*: 2 11

* *Ieremiæ* 35. 7.

* Companies of Tartars, and ſubiects of the great CHAM, liuing in Tentes in the wildernes, without Ciuilitie, togeither with their wiues, children, and cattle, neuer abiding in one place, but ranging and robbing vp and downe where they liſt.

* Sequor nil conſequor. dictum Arioſti.

Sapientiam

Fig. 2.4 Emblem of a Tent. Henry Peacham, *Minerva Britanna* (London, 1612). STC 19511. Houghton Library, Harvard University.

place without." Scolnicov distinguishes "everyday space"—the theater as an architectural structure—from "theatrical space"—the fictive locations rendered through a theatrical performance. Theatre space "exists independently of, and prior to, any performance"; "theatrical space"—a theatrical illusion, a fictive location—does not have to abide by natural laws and is therefore liberated from "the universal co-ordinates of time and space."[62] Each performance defines its "time-space structure," within which "its inner logic can function."[63] Scolnicov explains: "The theatrical space has a double nature: as it has visible extension in the theatre, and by extrapolation also beyond it, it is created by the performance; but to the extent that it is predetermined by the text, both in dialogue and stage directions, it is an inbuilt structural dimension of the play itself."[64] Theatrical space therefore encompasses both the visible scenery represented onstage, which Scolnicov calls "theatrical space within," and the invisible places from which the characters enter and to which they exit, as well as the unrepresented regions and locations to which they refer—the space that Scolnicov terms "theatrical space without."[65]

In *Othello*, Shakespeare masterfully juxtaposes theatrical space within and theatrical space without. The juxtaposition erodes and undermines domestic stability. Theatrical space within, whether Brabantio's house, the duke's council chamber, the fortress at Cyprus, or the bedchamber in Act 5, scene 2, appears to be "real" and "concrete" places; whereas, theatrical space without—namely, the fictive space at the borders, primarily associated with the African landscapes of Othello's ancestral home and earlier experiences in life—appear as part of vast, expansive, and blurry routes, leading to nameless destinations. As Paul Shepard maintains, "an environment without place names is fearful," and "landscapes without place names are disorienting."[66] Othello's domestic life seems caught between stability anchored in his marriage to a Venetian woman and the instability associated with ever-shifting fragmentary experiences of memory.

---

[62] Hanna Scolnicov, "Theatre Space, Theatrical Space, and the Theatrical Space Without," *The Theatrical Space*, (ed.) James Redmond (Cambridge: Cambridge University Press, 1987) 11–12.

[63] Scolnicov 11.

[64] Scolnicov 15.

[65] Scolnicov 13.

[66] Paul Shepard, *Man in the Landscape: A Historic View of the Esthetics of Nature* (College Station: Texas A&M University Press, 1991) 41, 43. For a discussion of this phenomenon in *The Tempest*, see my essay, "Alien Habitats in *The Tempest*," Patrick M. Murphy, (ed.), *The Tempest*: *Critical Essays* (New York and London: Routledge, 2001): 448–9.

Brabantio's Palazzo in Venice

Architects, developers, and the house dwellers "endow the house with meaning according to their culture's world view and ethos."[67] Extensive surveys of how people around the world perceive their domestic space reveals that home provides more than a shelter: "it is a world in which a person can create a material environment that embodies what he or she considers significant. In this sense the home becomes the most powerful sign of the self of the inhabitant who dwells within."[68] English travelers in Benin in 1553, for example, recognize the dignified status of the king by the audience room of his house: "the great hall, long and wide, the wals made of earth, the roofe of thin boords, open in sundry places, like unto lovers to let in the aire."[69] When viewed as the center of family life and hospitality and the stage upon which memorable personal events unfold, the house becomes a "home," which might be defined as a special kind of place to which one properly belongs and in which one's affections center or where one finds rest, refuge, or satisfaction.[70] I submit that the experience of dwelling in *Othello* seems initially to be the opposite of the African landscapes of Othello's childhood; yet eventually differences collapse, revealing a disturbing similarity between Venetian and alien spaces of residence. Similitude in this play carries a disturbing and unsettling valence, an ability to join and create geographical, cultural, and racial clusters.[71]

---

67 Robert M. Rakoff, "Ideology in Everyday Life: The Meaning of the House," *Politics and Society* 7 (1977): 85. See Sousa, "Unhoused in Othello," 133–4.

68 Mihaly Csikszentmihalyi, and Eugene Rochberg-Halton, *The Meaning of Things: Domestic Symbols and the Self* (Cambridge: Cambridge University Press, 1981) 123.

69 Hakluyt, *Principal Navigations*, 5:149.

70 This definition paraphrases and combines several *Oxford English Dictionary* definitions, as I did in my essay, "Unhoused in *Othello*" (134).

71 In *The Order of Things* (New York: Vintage Books, 1973), Michel Foucault argues that, in the Renaissance, knowledge was organized along a "semantic web of resemblance": *convenientia*, or adjacency, "a hinge between two things," through which "a resemblance appears"; *aemulatio*, a resemblance, as in a mirror image, freed from "the law of place," and requiring no contact between two things; "analogy," a form of "resemblances across space," yet still requiring adjacency, bonds, and joints; and "sympathy," a bond requiring no predetermined path and capable of traversing vast distances (17–25). The Latin word *convenientia* signified "meeting together, agreement, accord, harmony, conformity, suitableness, fitness" (*OED*). The *OED* defines sympathy as: "A (real or supposed) affinity between certain things, by virtue of which they are similarly or correspondingly affected by the same influence, affect or influence one another (esp. in some occult way), or attract or tend towards each other." In his translation of Plutarch's *Moralia* (London, 1603), Philemon Holland offers a glossary of "obscure words," in which he defines "sympathie" as "a fellow feeling, as is betweene the head and stomache in our bodies: also the agreement and natural amitie in divers senselesse things, as between iron and the load-stone" (sig. Aaaaaa^{v}). Ian Maclean, in "Foucault's Renaissance Episteme Reassessed: An Aristotelian Counterblast," *Journal of the History of Ideas* 59.1 (1998), deems this episteme "unreliable," since Foucault assumes that these forms of similitude come from the same field, rather

John Gillies traces disconcerting "patterns of 'intrusion' and 'exorbitance'" and "a glorious—yet unsettling—contradiction," associated with Venice, in *The Merchant of Venice* and *Othello*.[72] He cites Lewkenor's 1599 English translation of Gasparo Contarini's *Commonwealth and Government of Venice* to illustrate the paradox that Venice represented: a city that was planted in quagmires and "seated in the middle of the sea," yet had "palaces … reaching up to the clouds"; a democratic republic that was ruled by aristocrats; and a city that was governed by "unweaponed men in gownes," and yet was also a military and imperial power.[73] In another fascinating paradox, Venice, though a thriving commercial and cultural center, was a city governed by old men, the average age of doges, elected from 1400 to 1600, being 72; therefore, as Dennis Romano notes, the deliberations of Venetian councils, when compared to "the often rash decisions of more youthful Renaissance princes," tended to be slower and more deliberate. [74] Fynes Morison, who was in Italy in 1594, refers to the aging population of Venice: "I have never in any place observed more old men, or so many Senators venerable for their grey haires and aged gravity."[75] Othello, whom Iago calls "an old black ram" and who says "the young affects [are] / In me defunct" (1.3.263–4), might, perhaps, feel at home in the company of such geriatric leaders.[76]

Early modern maps offer "an idealized portrait of the city floating in the lagoon that protects its liberty and sustains its prestige as a trade emporium."[77] Visitors, such as Thomas Coryat, writing in 1611, comment on the status of

than from "the spheres of grammar, rhetoric or moral philosophy, dialectics, and natural philosophy or medicine" (153). Foucault also relies on Platonic theories, and—more to the point—he inexplicably excludes from consideration a large body of Aristotelian texts and commentaries.

72 John Gillies, *Shakespeare and the Geography of Difference* (Cambridge: Cambridge University Press, 1994) 122–3.

73 Paraphrased from Gillies, 122. The quotations, cited by Gillies, are from Gasparo Contarini, *The Commonwealth and Government of Venice*, trans. Lewes Lewknor (London, 1599).

74 Robert Finlay, *Politics in Renaissance Venice* (New Brunswick, NJ: Rutgers University Press, 1980) 37–43, 124–41; and Dennis Romano, "City-State and Empire," *Artistic Centers of the Italian Renaissance: Venice and the Veneto* (Cambridge: Cambridge University Press, 2007) 9.

75 Fynes Moryson, *An Itinerary* (Glasgow: James MacLehose and Sons, 1907) 1: 164–5.

76 In reality, however, Othello shows anxiety about old age, and, as Philip D. Collington argues, Othello, like Shakespeare's other old men, Lear and Prospero, employs "sexualized and misogynous language" "to conceal affective states ranging from insecurity and fear to bitterness and rage" (188). See Collington's article, "Sans Wife: Sexual Anxiety and the Old Man in Shakespeare," in Erin Campbell, (ed.), *Growing Old in Early Modern Europe: Cultural Representations* (Aldershot and Burlington: Ashgate, 2006) 185–207.

77 Bronwen Wilson, "Venice, Print, and the Early Modern Icon," *Urban History* 33.1 (2006): 46.

Venice as a glorious cosmopolitan center and a magnet attracting visitors, traders, and adventurers from all over the world: "Here you may both see all manner of fashions of attire, and heare all the languages of Christendome, besides those that are spoken by the barbarous Ethnickes."[78] Contarini praises the Venetians for their "humanitie towards straungers";[79] elsewhere, he praises Venice's welcoming of foreigners: "some forrain men and strangers have been adopted into this number of citizens, eyther in regard of their nobility, or that they had been dutiful towards the state, or else had done unto them some notable service."[80] Both Shylock's appeals to the city charter to uphold his bond, and Othello's confidence that his service to the state will be remembered, intimate an orderly and fair political hierarchy and perhaps what Contarini describes as Venice's "justice as pure and uncorrupted."[81] Obviously, Shakespeare also represents the other side: Venice as a city sharply divided along racial and religious lines. Contarini marvels at the abundance and variety of foreign commodities available for purchase in Venice, or Venetian and European merchandise for export by land and sea to far away regions, as if Venice "were a common and general market to the whole world."[82] The city functioned as a crossroads, where the trade routes intersected, and as a gateway between East and West. Through this intermediary role, Venice "negotiat[ed] the exchange and interchange of men, ideas, and especially goods between Europe and Asia."[83] Francesco Borri contends that the Plea of Rižana, a *placitum* written between 800 and 810, attests to the early network of connections between Venice's Latin-speaking elites and other population centers on the Istrian peninsula and along the Northern Adriatic arc.[84] In its long history, Venice played an intermediary role, and therefore rightly deserves to be known as the "hinge of Europe."[85]

Contemporary writers saw Venice as an architectural wonder and a miracle of human ingenuity. Visitors from Western Europe would have been struck by "a distinctly oriental atmosphere," the city having absorbed Byzantine, Islamic, and "Moorish architectural and urban characteristics."[86] Deborah Howard writes that

---

78 Thomas Coryat, *Coryats crudities* (London, 1611), quoted in Gillies 124.

79 Contarini sig. A2–A2^v.

80 Contarini sig. D1^v.

81 Contarini sig. A2^v.

82 Cantarini sig. B.

83 Romano, "City-State and Empire," 11.

84 Francesco Borri, "'Neighbors and Relatives': The Plea of Rižana as a Source for Northern Adriatic Elites," *Mediterranean Studies* 17 (2008): 1–26.

85 William H. McNeill, *Venice: The Hinge of Europe, 1081–1797* (Chicago: University of Chicago Press, 1974), qtd. in Romano, "City-State and Empire," 11.

86 Deborah Howard, "Venice and Islam in the Middle Ages: Some Observations on the Question of Architectural Influence," *Architectural History* 34 (1991): 59. See also, Patricia Fortini Brown, *Private Lives in Renaissance Venice: Art, Architecture, and the Family* (New Haven and London: Yale University Press, 2004), esp. chapter 8, "Theaters of the World," 217–51.

Fig. 2.5 Three views of Venice. Vicenzo Coronelli, 1650–1718. *Isolario: descrittione geografico-historica, sacro-profana, antico-moderna, politica*, Venice, 1696–1697. Summerfield H27. Courtesy of Special Collections, Spencer Research Library, University of Kansas Libraries.

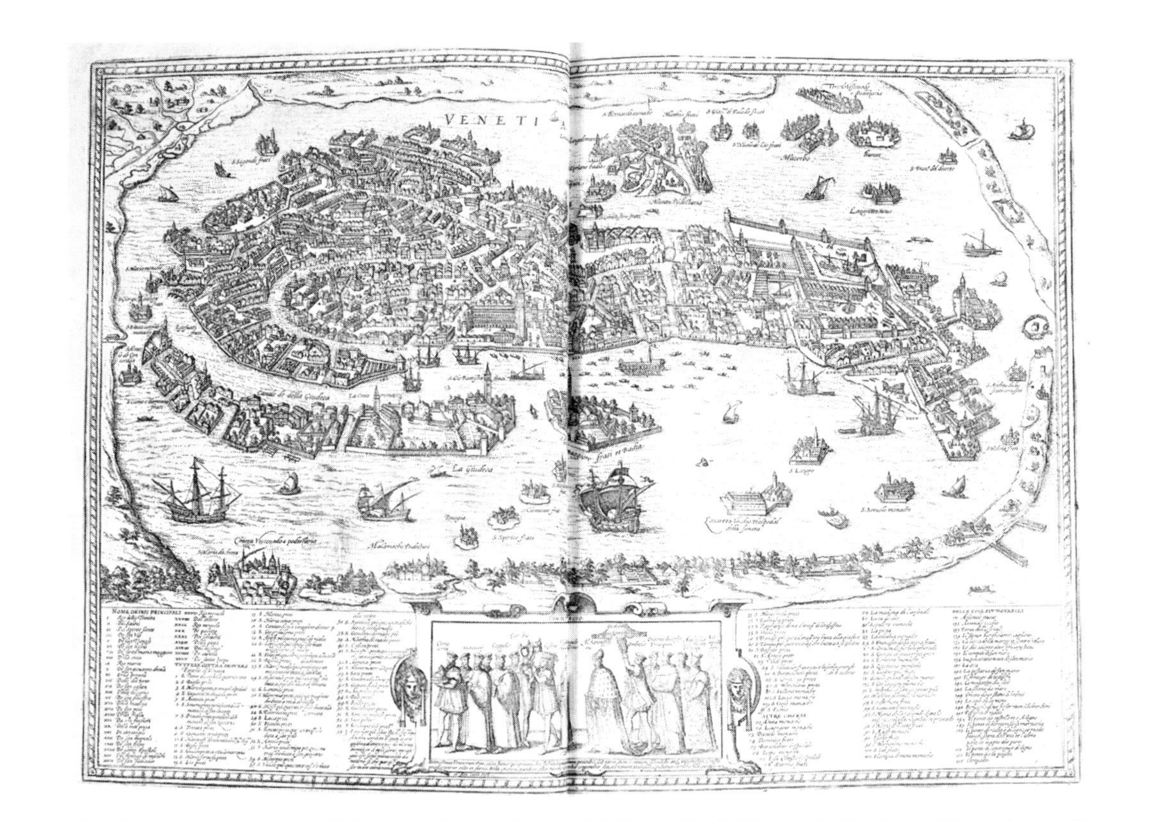

Fig. 2.6 A view of Venice. Georg Braun, 1540 or 41–1622, and Abraham Hogenberg, fl. 1608–58, *Civitates orbis terrarum* (Brussels, 1574–1618). Summerfield H9. Courtesy of Special Collections, Spencer Research Library, University of Kansas Libraries.

architectural historians have long remarked on "the resemblance between the early Venetian palace and the Arabic trading post, or *funduk*":

> Both in Venice and in the east the type is characterized by a two-storey, screen-like façade, perforated with arcades, often with corner towers, containing storage and (except in Venice) stabling below, and lodgings above. A central courtyard contained a well or fountain, fed by a cistern beneath.[87]

Excavations of Fatimid palaces of Cairo even bear resemblance to the palaces of Venetian patrician merchants.[88] According to Howard, Venetian manuscript illumination of Ptolemy in Alexandria offers "a delightful instance of the blurring of the boundaries between east and west" in the Venetian-style Gothic palace.[89] No wonder, yet again, that Othello seems to have felt so much at home in Brabantio's palazzo, although, as John Drakakis proposes, Othello also "internalizes" the "'orientalist' practices" of Venice and "inherits the lurid substance of Brabantio's dream."[90]

Lewes Lewkenor remarks on the fact that experienced travelers, who had been to "the farthest parts of Asia and Affrica," spoke of Venice as worthy of "the highest of all admiration" and as one of the "most infinitely remarkable" sites "that they had seen in the whole course of their travels."[91] Venice was and still is known for the beauty of its architecture, including "palaces, monasteries, temples, towers, turrets, & pinacles reaching unto the cloudes"; but the ingenuity and engineering skills of the builders were, as I noted earlier, particularly noteworthy, for the same buildings rise out of "quagmires," the muddy bottom of a lagoon.[92] Thomas Coryat, in his *Crudities* (1611), explains that the method of laying the foundation requires an extraordinary feat of engineering and technical skills:

> For whereas many of them [buildings] are situate in the water, whensoever they lay the foundation of any house they remove the water by certaine devices from the place where they lay the first fundamentall matter. Most commonly they drive long stakes into the ground, without the which they doe *aggerere molem*, that is, raise certaine heapes of sand, mudde, clay, or some other such matter to repell the water. Then they ramme in great piles of woodde, which they lay very deepe, upon the which they place their bricke or stone, and so frame the other parts of the building.[93]

---

87 Howard, "Venice and Islam," 68–9.

88 Howard, "Venice and Islam," 69.

89 Howard, "Venice and Islam," 69.

90 John Drakakis, "Shakespeare and Venice," in Michele Marrapodi, (ed.), *Italian Culture in the Drama of Shakespeare & His Contemporaries* (Aldershot, and Burlington, VT: Ashgate, 2007) 185. Drakakis is, of course, referring to Brabantio's line, "This accident is not unlike my dream" (1.1.140).

91 Preface "To the Reader" (sig. A1^{v}–A2).

92 Contarini sig. A2^{v}–A3.

93 Thomas Coryat, *Coryat's Crudities* (1611; Glasgow: James MacLehose and Sons, 1905) 1: 308.

Coryat reports that, while in Venice, he heard that the cost of laying the foundations, "contrived with so great labour," amounts to as much as 30 percent of the total costs of the construction.[94] In his *Itinerary*, Fynes Moryson confirms Coryat's report: "The foundations are laid of Oake in the waters, and the stone of Istria is much esteemed."[95] The Venetians spared no costs in building and furnishing their houses; as Moryson adds, even "the Pallaces of Gentlemen," though called "houses" "are and worthily deserve to be called Pallaces, some hundred of them being fit to receive Princes."[96] Such palaces, displaying "Princely magnificence," built upon costly, sturdy foundations, planted in a boggy lagoon, are, indeed, "monstrously strange," as Contarini puts it.[97]

Based on Othello's account of recent events, Brabantio's house seems to have represented stability and continuity and to fit almost perfectly the definition of the ideal home. We catch glimpses of what the house used to be like, and of Othello as a frequent dinner guest in Brabantio's house:

> Her father loved me, oft invited me;
> Still questioned me the story of my life
> From year to year—the battles, sieges, fortunes
> That I have passed. (1.3.128–31)

An atmosphere of warm hospitality emerges. As host, Brabantio provides food and drink; whereas Othello, as guest, provides entertainment; namely, narratives about his life. Desdemona takes an interest in his stories, as Othello notes:

> This to hear
> Would Desdemona seriously incline;
> But still the house affairs would draw her thence;
> Which ever as she could with haste dispatch,
> She'ld come again, and with a greedy ear
> Devour up my discourse. (1.3.145–50)

As house chores demanded, Desdemona would go in and out of the room, but she remained fascinated by her father's guest. In a metaphoric inversion, the houseguest provided the food, which Desdemona devoured with "a greedy ear." Eventually she asked for a private telling of his "pilgrimage" and then encouraged Othello to "woo" her. In its warmth, stability, hospitality, and domestic life, Brabantio's house may have come as close to a home as anything that Othello had ever experienced. If we take Othello's life-long perambulations and deracination as an experience in the wilderness, Brabantio's home seems like a peaceful retreat from the trials, tribulations, deprivation, and temptations of life on the go.

---

94 Coryat 1: 308.

95 Moryson 193.

96 Moryson 193.

97 Contarini sig. A2^{v}.

Brabantio's house may have a sturdy foundation, as construction in a boggy lagoon required, and may have seemed like a welcome refuge; however, ultimately it offers but an illusion of stability. At the beginning of the play, the house, enveloped in thick darkness, seems utterly empty: not because all the residents have moved out and taken away the furnishings, but because *one* of the dwellers, Desdemona, has already eloped with Othello, leaving behind a yet-to-be discovered empty bedchamber, a broken family, and a deeply hurt and disappointed father. I will discuss later the function of light and darkness in the play; suffice it to say here that the house has not always been so dark or so empty.

Brabantio had opened the house to a stranger, who stole his daughter's heart, and shattered the apparent atmosphere of domestic harmony and familial happiness. Francesco Sansovini writes of Venetian courtship: "The marriages among the nobility are for the most part always treated of by a third person, the bride neuer suffered so much as to behold her future husband, nor he her, till their marriage dower, and all thinges thereunto appertaining, bee fully agreed vpon and concluded."[98] By inviting Othello into the inner sanctum of his home, Brabantio allows Othello and Desdemona an unusual degree of access to each other, and therefore, ironically, makes possible this most unlikely marriage.

The laws of Venice frowned on biracial marriages, and other marriages of couples coming from different social strata. In the fifteenth century, the Venetian law emphasized patrilineal heredity: "among other things, it denied noble status to the sons of marriages between noblemen and slaves or other women of 'vile' status."[99] The *Serrata* laws (1497–1535) shifted the focus to "a man's maternal heredity," leading to the *Libro d'oro*, the Golden Book registry of noble births, which, as Stanley Chojnacki has uncovered, "fundamentally 'altered the meaning of nobility in Venice' by emphasizing the moment of birth rather than political adulthood as the central event in the attainment of noble identity."[100] In 1569, the *Libri d'argento* or "Silver Books of Citizen Families," became the register for *cittadini* to claim citizenship status.[101] Consequently, as Dennis Romano writes, "To a degree Venetian men used their female relatives in much the same way as they did their palaces. Women's bodies served as sites for demonstrations of family wealth and power," and "helped establish noble identity."[102] These laws help

---

98 Contarini sig. Cc^{v}.

99 Romano 9. Romano's conclusions are based on a study by Stanley Chojnacki, "Social Identity in Renaissance Venice: The Second *Serrata*," *Renaissance Studies* 8.4 (1994): 341–58.

100 Chojnacki 271, as quoted and paraphrased by Romano 16.

101 Romano 16–17.

102 Romano 17. In "Family Jewels: The Gendered Marking of Medici Women in Court Portraits of the Late Renaissance," *Mediterranean Studies* 17 (2008): 148–82, Heather L. Sale Holian argues that, for the Medici, jewels and other "priceless objects of personal adornment functioned as dynastic markers, 'branding' or 'marking' the female wearer as Medici, and as such are therefore comparable to the bold proprietary claims performed by the family's ubiquitous coat-of-arms displayed on Medici-owned villas, palaces, works of art, and even family pets" (148).

contextualize the possible consequences of Desdemona's elopement, and also of the Duke's indifference to Brabantio's concerns about his only daughter's strong-willed disregard for her family's plight. The Duke's tolerance might be explained as expediency: faced with the need to defend Cyprus and Venetian commercial interests, he needs Othello and is therefore willing to overlook Othello's action. Brabantio, however, seems fully aware of the consequences of Desdemona's actions for his family.

At the beginning of the play, the house is under siege; but, before long, the audience realizes that domesticity itself has been under assault from within and from without. Shakespeare suggests that the house fails on the most basic level to safeguard privacy and provide a refuge from the outside world. From Brabantio's perspective, his house is under frontal attack. Roderigo and Iago raise the alarm with shouts: "Awake! What, ho, Brabantio! Thieves! Thieves! / Look to your house, your daughter, and your bags!" (1.1.78–9). Iago asks questions to heighten Brabantio's and the audience's fear: "Signor, is all your family within?" and "Are your doors locked?" He informs the Venetian senator: "Zounds, sir, you're robbed!" (1.1.85). Burglary, as Heather Dubrow notes, particularly inspired fear and anxiety in the early modern period, and "by and large Shakespeare's culture punishes burglars especially severely and Shakespeare's texts represent them especially darkly."[103] Burglars behaved like beasts, violating the laws of nature and of man; they were particularly feared because they operate at night and therefore "violate place in the sense of literally sneaking in where they do not belong." [104] Furthermore, outsiders—rogues, vagabonds, and Gypsies—are associated with "fear of stealth," secrecy intensifying transgressiveness; consequently, the assizes records suggest that "an outsider was more likely to be prosecuted and sentenced harshly than the neighbor."[105]

Roderigo observes that Othello, behaving like a burglar, has violated the privacy of the house and stolen valuable movables, and, even more outrageously seduced Desdemona, who has been carted away "at this odd-even and dull watch o' th' night," by "a common knave, a gondolier" into "the gross clasps of a lascivious Moor" (1.1.120–28). In a state of panic, Brabantio wonders, "How got she out?" (1.1.167), and like Lear, suspects "treason of the blood" (167). He wants to summon his brother (173), and wake up "every house" (178). Iago's allusions to "Barbary horse" and a "black ram tupping a white ewe" compound to form the startling racist image of "your daughter and Moor are making the beast with two backs" (115–16). References to both domesticated animals and wild animals, such as haggard, guinea hen, and baboon, crop up frequently throughout the play, and such images together connect the Venetian world to the wilderness, suggesting that even a highly civilized and sophisticated place has become something wild and alien. Brabantio concludes that if Othello gets away with stealing Desdemona, then "Bondslaves and pagans shall our statesmen be" (1.2.99). Anxiety about

[103] Dubrow 23.

[104] Dubrow 30–31.

[105] Dubrow 29.

burglary and fear of the outsider come together. The burglar, as Dubrow remarks, violates and "erodes social boundaries": " … the burglar literally transgresses by crossing the threshold of a house."[106] The events at the beginning of the play strike the ominous note that family life, security, and trust all collapse.

When the Senate orders Othello to set sail for Cyprus, for he best knows "the fortitude of the place" (1.3.222), Desdemona's own "unhousèd" condition becomes apparent. Desdemona has no place to stay during his absence. Even while residing in Venice, Othello does not have a permanent home, as Cassio points out: "You have been hotly called for; / When being not at your lodging to be found, / The Senate hath sent about three several quests / To search you out" (1.2.44–7). "Lodging" suggests temporary quarters, such as one finds in a boarding house, where Othello presumably lived before he married Desdemona. However their decision to elope came about, Othello takes Desdemona from her father's house and seeks shelter for the night at some other place, as Othello's statement to Cassio implies: "'Tis well I am found by you. / I will but spend a word here in the house, / And go with you" (1.2.47–9). He will go inside the house, tell Desdemona that the Duke and the senators require his presence, and then proceed to the Senate. The text makes clear that this house provides only temporary accommodation.[107] Having defied her father and severed her ties to her family, she cannot return to her father's house, and Othello has neither bought nor rented a house in Venice; therefore, she has little option but to follow him to Cyprus. Even Jessica and Lorenzo, in *The Merchant of Venice*, at least have Portia's house in Belmont, where they take refuge. For all practical purposes, Desdemona has become unhousèd, homeless. Therefore, the move to Cyprus may offer new opportunities for possible happiness, but it leaves behind the shattered foundation of Desdemona's relationship to her father and, without her presence, his dark and empty house.

A Mighty Fortress in Cyprus

In Act II, the principal characters of the play arrive at a port, presumably the fortified town of Famagusta, which came under Turkish attack in 1569 and 1571. Words such as "battlements," "citadel," "castle," and fortification, all associated with Cyprus, underscore that Cyprus is a heavily armed fortress, with strong foundations and fortified walls. Othello and Desdemona move into state apartments in this fortification. References to military storehouses, works, and garrison, presumably located on high ground, provide defense for the "town."

---

106 Dubrow 32.

107 In *Speaking of the Moor: From Alcazar to Othello* (Philadelphia: University of Pennsylvania Press, 2008), Emily C. Bartels argues that "in a world where everyone seems to have a place to be, the Moor is no exception, appearing no less (if also no more) embedded on the homefront than his Venetian, Florentine, or Cypriot peers" (172). Bartels is arguing for Othello's "embeddedness in Venice on more than just military grounds" (173). My point differs substantially from hers, in that I am arguing for Othello's "unhousèd" condition, not his "embeddedness."

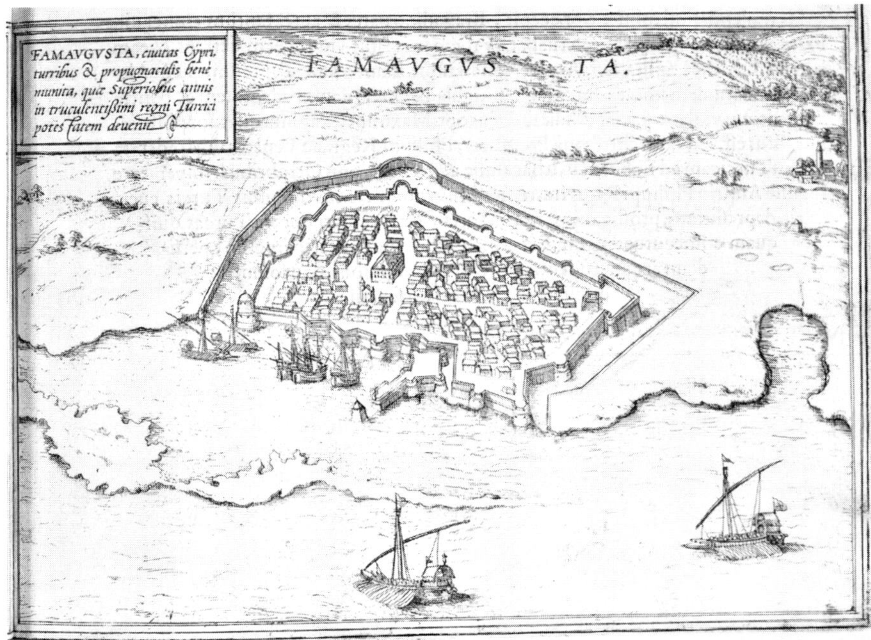

Fig. 2.7 A view of Famagusta, Cyprus (detail). Georg Braun, 1540 or 41–1622, and Abraham Hogenberg, fl. 1608–58, *Civitates orbis terrarum* (Brussels, 1574–1618). Summerfield H9. Courtesy of Special Collections, Spencer Research Library, University of Kansas Libraries.

Doubtless this place, to which Othello refers as "home," does serve as home for him and Desdemona. They settle down here and entertain important guests, such as Lodovico, for dinner in Act IV, scene 1.

While the play labels the living quarters of Iago, Emilia, and Cassio as lodgings, Bianca, on the other hand, owns a house, and seems well off. Like Othello and Desdemona, she receives Cassio as a dinner guest, and perhaps under different circumstances might have provided a shelter for abused wives, such as Emilia and Desdemona. We know that Veronica Franco (1546–91), Julia Lombardo, and Modesta Fonte, among the best known Venetian courtesans, were not only patrons of the arts but also benefactors for institutions for the protection of women. Franco, for example, "petitioned the government to establish an institution for impoverished young women who were at risk of slipping into prostitution," and the state established the Casa dell Soccorso, "a refuge for unmarried women and for wives fleeing unhappy or abusive marriages,"[108] an option apparently neither available for nor entertained by Emilia or Desdemona in Cyprus.

---

[108] Romano, 17–18, refers to Margaret F. Rosenthal's study, *The Honest Courtesan: Veronica Franco, Citizen and Writer in Sixteenth-Century Venice* (Chicago: University of Chicago Press, 1992).

As the scene shifts to Cyprus, the storm scatters and destroys the Turkish fleet; therefore, the change of location might promise more permanence, stability, and tranquility than Othello and Desdemona had experienced in Venice. Sent on a military mission, Othello engages in no combat. Ironically, the sea voyage separates Desdemona from Othello and places her under Iago's guardianship; likewise, the destruction of the Turkish fleet opens the path for Iago to assail Othello's domestic happiness. Instead of finding an opportunity for conjugal happiness, Othello and Desdemona face new challenges.

Othello, although he takes Desdemona from her father's house, gives her a castle in Cyprus; yet the castle, like the house, offers but an illusion of stability. In fact, Montano and two gentlemen underscore the fragility of even the sturdiest battlements in Cyprus, let alone the ships on the high seas:

> Methinks the wind hath spoke aloud at land;
> A fuller blast ne'er shoot our battlements.
> If it hath ruffianed so upon the sea,
> What ribs of oak, when mountains melt on them,
> Can hold the mortise? (5–9).

The Turkish fleet has been segregated and destroyed, and the Venetians have emerged unscathed; but the storm reveals that the "mortise" [joints] of the strongest man-made structures may give way in tempestuous weather, an indication that Othello and Desdemona's house, or "castle," in Cyprus cannot withstand the storm that lies ahead. Montano and the gentlemen suggest that a fierce storm can shake a strong foundation and batter even a well-built fortification, a fitting reminder that Iago's malice could undermine and destroy the foundation of Othello and Desdemona's marriage.

Turmoil temporarily gives way to calm. When Othello finally arrives in Act II, scene 1, allaying fears that he might have perished at sea, and observes Desdemona, his heart fills with joy: "If after every tempest come such calms, / May the winds blow till they have wakened death!" (2.1.184–5); he adds: "Come, let us to the castle" (200). In scene 2, through the herald, Othello decrees a general double celebration of his nuptial and of the defeat of the Turks, ordering that "every man put himself into triumph; some to dance, some to make bonfires, each man to what sport and revels his addition [rank] leads him" (2.2.3–6). A night brawl between the drunken Cassio and Montano interrupts the celebration and disrupts Othello and Desdemona's honeymoon. By scene 3, Othello and Desdemona have already retired to bed. The play's attention turns to this inner sanctum of their marriage, where new sources of danger await the newly-married couple.

In ancient times, Cyprus, especially Paphos, was known as the birth place of Aphrodite/Venus, the goddess of love, often referred to as "*diva potens Cypri*."[109] The drama of the period abounds with references to Cyprus as the land of love, as Aurelia's speech to her sister in Jonson's *Case Is Altered* makes clear: "I

---

[109] Sugden 142.

thought you'd dwell so long in Cypres isle, / You'd worship Madam Venus at the length."[110] The island was also of military and strategic importance. Venice acquired Cyprus in 1487 and maintained control over the island until 1571, when the Turks conquered it. In Shakespeare's play, Othello and Desdemona presumably arrive in Cyprus in the middle of that military contest. For Alvin Kernan, *Othello*'s Cyprus stands between "two reference points": "out at the far edge are the Turks, barbarism, disorder, and amoral destructive power; closer and more familiar is Venice, *The City*, order law, and reason."[111] As a frontier, Cyprus "is rather an outpost, weakly defended and far out in the raging ocean, close to the 'general enemy' and the immediate object of his attack," a "'town of war yet wild' where the 'people's hearts [are] brimful of fear.'"[112] Kernan's analysis oversimplifies the cartography of Shakespeare's play; but, as John Drakakis aptly notes, Cyprus functions as "a geopolitical frontier where the marriage between 'Moor' and 'Christian', Venetian and Turk, is to be tested."[113] Kernan's view fails to account for the extent to which seemingly incompatible modes of dwelling intermingle and modify each other. Fortunatus, in Thomas Dekker's *The Pleasant Comedie of Old Fortunatus* (1600), reminds us that in Cyprus no one can get sleep or rest in peace: "the great bell of S. Michaels in Cyprus … keeps most rumbling, when men would most sleepe."[114] In Cyprus, the birthplace of the Goddess of Love, no one can sleep in peace, an ominous sign of what awaits Desdemona and Othello during their sojourn on the island.

The Edge of Darkness

In *Othello*, the characters seem to stand on the edge of darkness, and Shakespeare may have borrowed lighting effects, well known to painters, to create illusions of distance. In *The Painting of the Ancients* (1638), Franciscus Junius writes that the viewer perceives white objects to be nearer, whereas black objects and objects enveloped in darkness to lie further away; therefore, painters make use of light and dark shades to create illusions of depth and of distance because "The white shall always seeme to be nearer, and the blacke further off." Consequently, painters use shades of black or brown to make something like a well, a ditch, or cave seem "hollow"; he adds, darker shades suggest greater depth: "for whatsoever is extreme

[110] Sugden lists many of these references (143).

[111] Alvin Kernan, "*Othello*: An Introduction," *Shakespeare: The Tragedies: A Collection of Critical Essays*, (ed.) Alfred Harbage (Englewood Cliffs, NJ: Prentice-Hall, 1964): 77–8.

[112] Kernan 77–8.

[113] Drakakis, "Shakespeare and Venice," 183.

[114] Thomas Dekker, *The pleasant comedie of old Fortunatus* (London, 1600), sig. A4. STC 6517.

blacke, the same worketh in us an apprehension of a bottomlesse deepnesse.[115] Renaissance artists were, of course, very much aware of this effect. For example, Michelangelo Merisi da Caravaggio (1573–1610) and his followers, such as Giuseppe de Ribera (1591–1652), known as *tenebrosi*, employed a characteristic style of extreme contrasts between light and shadows to create dramatically accentuated and intense chiaroscuro effects.[116] Members of this school were known to favor "*i chiaroscuri intensi, i fondi scuri, i colori cupi*" [intense chiaroscuro, dark background, and gloomy colors].[117]

As is well known, productions in the London public theaters of Shakespeare's time took place in daylight. However, despite the absence of tools to create "variable lighting," the plays include numerous night scenes. As Alan Dessen notes, the playwright indicates the illusion of on-stage darkness by stage directions, dialogue, props (tapers, torches, and candles), and costume, "especially the nightgown, to denote night or interrupted sleep."[118] Some scenes require "silence, stealth, even tiptoeing."[119] Other subtle markers of variable lighting conditions were also possible, such as, "for example, if a torch or candle was cited as the only source of light in a given scene, to extinguish that light was to indicate stage darkness."[120] As R.B. Graves remarks, type of lighting utensils determined and signaled indoor or outdoor location: tapers for indoors; torches and lanterns for outdoors.[121] I submit that, by using stage conventions of imaginary darkness, Shakespeare in *Othello* employs tenebrist lighting effects and generates a darkness that blurs boundaries of perception, reconfigures architectural space, and racializes and redefines family life in the play. In fact, Shakespeare conducts a visual experiment with light and darkness. The play often calls for special lighting effects—scenes that are to be staged *a lume di notte* (by candlelight)— or in a mode that approximates tenebrism—to reveal multiple layers of represented reality, manipulate actual and fictive space, transform architectural space, and to reveal a dynamic interplay of space, vision, and race.[122]

---

[115] Franciscus Junius, *The Painting of the Ancients* (London, 1638), 276. STC 7302. See "How to Draw Distance," in David Park, *The Fire Within the Eye: A Historical Essay on the Nature and Meaning of Light* (Princeton; Princeton University Press, 1997) 130–36.

[116] The *OED* traces the English usage of *tenebroso* to an article by W.M. Rossetti in 1886, although the term can be documented in much earlier usage in Italian and Spanish.

[117] Salvatore Battaglia, *Grande Dizionario della Lingua Italiana* (Turin: Unione Tipografico-Editrice Torinese, 2001).

[118] Dessen, *Elizabethan Stage Conventions*, 70.

[119] Dessen, *Elizabethan Stage Conventions*, 71.

[120] Dessen, *Elizabethan Stage Conventions*, 72.

[121] R.B. Graves, *Lighting the Shakespearean Stage, 1567–1642* (Carbondale and Edwardsville: Southern Illinois University Press, 1999) 205–207.

[122] In "Caravaggio Reloaded: Neo-Baroque Poetics," Angela Ndalianis notes the ways in which "The neo-baroque articulates the spatial, the visual and the sensorial," especially "its delight in spectacles that playfully immerse the viewer in multiple layers of representational realities" (73). Her article appears in *Caravaggio & His World: Darkness & Light* (Sydney, N.S.W.: Art Gallery of New South Wales; Melbourne: National Gallery of Victoria,

Shakespeare and Caravaggio were near contemporaries, the playwright being seven years older than the painter. Francine Prose draws attention, in passing, to a similarity between them: "Indeed an intensely Shakespearean spirit—theatrical, compassionate, alternately and simultaneously comic and tragic—suffuses Caravaggio's art."[123] Shakespeare and Caravaggio have much in common. Dramatic intensity pervades Caravaggio's paintings, as Prose adds: "For Caravaggio, the lives of saints and martyrs and their dramas of suffering and redemption were played out among real men and women, on earth, in the here and now, and in almost total darkness."[124] Caravaggio found inspiration in public executions, Roman street life, hagiographical narratives, and mystery plays.[125] Caravaggio tapped into the "grotesque and the extreme," as in *Boy Bitten by a Lizard* or *Medusa*; or in *The Death of the Virgin*, in which the Virgin looks "too much like the bloated corpse of a real woman."[126] I will not, however, claim that one artist influenced the other; rather, Caravaggio and Shakespeare, apparently independent of each other, employ similar techniques involving the use of lighting and visual effects. Shakespeare, however, could have read the 1598 English translation of the Italian treatise, *A Tracte Containing the artes of curious painting caruinge buildinge*, by Giovanni Paolo Lomazzo, the same treatise that may have influenced Caravaggio.[127] Even Milton in an academic exercise considers "Whether Day is better than Night."[128]

2003), 72–7. Caravaggio, for her, represents "strategically orchestrated levels of reality." Caracci devises, in her words, an open and limitless two dimensional space. Likewise, Caravaggio wants to collapse "the frame that separates illusion from reality, fictive space from actual space." I think that these ideas are particularly helpful in trying to analyze Shakespeare's own experiments with lighting and special effects in *Othell*o. In "*Othello* and Perception," James Hirsh argues that "*Othello* dramatizes the processes by which people perceive one another and their situations," and that the play dramatizes "a change in Othello's perception of Desdemona," as well as "playgoers' perception of Othello" (Orlin, *New Casebooks: Othello*, 135). My focus here is, rather, on lighting effects and Shakespeare's manipulation of lights, darkness, and shadows to create a uniquely Caravaggesque effect.

123 Francine Prose, *Caravaggio: Painter of Miracles* (New York: HarperCollins, 2005) 16–17.

124 Prose 29.

125 Sergio Benedetti, "Darkness and Light," *Caravaggio & His World: Darkness & Light* (Sydney, N.S.W.: Art Gallery of New South Wales; Melbourne: National Gallery of Victoria, 2003) 28–32, 32.

126 Prose 50, 102.

127 The study of perspective, including Lomazzo's book, had an influence on English landscape painters, and Shakespeare uses linear and aerial perspective. See James Turner, "Landscape and the 'Art Prospective' in England, 1584–1660," *Journal of the Warburg and Courtauld Institutes* 42 (1979): 291–2.

128 Donald Lemen Clark, "Ancient Rhetoric and English Renaissance Literature," *Shakespeare Quarterly* 2.3 (1951): 200. I am grateful to Professor Richard Hardin, University of Kansas, for bringing this example to my attention.

In his well-known biography of the painter, Howard Hibbard suggests that Caravaggio, "notorious as a painter-assassin," must be considered "the most important painter of the entire seventeenth century," although Caravaggio died in 1610 at the age of 39.[129] "Caravaggio's paintings," adds Hibbard, "speak to us more personally and more poignantly than any others of his time."[130] Caravaggio's revolutionary method involved accentuating and sharpening the stark contrasts between light and darkness. Earliest commentators, both admirers and detractors, remark on the style. For example, Giulio Mancini, *Considerazioni sulla pittura* (c. 1617–21), states that Caravaggesque tenebrism characteristically employs "lighting from one source only, which beams down without reflections," as if "in a dark room with one window and the walls painted black," therefore creating very deep shadows and a "powerful relief."[131] Mancini thinks that this method works well for single figures, but not for narrative compositions, "since it is impossible to put in one room a multitude of people acting out the story, with that light coming in from a single window, having to laugh or cry or pretending to walk while having to stay still in order to be copied."[132] Writing in 1672, Giovanni Pietro Bellori, *Le vite de'pittori e architetti moderni*, mentions Caravaggio's ability to "give relief to the forms" by placing the figures in the darkness of a closed room, and by "placing a lamp high so that the light would fall straight down, revealing the principal part of the body and leaving the rest in shadow so as to produce a powerful contrast of light and dark."[133]

Sergio Benedetti suggests that Caravaggio's painting, *Taking of Christ* (1602, oil on canvas, National Gallery of Ireland, Dublin), encapsulates Caravaggio's innovations, including a "background stripped to its essentials," "reduction of space around the figures," and an "idealized source of light," falling from above; this light illuminates Christ and the other figures, contrasting Jesus' calm and gesture of self-sacrificial resignation to save mankind, Judas's lack of expression, St John's terror, and the face of a man holding a lantern, which scholars take to be a self-portrait of Caravaggio.[134] Edmund Capon puts it best, when he writes that "the abyss of blackness against which the figures are invariably set lends both mystery and profundity to the occasion."[135] In *Saint John the Baptist* (c. 1604/5), a painting at the Nelson-Atkins Museum of Art in Kansas City, Missouri, Caravaggio manipulates lighting to reveal a pensive youthful John the Baptist, whose smooth white body pierces through the shadows, not unlike the figure of Desdemona lying in the nuptial bed in Act V, scene 2.

---

[129] Howard Hibbard, *Caravaggio* (New York: Harper & Row, 1983) vii.

[130] Hibbard vii.

[131] The passage has been translated by Hibbard, 350. All translations, unless indicated otherwise, are by Hibbard.

[132] Hibbard 350.

[133] Hibbard 363–64.

[134] Benedetti, "Darkness and Light," 32.

[135] Edmund Capon, "Why Caravaggio?" in *Darkness & Light*, 14–15, 15.

Fig. 2.8 Michelangelo Merisi, called Caravaggio, Italian (1571–1610). *Saint John the Baptist in the Wilderness*, 1604–05. Oil on canvas, 68 x 52 inches (172.7 x 132.1 cm). The Nelson-Atkins Museum of Art, Kansas City, Missouri. Purchase: William Rockhill Nelson Trust, 52–25. Photograph by Jamison Miller.

Caravaggio received his training in Milan, an artistic tradition known for "empirical experiments in lighting effects": "The painters of Lombardy and the Veneto produced numerous examples of this type during the sixteenth century, and nocturnal subjects illuminated by artificial light had been extensively developed in the studio of the Bassano family."[136] Caravaggio may have been acquainted with *Trattato dell'arte de Pittura, Scultura, et Architectura*, by Giovanni Paolo Lomazzo (1538–1600), published in Milan in 1585.[137] As mentioned above, Lomazzo's book was also available in an English translation.[138] Even if Shakespeare did not consult this particular treatise, other studies of perspective, light, shadows, and mirrors circulated in Shakespeare's time, as for example, Salomon de Caus's *La perspective, avec la raison des ombres et miroirs*, dedicated to Henry, Prince of Wales, and published in Oxford in 1611. Inigo Jones, influenced by Italian theater design and the visual arts, worked in a variety of projects, including stage design for Ben Jonson's *Masque of Blackness*, performed at Whitehall on Twelfth Night, 1605. Certainly, his drawings connect theatrical design to "all the visual arts."[139]

Lomazzo covers a variety of subjects including proportions, actions and gestures, color, light and shadows. In the section on gestures, Lomazzo writes that figures who embody "Malice," for example, must be represented "with hollowe eiebrowes and eager lookes, discouering their venomous stomacke against the truth"; "envie," he writes, "causeth a man to drawe backe all his limmes [limbs], plucke in, and as it were shadowe his eie-liddes, grinde his teeth, wry his mouth, turne himself with a passionate kinde of lookes, as if he meant to prie into other mens actions, being ever talking of other men."[140] To represent motion, Lomazzo suggests that human figures, anatomically and proportionally drawn, must also be "very painefully lightned and shadowed."[141] He analyzes the nature of primary and

---

136 Benedetti, "Darkness and Light," 28–32, 30. Benedetti writes: "Other artists such as Savoldo, Romanino and Antonio Campi had executed works on similar themes, and Giovan Paolo Lomazzo had even published a theoretical treatise on the subject" (30).

137 Giovanni Paolo Lomazzo, *Trattato dell'arte de la pittura, scultura, et architectura* (Milan, 1585), available at Spencer Research Library, University of Kansas (Shelfmark: Summerfield C 29). On Caravaggio's possible acquaintance with Lomazzo's treatise, see Benedetti, 30; Hibbard, *Caravaggio*, 42; and John Varriano, *Caravaggio: The Art of Realism* (University Park, PA: Pennsylvania State University, 2006) 118.

138 Giovanni Paolo Lomazzo, *A tracte containing the artes of curious paintinge caruinge buildinge*, trans. Richard Haydocke (Oxford, 1598), STC 16698. I am grateful to Margaux DeRoux, University of Kansas, for bringing to my attention Alison Thorne's discussion of Lomazzo's influence in England, through Haydocke's translation, especially the "commerce between verbal and visual modes of expression." See Thorne's *Vision and Rhetoric in Shakespeare: Looking through Language* (New York, NY: St Martin's Press, 2000) 58–9; 103.

139 Stephen Orgel and Roy Strong, *Inigo Jones: The Theatre of the Stuart Court*, 2 vols. (London: Sotheby Parke Bernet; Berkeley: University of California Press, 1973) 1: xiv.

140 Lomazzo fol. 26–7.

141 Lomazzo Book 2, fol. 5.

Fig. 2.9 Bedchamber. Salomon de Caus, *Perspective avec la Raison* (London 1611). STC 4868.7. Typ 605.11.264 F. Houghton Library, Harvard University.

secondary light, the use of mirrors for indirect illumination, and special effects. He also analyzes "sciography," the science of shadows, the study of their causes and effects. He warns painters that if the lighting source comes from above, eyebrows cast shadows over the cheeks; the nose over the chin, and the chin over the breast; therefore, strategically placed mirrors to reflect light would be necessary if "the bodie" is to be "most sweetelie lightned."[142] He adds the advice that "Now the light taken from aboue, is imagined to stand on the one side of the picture."[143] Lomazzo's treatise helps us contextualize Caravaggio's and Shakespeare's own experiments with varying lighting conditions and special visual effects.

The Three Nights of Othello

In *Othello*, Shakespeare, to make maximum use of lighting effects and to accentuate the power of darkness and shadows, compresses the action into three crucial nights. The first night, set in Venice, encompasses all of Act I, and represents Brabantio's discovery of his daughter's elopement and his accusation against Othello, as well the Venetian council's preparation to send Othello to defend Cyprus from an impending Ottoman invasion.

The second night, centering on the fall of Cassio in Act II, scenes 2 and 3, takes place in Cyprus, presumably several days later. The third night extends approximately from Lodovico's arrival from Venice in Act IV, scene 1 to the end of the play. The staging of the events of these three nights calls for special lighting effects, as if to suggest that the characters stand on the edge of darkness. Shakespeare deploys images of night and darkness as powerful symbols. Thomas Nashe, in "Terrors of the Night or A Discourse of Apparitions" (1594), views the night as "the devil's Black Book, wherein he recordeth all our transgressions."[144] In *A Midsummer Night's Dream*, Theseus reveals an awareness of the effects of shadows: "Or in the night, imagining some fear, / How easy is a bush supposed a bear!" (5.1.21–2). Nashe suspects that the darkness of the night, especially when allied with dreams, disturbs the human mind: "To nothing more aptly can I compare the working of our brains after we have unyoked and gone to bed than to the glimmering and dazzling of a man's eyes when he comes newly out of the bright sun into the dark shadow."[145]

The play, in fact, begins with the powerful image of a house enveloped with thick darkness. Lurking in the shadows, Iago and Roderigo stand in front of Brabantio's house. Darkness collapses the distinction between outside and inside, safe and unsafe, thief and guest, concealing the elopement yet magnifying and heightening the perception of it. Night draws a mantle of darkness over the entire house and

---

142 Lomazzo fol. 170.

143 Lomazzo fol. 170.

144 Thomas Nashe, "Terrors of the Night or A Discourse of Apparitions," in *Pierce Penniless*, (ed.) Stanley Wells (London: Edward Arnold, 1964) 146.

145 Nashe 153.

Fig. 2.10 Venetian Gondolas. Cesare Vecellio, ca. 1521–1601. *De gli habiti antichi, et moderni di diuerse parti del mondo*. Venetia, 1590. Summerfield B1840. Courtesy of Special Collections, Spencer Research Library, University of Kansas Libraries.

creates intense blackness. Later in the first Act, candles, torches, and tapers create the illusion of stage darkness. Venice is astir with Desdemona's elopement, the summoning of Othello to the Council chamber, and then the events in the council, which combine both preparation for defending Cyprus and Brabantio's complaint against Othello. As I have argued above, Desdemona's elopement intertwines with images of thieves robbing the house, racial fears, animals copulating in the night ("a black ram tupping the white ewe"), loss of security, and danger posed by the vast Ottoman empire. The first Act situates Brabantio's house against an abyss of darkness.

The second Act opens in daylight, but a furious storm has raged through the island the previous night, and still darkens the sky above the sea. As discussed above, the dark, stormy, menacing sky will lead to the second night, presented in scenes 2 and 3 of Act II. Upon Desdemona's landing in Cyprus, Iago immediately introduces the matter of household management, betrayal, and adultery, as he teases Desdemona about the nature of all women:

> Come on, come! You are pictures out of doors,
> Bells in your parlors, wildcats in your kitchens,
> Saints in your injuries, devils begin offended,
> Players in your housewifery, and housewives in your beds (2.1.109–12).

When Desdemona calls him "slanderer," he replies: "You rise to play, and go to bed to work" (115). When Othello arrives, he and Desdemona retire to their private quarters, and through the Herald, he decrees a general double celebration of his nuptial and of the defeat of the Turks.

We next see Othello and Desdemona in Act II, scene 3, a night scene. The sword fight between the drunken Cassio and Montano stirs Othello and Desdemona to leave their bed and come out into the courtyard of the castle. Othello must deal with a scene of confusion and unpredictable behavior. Two-faced Iago, having gotten Cassio to drink and in trouble, suggests that the fight came out of nowhere. One minute Cassio and Montano were friends, "like bride and groom / Divesting them for bed" (170–71); the next Cassio turns into a "night-brawler" (186). Othello fears that people will question his own ability "to manage private and domestic quarrel" (II.3.205). When Desdemona enters, Othello complains: "Look if my gentle love be not raised up!" (II.3.240); and turning to Desdemona, he states: "All's well now, sweeting; come away to bed" (II.3.242). Ironically, he points out to her that soldiers expect "to have their balmy slumbers waked with strife" (II.3.148). Iago encourages Cassio to seek Desdemona's help, which will arouse Othello's suspicion. The events of the wild night, however, suggest that we stand on the brink of another abyss—Othello's inner world of tumultuous passions and jealousy,[146] which become apparent in Act III, scene 3, leading eventually to his and Iago's plan to kill Desdemona and Cassio.

---

[146] On Othello's change from "self-contained man" to his wife's murderer, see Gail Kern Paster, *Humoring the Body: Emotions and the Shakespearean Stage* (Chicago and London: University of Chicago Press, 2004) 117–18. Paster argues that the transformation

The third and last night, beginning with Lodovico's arrival from Venice, represents another significant moment in Othello and Desdemona's domestic life focused on the conjugal bed. Desdemona instructs Emilia to "Lay on my bed my wedding sheets" (4.2.105). In the next scene, Emilia reports that she has done as requested: "I have laid those sheets you bade me on the bed" (4.3.21). As she undresses for bed, Desdemona and Emilia talk about home life. Desdemona remembers her mother's home and servant Barbary, who was in love, but whose lover "proved mad / And did forsake her" (4.3.26–7). Barbary died, singing the willow song about another "poor soul" who lamented her fate under a sycamore tree. Desdemona wonders whether such women exist who betray their husbands; Emilia thinks that there are many, but she thinks that "it is their husbands' faults / If wives do fall" (4.3.85–6). Desdemona remembers her mother's house, which had become a site for conjugal strife and tragedy, a reflection of what her home in Cyprus has turned into. Emilia speaks of abusive husbands and revengeful wives, reinforcing the idea of home not as a site of happiness but of violence and tragedy. Darkness connects Othello and Desdemona's new abode in Cyprus to Brabantio's house, which they had left behind, shattered and enveloped in darkness.

A lume di notte

The text of *Othello* calls for special lighting effects, including torches, candles, tapers, and light.[147] In Act V, scene 2, the 1622 Quarto text reads, "Enter Othello with a light, and Desdemona in her bed." More frequently, however, Shakespeare sprinkles stage directions through the dialogue. As Brabantio begins to search his house for Desdemona, who has eloped with the Moor, he says:

> Strike on the tinder, ho!
> Give me a taper! Call up all my people!
> This accident is not unlike my dream.
> Belief of it oppresses me already.
> Light, I say! Light! (1.1.139–41).

Likewise, Cassio, stabbed in the dark by Iago, shouts: "O, help, ho! light! a surgeon!" (5.1.30). A large number of the night scenes are to be staged *a lume di notte* (lit by candlelight, torches, or tapers). However, the nature of the light seems to change, starting in Act IV, scene 3, as Emilia helps Desdemona undress for bed. Here, as I will argue, the lighting resembles Caravaggio's own use of lighting effects.

can be attributed to "such environmental factors as geohumoralism and the passions becoming increasingly associated with black skin" (117). See also Mary Floyd-Wilson, *English Ethnicity and Race in Early Modern Drama* (Cambridge: Cambridge University Press, 2003) 132.

[147] See 1.1.139–40; 1.1.157–8, stage direction; 1.2.1, stage direction; 1.2.154, etc.

The play signals this switch when Desdemona wonders about the nature of women, vouching that she would not commit adultery: "No, by this heavenly light!" (64); Emilia retorts: "Nor I neither by this heavenly light. / I might do't as well i'th'dark" (65–6). For a while in Act V, both kinds of lighting—that is, scenes lit by candlelight, and scenes lit by a more heavenly kind of light—continue to be used. One light comes from a physical source—a candle, a taper, a torch; the other serves as a metaphor for a divine kind of light, which reveals the truth. Cassio, having been stabbed in the dark, calls for light and a surgeon. No one can rely on sight, as they hear cries in the night, until Lodovico, Gratiano, and Bianca arrive and bring torches. The flickering light of the torches distorts Bianca's facial expressions, as Iago notes to Lodovico and Gratiano: "Do you perceive the gastness [ghastly look] of her eye?" (5.1.107). At the same time, Othello, lurking in the shadows, praises Iago for stabbing Cassio and imagines Desdemona's dark bedroom, which he is about to enter. In his mind's eye, he can see in the dark: "Strumpet, I come, / Forth of my heart those charms, thine eyes, are blotted. / Thy bed, lust-stained, shall with lust's blood be spotted" (5.1.34–6).

Michael Neill argues that the "bed" in *Othello* symbolizes the play's preoccupation with a sensational, scandalous bi-racial marriage; therefore, a "lurid vision of the bed" looms large in the audience's imagination throughout the play, until the bed finally appears in Act V. He adds, "The appearance of the bed from within the curtained alcove at the rear of the stage envisioned in the Folio direction signals a moment of quite literal discovery, when the hidden object of the play's imaginative obsession at last stands revealed."[148] I suggest that Shakespeare carefully manipulates lighting here to reveal two parallel, yet contradictory realities, juxtaposing interior and exterior realities: Desdemona's innocence and Othello's grotesque obsession and murderous intent. Shakespeare paints a tableau, reminiscent of Caravaggio's *Taking of Christ* and *Saint John the Baptist*, in the manipulation of lighting effects.

Act V, scene 2 calls for a physical source of light, such as a candle or taper. The stage direction in the 1622 Quarto calls for Othello to enter with "a light." In his soliloquy, however, Othello refers to another kind of light, to a non-physical, heavenly light that shines on Desdemona as she lies in bed and reveals her skin to be whiter than snow and "smooth as monumental alabaster" (5.2.5). Similarly, Othello states that he will "Put out the light, and then put out the light" (5.2.7), extinguishing the "flaming minister," the taper or candle lighting the room, as well as the "Promethean heat" of life, the heavenly light that shines in us and give us the breath of life. An account of a production at Oxford University in 1610 makes clear that the staging called for the creation of a tableau[149]:

[148] For a fascinating study of the bedroom scene, see Michael Neill, "Unproper Beds: Race, Adultery, and the Hideous in *Othello*," *Shakespeare's Middle Tragedies: A Collection of Critical Essays*, (ed.) David Young (Englewood Cliffs, NJ: Prentice Hall, 1993) 133.

[149] In her introduction to her collection of essays, *Caravaggio: Realism, Rebellion, Reception* (Newark, DE: University of Delaware Press, 2006), Genevieve Warwick remarks

> At vero Desdemona illa apud nos a marito occisa, quanquam optime semper causam egit, interfecta tamen magis; cum in lecto decumbens spectantium misericordiam ipso vultu imploraret. [But truly that Desdemona was killed among us by her husband, although she always pleaded her case well, for all the more she was slain; when resting on her bed she called with her very countenance the pity of those watching.][150]

The conditions, under which this night scene took place, made it possible for the spectators to observe Desdemona's facial expressions closely. According to the 1610 eyewitness, Desdemona "called with her very countenance the pity of those watching"; likewise, in the text of the play, Desdemona calls attention to Othello's distorted facial expressions: "And yet I fear you; for you're fatal then / When your eyes roll so" (5.2.37–8); and she adds, "Alas, why gnaw you so your nether lip? / Some bloody passion shakes your very frame" (5.2.43–4). Like Caravaggio, Shakespeare seems fully aware that lighting serves both to reveal and to conceal, as he orchestrates layers of reality, which oscillate between the physical and the metaphorical, the human and the divine, and interior and exterior space. A physical source of light distorts and envelops the figure in shadows; a heavenly kind reveals the truth.

Shakespeare suggests that the bedroom door reinforces two levels of reality: Othello's isolation from the world and the truth, but out of this confined dark room emerges the truth. The 1999 RSC production of *Othello* in Stratford, for example, underscored how Othello's world symbolically shrinks. Several doors in earlier scenes gradually disappeared until only one door remained: the door that Othello closes behind himself as he enters the conjugal bedroom to kill his wife in Act 5, scene 2. Othello approaches the conjugal bed; for the first 22 lines, he seems on the verge of turning his murderous errand into lovemaking. That one door opens, however, to allow other characters to enter. These characters bring more lights and the truth. Nonetheless, a profound sense of emptiness, disturbingly reminiscent of Brabantio's house in the opening scene, pervades the closing scene.

Othello realizes that he has reached his "journey's end" (5.2.268), and he asks himself, "Where should Othello go?" (272). He has no place to which to return. All the routes of his life have finally ended in this claustrophobic place. For the first time, we have a sense that we are in a completely enclosed space, isolated from the outside world. The scene has become a tableau: the background is hidden in deep darkness and shadows; a single source of light illuminates Othello's distorted facial expression, and yet reveals the white, alabaster-like skin of Desdemona and her martyr-like pleading countenance. Shakespeare uses light and shadows to reveal multiple layers of reality.

---

that the tableaux vivants, used in medieval mystery plays, survived well into the early modern period, and even evolved into the "*oratorio sacro* favored by Filippo Neri," which "conjoined music to the reading of sacred texts" (19). This tradition of tableaux vivants "formed part of Caravaggio's visual inheritance" (19).

[150] Geoffrey Tillotson, "*Othello* and *The Alchemist* at Oxford in 1610," *TLS*, July 20, 1933: 494.

Using painting techniques, Shakespeare represents two planes of reality: a story of love, jealousy, and passion drops off into the mysterious background of Othello's past. Shakespeare juxtaposes the concrete, poorly lit indoors to the vast, limitless darkness, which symbolizes Othello's past, mysterious and exotic life, fantastical experiences. As Gilles Deleuze observes, "Clarity endlessly plunges into obscurity."[151] Deleuze poses a pivotal question: "Does the line of light—or fold of the two levels—pass between the shadows and the dark background being withdrawn from it?"[152] Light and shadows intersect in Othello and Desdemona's bedroom. A tension emerges between physical and experiential space, a tension that eventually breaks apart what Iago describes as "a frail vow betwixt an erring barbarian and [a] supersubtle Venetian" (1.3.353). Shadows and darkness overpower clarity and, for a while, even the truth of Desdemona's virtue.

Shakespeare veils Othello's origins in obscurity and wraps Othello's life in Venice and Cyprus in thick darkness. Shadows fall. Tragedy unfolds. The Moor, Eleazar, in Thomas Dekker's *Lust's Dominion*, refers to tragedy as the "Minion of the night, / Rhamnusias pew-felow" (5.3.48–9), and as a black man, he claims his rightful place: "Mine is the stage, thine is the Tragedy" (60).[153] As I have argued elsewhere, in Veronese's *Cena in Casa de Levi* (1573; Oil on canvas, Gallerie dell' Accademia, Venice), the face of an African emerges from behind a column, as if "in Veronese's imagination, an African face will emerge wherever shadows are to be found"; likewise, the portrayal of Aaron in *Titus Andronicus* depends not only on ethnographical fantasies of the age but also on images associated with the color black.[154] In fact, popular manuals contained recipes for special effects that could be conducted at home in order to generate shockingly racist and insulting representations of Africans. The 1586 *Booke of Prittie Conceits* gives these directions: "To make folke seeme blacke: Put oyle oliue into a lampe, and put therein fine powder of ground glasse, & light it, and all those that bee about it will seeme blacke as Egyptians."[155] The work of St Albertus Magnus, widely popular, gives the following directions, in the 1565 translation, bearing the title *The Booke of Secretes*: "Take a greene frog, and cut of the head of it upon a grene cloth, maket it wette with the Oyle of a buctree or eldertree, and put in the wicke and lighte it in a greene lampe, & see a black man standing, betweene whose handes there shalbe a lampe, and a meruilous thing."[156] Art and these homemade special effects reinforce racial attitudes, and the iconography of tragedy as a creature of darkness.

---

151 Deleuze 32.

152 Deleuze 32.

153 Thomas Dekker, *Lust's Dominion*, in Fredson Bowers, (ed.), *The Dramatic Works of Thomas Dekker* vol. 4 (Cambridge: Cambridge University Press, 1961).

154 Sousa, *Shakespeare's Cross-Cultural Encounters*, 100–101.

155 Anonymous, *The Booke of Pittie Conceits*, STC 3351 (London, c. 1586), sig. A2^{V}. Other editions include STC 3352 (1599), 3353 (1612), 3354 (1626).

156 St Albertus Magnus, *The Booke of Secretes* (London, c. 1565), sig. K4. There were also the proverbial Cimmerians of the ancient world: "People inhabiting the furthest part of Europe, not farre from the fennes called Paludes Meotidis, aboute the sea Bosphorus Cimmerius, Northeast from Græcia. Plinie and other affirme, that by the farre distaunce

As such, Othello ironically embodies tragic forces, traditionally associated with female mythological figures: maenads, the female votaries of Dionysus, and the Furies—Megaera (jealous), Tisiphone (blood avenger), and Alecto (unceasing in pursuit)—born of Uranus, when his young son, Kronos, castrated him.[157] Gæa, the Earth, incited Kronos and her other sons, to seek revenge on their father for not allowing them to see the light by keeping them concealed in the depths of the earth. As Richard Seaford points out, Furies and maenads share similarities in aggressiveness, kin-slaughtering frenzy, appearance, and "accoutrements" such as "snakes, wands, or torches."[158] The chorus, in Aeschylus' *Seven against Thebes*, warns Eteocles, "The Fury of the black goatskin will go out from the house when the gods receive sacrifice from hands" (*Melanaigis exeisi domōn Erius hotan ek kherōn theoi thusian dekhōntai*).[159] The black goatskin evokes darkness as a central theme and obviously connects Dionysus, Dionysus' maenads, and the Fury: "The designation of the Fury as Melanaigis is facilitated by the Furies' black appearance and black clothes, which Aeschylus refers to several times in the *Oresteia*."[160] *The Misfortunes of Arthur*, a play written by Thomas Hughes and others, and performed on February 28, 1588 by the members of Gray's Inn before Queen Elizabeth at Greenwich, provides a clear sense of how the Furies were represented on the English stage, as the "First Dumbe Shewe" indicates:

> Sounding the musicke, there rose three furies from vnder the stage appareled accordingly with snakes and flames about their blacke haires and garments. The first with a Snake in the right hande and a cup of wine with a Snake athwart the cup in the left hand. The second with a firebrand in the right hande, and a *Cupid* in the left: The thirde with a whippe in the right hande and a *Paegasus* in the left.[161]

---

of the sunne from it, that country is alway verie darke: wherof happened this prouerbe. *Cimmerijs tenebris atrior,* Blacker than the darkenesse of Cimmeria: applyed to much darkenesse, dulnesse of witte, or lacke of wisedome"—Thomas Cooper, *Thesaurus Linguae Romanae et Britannicae* (London, 1565); and as an adjective: "Of or belonging to the legendary Cimmerii. Hence, proverbially used as a qualification of dense darkness, gloom, or night, or of things or persons shrouded in thick darkness" (*OED*).

[157] *The Columbia Encyclopedia*, fifth edition (New York: Columbia University Press, 1993), 1028; Oskar Seyffert, *A Dictionary of Classical Antiquities* (New York: Meridian Books, 1956), 664; Linda Woodbridge, *The Scythe of Saturn: Shakespeare and Magical Thinking* (Urbana: University of Illinois Press, 1994) 22; and Robert S. Miola, "Othello *Furens*," *Shakespeare Quarterly* 41.1 (1990): 49–64. Miola argues that Seneca's *Hercules Furens* supplies "a mythic archetype that enables Shakespeare to transform the loose melodrama of Cinthio's *Gli Hecatommithi* into compelling tragedy" (51).

[158] Seaford, "Dionysus as Destroyer of the Household," 140.

[159] Seaford, "Dionysus as Destroyer of the Household," 141.

[160] Seaford, "Dionysus as Destroyer of the Household," 141. *Othello* contains three references to goats, obvious symbols of lechery, but goats were, of course, associated with Dionysus.

[161] Thomas Hughes et al., *The Misfortunes of Arthur*, (ed.) Harvey Carson Brumbine (Berlin: Verlag Von Emil Felber, 1900), 115. See also E.K. Chambers, *The Elizabethan Stage* (Oxford: Clarendon Press, 1961), 3: 348–9. According to Chambers, seven collaborators worked on the text of the play.

The Furies appear in some 33 printed play texts of the period, including *Gorboduc* (c.1562–65) and *A Warning for Fair Women*, printed in 1599, and became recognizable stock and emblematic stage figures.[162]

Evoking the Furies and the maenads, Othello threatens to tear Desdemona "all to pieces" (3.3.431); and later he reiterates: "I will chop her into messes!" (4.1.196). He explicitly conjures the Furies to rise with their "aspics' tongues": "Arise, black vengeance, from the hollow hell!" (3.3.450; 447). Iago, however, apparently not wanting a blood-bath, shapes and moulds the "savage madness" (55) of an Othello intent on dismembering Desdemona as in a maenadic ritual (*sparagmos*) to a Fury, who does not dismembers but strangles her "in her bed, even the bed that she has contaminated" (4.1.203–204). In the process, Othello attempts to regain his masculinity in casting the ritual strangulation of his wife into the extinguishing of the "Promethean heat," the breath of life, the fire stolen from Zeus as a gift to humankind. He mistakes Desdemona for Pandora—a woman made out of clay, all-gifted with charms and adornments "coupled however with lies, flattering words, and a crafty mind," ironically, attributes that fit Iago rather than Desdemona.[163]

In *Hecatommithi*, one of the principal sources for Shakespeare's *Othello*, Giraldi Cinthio depicts the characters' experience of home in a memorable way. He explains that Disdemona and the Moor felt a strong mutual bond of love and were united in marriage, although "the Lady's relatives did all they could to make her take another husband."[164] After a period of marital bliss in Venice, the Moor becomes commandant of the soldiers in Cyprus, where he and his wife settled down in a house. The Corporal, Cassio's prototype, regularly frequents their house as a dinner guest. Iago's counterpart, the wicked Ensign, falls in love with Disdemona, who rejects his advances. In turn, the Ensign, imagining that Disdemona loved the Corporal, sets out on a path of revenge against the Corporal and Disdemona. When she comes to the Corporal's defense, the Ensign suggests to the Moor that "Perhaps Disdemona has good cause to look on him so favorably," advising the Moor, "if you keep your eyes open you will see for yourself."[165] The Ensign steals the handkerchief from Disdemona and persuades the Moor to use a sand-filled stocking to beat Disdemona to death, and then, since "the house where you are staying is very old, and the ceiling of your room has many cracks in it,"

---

162 For a complete list, consult Thomas L. Berger, William C. Bradford, and Sidney L. Sondergard, *An Index of Characters in Early Modern English Drama Printed Plays, 1500–1660*, revised edition (Cambridge: Cambridge University Press, 1998), 48. In *A Warning for Fair Women*, (ed.) Charles Dale Cannon (The Hague: Mouton, 1975), the Furies accompany the personified figure of Tragedy, which enters "with a bowle of bloud in her hand" (*Dumb Show I*, stage direction, l. 771).

163 Seyffert 520.

164 Geoffrey Bullough, (ed.), *Narrative and Dramatic Sources of Shakespeare* (London: Routledge, 1973), 7: 242.

165 Bullough 7: 244.

he adds, "when she is dead, we shall make part of the ceiling fall; and we'll break the Lady's head, making it seem that a rafter has injured it in falling, and killed her."[166] That is precisely what they do. After her funeral, the Moor searches the empty house for his Disdemona. Filled with regret and kindling his hatred for the Ensign, the Moor can no longer contain his feelings. In the source, "unhousèd" has a much more literal meaning: the ceiling of the house comes tumbling down, as does the Moor's marriage. The specter of this unhousing haunts Shakespeare's representation of space in *Othello* and defines the central character's identity.

In Shakespeare's play, Othello neither searches the empty house for his dead wife nor returns to Venice to be punished. Yet Othello seems linked to the house, at first in Iago's imagination, as the guest turned thief who steals the most precious possession of the house, and then as a noble but extremely jealous exile who robs himself of the home that he and Desdemona tried to build together. Not in a literal but in a figurative sense, Othello's house tumbles down as he unhouses himself with the help of Iago. His family, home, past experiences, and childhood memories have become a blur of half-remembered, half-forgotten images, full of fundamental contradictions and fantasies. To tragic ends, Iago recognizes that Othello's emotional realm revolves around Desdemona; their bedroom is Othello's anchor in the European world.

The destroyer of household also becomes the thick darkness that envelops, penetrates, and transforms the house into something mysterious, exotic, and strange. As we see throughout the play, Shakespeare uses darkness to reduce the space around his characters, while simultaneously implying that the darkness that envelops them breaks the boundaries of space and connects them to a world elsewhere. Michel de Certeau argues that ironically the discourse that attempts to reconstruct the space of the Other also produces "the status of the strange";[167] and, as Syed Mansurul Islam writes, such a discourse in fact offers "the performative enactment of becoming other,"[168] which Iago exploits to destructive ends. Othello's storytelling reinforces his displacement from the European community to which he aspires to belong, and reenacts his Otherness, rooted in racial difference and life experiences in the mysterious *terra incognita* of his birth and of his travels.[169]

---

[166] Bullough 7: 250.

[167] Michel de Certeau, *Heterologies: Discourse on the Other*, trans. Brian Massumi (Manchester: Manchester University Press, 1986) 67.

[168] Syed Mansurul Islam, *The Ethics of Travel from Marco Polo to Kafka* (Manchester: Manchester University Press, 1996) vii.

[169] Russ McDonald writes: "Othello is a man of extremes, an African prince who has spent his life in 'the tented field', without a permanent home" (1394).

Chapter 3
At Home in *Hamlet*

Omne animal, simul atque natum sit, voluptatem appetere eaque gaudere ut summo bono, dolorem aspernari ut summum malum et, quantum possit, a se repellere, idque facere nondum depravatum ipsa natura incorrupte atque integre iudicante

—Cicero, *De Finibus bonorum et malorum liber primus*.[1]

I have not art to reckon my groans

—Hamlet, 2.2.120–21

The knowledge we have as individuals and as members of a particular society remains very limited, selective, and biased by the passions of living

—Yi-Fu Tuan.[2]

Whether we examine houses as material objects, made of stone or brick and mortar; as cultural constructions, endowed with meaning; or as phenomena of perception, charged with emotions and the experiences of life, dwelling-places are, as Robert M. Rakoff puts it, "part of an ordered human world."[3] Houses—whether a castle or a shack—serve to provide shelter and demarcate space, define areas of cultural activity, reveal habits of minds and social processes, and express feelings.[4] Further, the house expresses the "uses and purposes of intimate space."[5] Gaston Bachelard cautions that as a body of images the house can either provide "proofs" or mere "illusions of stability."[6] As I have argued in the previous chapter, the house in *Othello* provides but an illusion of stability inasmuch as the "reality" or "psychology" of the house can be constantly reimagined, and relocated along the imaginative and emotional spectrum of human experience. In *Hamlet*, Shakespeare

---

[1] Cicero, *De finibus bonorum et malorum liber primus*, 30: "Every living being from its moment of birth seeks pleasure, enjoying it as the ultimate good while rejecting pain as the ultimate adversity and, insofar as is possible, doing his best to avoid it; he behaves in this fashion to the extent that he has not yet been conditioned and insofar as his basic nature has been left intact to judge naturally and with integrity," quoted in Roselyne Rey, *The History of Pain*, trans. Louise Elliott Wallace, J.A. Cadden, and S.W. Cadden (Cambridge, MA and London: Harvard University Press, 1995) 1.

[2] Yi-Fu Tuan, *Space and Place*, 85.

[3] Robert M. Rakoff, "Ideology in Everyday Life: The Meaning of the House," *Politics and Society* 7 (1977): 85.

[4] Rakoff 85.

[5] Rakoff 85.

[6] Bachelard, *Poetics of Space*, 17.

represents home as a place that the residents reimagine, inscribe, and transform, according to their own experiences and perceptions.

When Hamlet asks Ophelia where her father is, she does not vacillate in her response, "At home, my lord" (3.1.151). She knows that Polonius and Claudius, from a hiding place nearby, are, in fact, surreptitiously listening to the conversation. Although the characters' precise living accommodations in Elsinore remain undisclosed, Hamlet implies, at least on the level of metaphor, that Polonius and his family reside in a house: "Let the doors be shut upon him, that he may play the fool nowhere but in's own house" (3.1.132–3). The passage, rather cruelly, recommends that Polonius be locked up in a house with those who abuse, torment, mock, or make a fool of him. Elsewhere in the play, "home" also occurs in the context of a "return" to one's dwelling-place or country. Claudius welcomes Voltemand and Cornelius home from Norway (2.2.89), and also explains his intentions to Laertes: "Hamlet returned shall know you are come home" (4.7.130–31). In fact, the play dramatizes various homecomings: Hamlet and Laertes return home for a royal funeral, a coronation, and a royal wedding; as ghost, old Hamlet, breaching the barriers of nature, makes a comeback, first dressed in full armor on the battlements and later dressed in a nightgown in Gertrude's closet; Hamlet, escorted to England, manages to escape certain execution and returns home; after Polonius's death, Laertes returns from France once again, this time to triumphal cheers of the common people who would like to see him crowned king; and Fortinbras, on his voyage of return to Norway in Act V, chances upon the ruins of the Danish court and claims his "rights of memory" to the Danish throne.

Throughout the play, Shakespeare connects and intertwines house and body, a physical place of dwelling and a space transformed and reimagined through individual perception and experience. This meaning occurs metaphorically in Act III, scenes 3 and 4, which George Hibbard considers to be "the centre of the play's action" and "its emotional centre," respectively.[7] Polonius hopes that in her closet Gertrude will "tax [Hamlet] home" (3.3.29) or "lay home to him" (3.4.1). These synonymous expressions carry the meaning of taking to task—reproaching and demanding of an account for his behavior.[8] The *OED* records numerous early 1600 datings for attributive and metaphorical extensions.[9] "Home," in adverbial usage, here means to the very heart, deeply, intimately, poignantly. Either in relation to physical action or in a figurative sense, to tax or lay home involves an attempt to reach, touch, penetrate, or affect intimately, closely, and directly.[10] Therefore, I

---

[7] George R. Hibbard, (ed.), *Hamlet*, Oxford World's Classics (1987; Oxford: Oxford University Press, 2008) 276n.

[8] Ann Thompson and Neil Taylor, (eds), *Hamlet, The Arden Shakespeare* (London: Cengage Learning, 2006) 328n; and in his edition, A.R. Braunmuller simply notes, "reprimand him severely" (85n).

[9] I am grateful to Prof. James Hartman, University of Kansas, for bringing this to my attention in a personal email dated March 25, 2009.

[10] Definitions derived from the *OED*.

submit, the emplacement of the body serves as a focal point for gauging perception of home, as a physical space, and of domestic life. Hamlet's homecoming reveals that a barrier has been breached between mourning and celebration, occasions that normally require opposing emotional responses. Hamlet takes it upon himself to erect a barrier between his uncle and mother's pursuit of pleasure and his own intense suffering.

In Shakespeare's play, habits of everyday life help define specific places. Northrop Frye suggests that the Ghost "squeezes Hamlet's life into narrowing limits" and interrupts "the habits, such as they are, of Hamlet's life."[11] For Frye, the Ghost entreats Hamlet to refocus his attention and redirect his course of action. Yet one might argue that both Hamlet and Claudius similarly face what at times seems a narrowing, at times a broadening of the limits of their lives. In this patriarchal domain, Claudius wants to erase reminders of his brother's ownership and presence; Hamlet wants to reassert his father's claim to the house, wife, throne, and family.

Habit and Location

A Google Earth flyover of Helsingør, Denmark, shows the strategic location of Helsingør's Kronborg Castle, formerly known as Krogen (*krog*, "hook"; *Krone*, "crown"), which stands guard over the narrow strait known as the Øresund connecting the Kattegat and the Baltic.[12] Erik of Pomerania, adopted son of queen Margrete, chose Helsingør for a fortress because in this strategic location the guns stationed on the castle's ramparts could "cover the surrounding waters through an impressively sweeping arc of 265°."[13] Finished in 1427, the castle, for over a hundred years, guarded the Øresund and generated revenue through the lucrative toll collected from passing vessels.[14] In the sixteenth century, the medieval fortress,

---

[11] Robert Sandler, (ed.), *Northrop Frye on Shakespeare* (New Haven and London: Yale University Press, 1986) 87. This may be linked to Jan Kott's notion of tragically imposed situations in the play (*Shakespeare Our Contemporary* [New York: Doubleday, 1966]).

[12] David Hohnen, *Hamlet's Castle and Shakespeare's Elsinore* (Copenhagen: Christian Ejlers, 2000) 16. Cincinnati, Ohio, has its own Elsinore Castle. The *Hamlet*-inspired design of the Cincinnati structure, by the architect Samuel Hannaford (1860–1936), won the Water Works Department's competition. Erected in 1883, Cincinnati's Elsinore, which looks more like a stage set, consists of a round and a square tower, connected by a bridge. A vault under the towers houses the reservoir valves. See Geoffrey J. Giglierano and Deborah A. Overmyer, *The Bicentennial Guide to Greater Cincinnati: A Portrait of Two Hundred Years* (Cincinnati: Cincinnati Historical Society, 1988) 162. I am grateful to Susanne Clement, Utah State University, for her help with the Danish language.

[13] Hohnen 16.

[14] Hohnen 26.

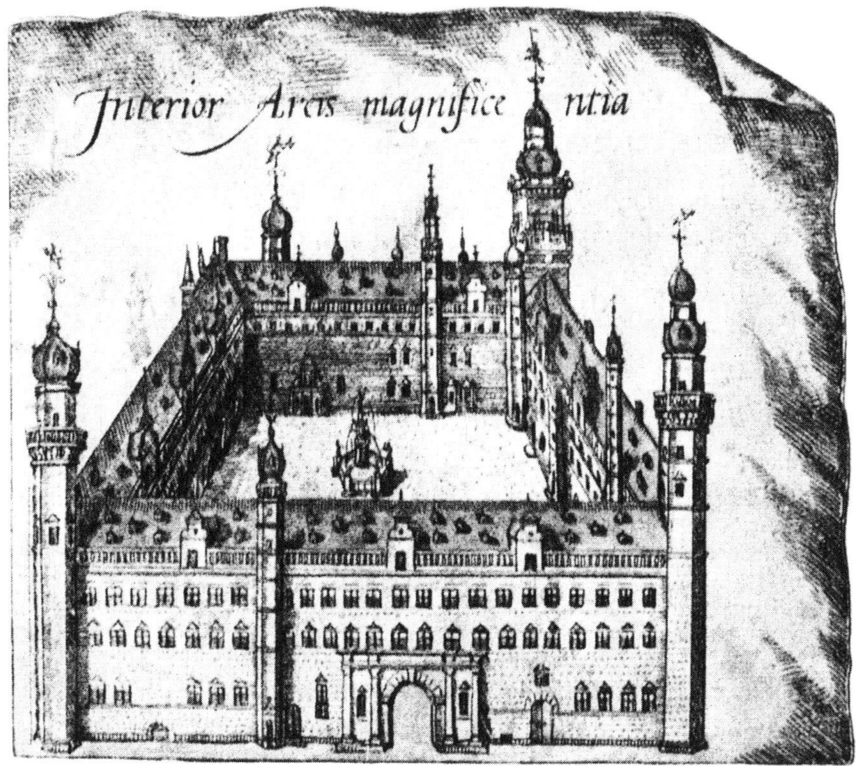

Fig. 3.1 Kronborg Castle, Elsinore (detail). Georg Braun and Abraham Hogenberg, *Civitates orbis terrarum*, vol. 4 (Brussels, 1574–1618). Courtesy of Special Collections, Spencer Research Library, University of Kansas Libraries.

under Frederick II, underwent considerable modernization and renovation.[15] Braun and Hogenberg, in *Civitates Orbis Terrarum* (1585–1586), describe the new structure as "a splendidly beautiful building whose roofs and spires glow in the sunshine like gold, and where elaborate tapestries, a magnificent fountain and royal tournaments inevitably fill the beholder with astonishment."[16] In 1629 a fire destroyed this building, and subsequently the current structure, which underwent renovation in the twentieth century, was erected.

Helsingør of Shakespeare's time failed to impress Fynes Moryson during his visit in 1593. He thought Helsingør was a "a poore village," although "much frequented" by sailors because of its location. However, he deemed the castle,

---

[15] Hohnen 32.

[16] Braun and Hogenberg, *Civitates Orbis Terrarum* (Cologne, 1572–1617), as quoted by Honnen 10.

lying "upon the mouth of the Straight," to be "strong": "[the castle] was built foure square, and hath only one gate on the East side, where it lies upon the straight. Above this gate is a chamber in which the King useth to eat, and two chambers wherein the King and Queene lie apart."[17] He visited the stables, chapel, a "faire gallery, in which the King useth to feast at solemne times,"[18] and the apartments, where James VI of Scotland had stayed in 1589–1590. Moryson caught a glimpse of the castle's multiple functions: it could accommodate the royal family, foreign visitors, and a large royal household. It also retained its strategic military function. Based on what we know about the English royal household, especially through E.K. Chambers's thorough survey, we learn that it had various departments whose functions changed over time, and a complex organization, with domestic and political functions: on the one hand, the royal household "ministered to the material well-being and splendor of the Sovereign himself"; and on the other, it served as "an instrument of central executive government."[19] Elsinore of the play, too, in addition to its military function, provides lodging for the sovereign and courtiers and serves as seat of executive power, but Shakespeare also infuses this place with emblematic and symbolic function.

Castles serve many powerful emblematic purposes. Charles Ross examines the "custom of the castle" in medieval and Renaissance literature. The knight-errant, seeking hospitality in an unknown castle, comes into contact with strange traditions and customs; his experience in this "community of strangers" functions as a stage of the chivalric quest.[20] These customs, representing a transition between the old and the new, give rise to "ghost fear," an intense cultural anxiety that "the ghosts of ancestors would be angry if the living should change the ancient folkways."[21] Ross argues that *Hamlet* presents "the anxieties of a culture caught in a moment of painful transition," undermining or questioning "the patterns of customary behavior."[22] James Black focuses on warfare imagery, rituals of combat, and siege tactics associated with the castle; he suggests, however, that siege warfare, which requires waiting, watching, listening, and gathering intelligence, shapes the dynamics of interaction between Hamlet and his uncle.[23] Further, Elsinore embodies

---

17 Moryson, I: 124–5.

18 Moryson, I: 124.

19 E.K. Chambers, *The Elizabethan Stage* (Oxford: Clarendon, 1961), 1: 27–70. Also of interest here is David Starkey, (ed.), *The English Court: From the Wars of the Roses to the Civil War* (London and New York: Longman, 1987), especially Starkey's own essay, "Intimacy and Innovation: The Rise of the Privy Chamber, 1485–1547," 71–118.

20 Charles Ross, *The Custom of the Castle: From Malory to Macbeth* (Berkeley: University of California Press, 1997) 5.

21 William Graham Summer, *Folkways: A Study of the Sociological Importance of Usages, Manners, Customs, Mores, and Morals* (Boston: The Athenaeum Press, 1913) 28–9, 67, qtd. in Ross 104.

22 Ross 108.

23 James Black, "Hamlet Hears Marlowe; Shakespeare Reads Virgil," *Renaissance and Reformation* 18.4 (1994): 24.

Petrarchan elements related to the castle of the beloved as a "stronghold defeated from within."[24] A miniature illumination from the *Roman de la Rose* (c. 1490), known as "the Castle of Jealousy," represents the castle as an emblem combining the woman's body and symbols of male sexual desire.[25] Medieval drama gives us hell-castles. A "hell-castle," according to Glynne Wickham, consists of "an edifice, which viewed from outside, resembles a castle and, viewed from inside, a sequence of dark dungeons and torture chambers pervaded by stench and heat."[26]

Shakespeare's Elsinore combines and transforms these traditions associated with the castle. When Hamlet returns home from Wittenberg, his former home has transformed into a community of strangers. The cat-and-mouse game that he and Claudius play, in fact, resembles medieval siege tactics. In the beginning of the play, the castle retains its function as a military stronghold; sentinels on the battlements stand guard against enemy assault. As Horatio explains, they stand in readiness to repel a Norwegian assault—"the main motive of our preparation, / The source of this our watch, and the chief head / Of this posthaste and rummage in the land" (1.1.105–107). As in *Othello*, despite urgent preparation, no military combat occurs. Instead, the play intimates that Elsinore has already been conquered from within: Claudius has gained the throne and conquered the queen's heart. As new lord of the castle, he wants to leave his imprint on his house, household, and country.

In *Hamlet*, walls seem to shift: space expands or contracts, as a matter of perception. In the 1623 Folio text, Hamlet says to Rosencrantz: "O God, I could be bounded in a nutshell and count myself a king of infinite space, were it not that I have bad dreams" (2.2.254–56). Home, for him, has become a "prison," a place with "many confines, wards and dungeons" (246–7); but it has also become a boundless space. The short story, "Carmilla," by Sheridan Le Fanu (1814–73), offers a parallel to the phenomenon in *Hamlet*. Laura, the narrator of the story, notes that, after the mysterious Carmilla's arrival, solid walls and locked doors can no longer protect her from the dream-like intimate embraces of her houseguest: "But dreams come through stone walls, light up dark rooms, or darken light ones, and their persons make their exits and their entrances as they please, and laugh at locksmiths."[27] As in Le Fanu's story, the apparition in Shakespeare's

---

24 Anne Lancashire, "The Emblematic Castle in Shakespeare and Middleton," in *Mirror up to Shakespeare: Essays in Honour of G.R. Hibbard*, (ed.) J.C. Gray (Toronto: University of Toronto Press, 1984) 228–9. See also Thomas L. Berger, "The Petrarchan Fortress of *The Changeling*," *Renaissance Papers* (1969): 37–46; and Glynne Wickham, "The Hell-Castle and Its Door-Keeper," *Shakespeare Survey* 19 (1966): 68–74.

25 Guillaume de Lorris et Jean de Meun, *Le Roman de la Rose*, British Library Harleian MS 4425, Fol. 39. See the discussion of this image in Matilde Battistini, *Symbols and Allegories in Art*, trans. Stephen Sartarelli (Los Angeles: The J. Paul Getty Museum, 2002) 273.

26 Wickham, "Hell-Castle," 71.

27 Sheridan Le Fanu, "Carmilla," in *A Glass Darkly*, (ed.) Robert Tracy (Oxford: Oxford University Press, 1993) 277.

play also undermines the security of boundaries. Stephen Greenblatt notes that the appearance of the ghost "triggers some elements of the traditional rituals in response to hauntings."[28] For Aleida Assmann, early modern representations of supernatural phenomena constitute "remnants of a religious prehistory" and serve as "heterodox agents of an obsolete, forgotten and repressed world."[29] I don't think that Elsinore is simply a haunted castle; rather, Elsinore embodies Bachelard's concept of home as a fulcrum, where "intimate space and exterior space keep encountering each other."[30]

Embodied Space

The play focuses on the intertwined lives of Claudius, who forges a physical, bodily, sexual alliance with Gertrude, and Hamlet, who forms an alliance with the spectral presence of his father. Both compete for control of Elsinore as a physical place of dwelling; and both attempt to reimagine and reinscribe Hamlet's father's house and household. I proceed on the assumption that "bodied spatiality is at the heart of dramatic presentation, for it is through the actor's corporeal presence under the spectator's gaze that the dramatic text actualizes itself in the field of performance."[31] For my purposes here, I will adapt William Cohen's definition of "embodiment," in his book *Embodied* (2009), which attempts to "articulat[e] a relation between inner self and outer form by emphasizing both the surface elements of the body and the incorporative capacities of sensory perception."[32] In *Hamlet*, the audience enters a world sharply demarcated along two competing centers of perception: Claudius resorts to a politics of pleasure to gain supporters and to strengthen his hold on the throne; Hamlet counters his uncle's move by underscoring his pain and suffering.[33] Unlike Hamlet, Claudius negotiates the transition from mourning

---

[28] Stephen Greenblatt, *Hamlet in Purgatory* (Princeton: Princeton University Press, 2001) 245.

[29] Aleida Assmann, "Spirits, Ghosts, Demons in Shakespeare and Milton," in Andreas Höfele and Werner von Koppenfels, (eds), *Renaissance Go-Betweens: Cultural Exchange in Early Modern Europe* (Berlin and New York: Walter de Gruyter, 2005) 202.

[30] Bachelard 201.

[31] Stanton B. Garner, Jr., *Bodied Phenomenology and Performance: Spaces in Contemporary Drama* (Ithaca: Cornell University Press, 1994) 1.

[32] William A. Cohen, *Embodied: Victorian Literature and the Senses* (Minneapolis: University of Minnesota Press, 2009) 13–14. Although Cohen does not, of course, discuss Shakespeare, I find his approach to questions of embodiment to be particularly pertinent to my argument about *Hamlet*. I should add that Cohen's definition appears in a discussion of Wilkie Collins's novel *Poor Miss Finch* (1872), in which, quite appropriately for my argument, the wicked identical twin takes the place of his brother as Miss Finch's lover (14).

[33] It is not my goal to provide a psychoanalytic reading of these entangled alliances, although the play permits such a reading as Ernest Jones, in *Hamlet and Oedipus* (New York: W.W. Norton, 1976) and Janet Adelman, in *Suffocating Mothers: Fantasies of Maternal*

to celebration, pain to pleasure—aptly expressed in what becomes the defining hendiadys of his life, "with mirth in funeral and with dirge in marriage" (1.2.42), or in Hamlet's words, "The funeral baked meats / Did coldly furnish forth the marriage tables" (1.2.180–81). The unspeakable pain of his father's funeral and the unseemly pleasure of his mother's wedding tear at Hamlet. The play explores fundamental and defining contradictions, something with which Hamlet struggles to the end of the play when he entreats Horatio to live on, "And in this harsh world draw thy breath in pain, / To tell my story" (5.2.336–7). To tell the story of these parallel lives, Shakespeare represents an experiential discontinuity between the pleasure-seeking Claudius and the mournful, sorrowful Hamlet. For Hamlet, home intertwines pleasure and pain, and seemingly splits his world into competing domestic arrangements, associated with a house of pleasure and one of sorrows.

The House of Pleasure

Polonius worries that Laertes will become a wild "Dansker" in Paris, borrowing or lending freely, drinking, gambling, and frequenting "a house of sale," a brothel (2.1.60). As he puts it, "such wanton, wild, and usual slips / … are companions most known / To youth and liberty" (2.1.22–4). Henry Peacham, in *The Art of Living in London* (1642), envisioned similar dangers associated with city living, such as idleness, lavish spending, drunkenness, playing cards and dice, and above all "these over-hot and crafty daughters of the Sunne, your silken and gold-laced harlots everywhere (especially in the Suburbs) to bee found."[34] Indeed, a number of contemporary treatises warn of the dangers of pleasure. Richard Barckley, for example, describes the lecherous Muleasses, king of Tunis, who being "so drowned in pleasures" was "expelled from his kingdome for whordome": "his Sonne or brother dispossessed him of his kingdom" and caused "his eyes to be put out with a burning hote iron."[35] The anti-theatrical treatise *A mirrour of monsters* (1587), by William Rankins, inveighs against the theater, a house specializing in the presentation of "murders, mischiefs, adulteryes, ingratitude, idlenes, dissention, impudence, and all kynde of villany, that eyther can be thought upon or practiced in a Commonweath," culminating in what he calls the marriage of Faustus and Luxuria.[36] In *The Passions of the Minde in General* (1604), Thomas Wright writes:

Origin in Shakespeare's Plays (New York and London: Routledge, 1991), among others, ably demonstrate. Adelman argues that "*Hamlet* thus defines the son's position between two fathers by relocating it in relation to an indiscriminately sexual maternal body that threatens to annihilate the distinction between the two fathers and hence problematizes the son's paternal identification; at the same time, the play conflates the beloved with this betraying mother, undoing the strategies that had enabled marriage in the comedies. The intrusion of the adulterous mother thus disables the solutions of history and comedy as Shakespeare has imagined them; in that sense, her presence initiates the tragedy" (14–5).

34 Henry Peacham, *The Art of Living in London* (London, 1642) sig. A1–A3.

35 Richard Barckley, *A Discourse of the Felicie of Man* (London, 1603) sig. C4.

36 William Rankins, *A mirrour of monsters* (London, 1587) fol. 23–4.

"Aristotle reduceth all passions to pleasure and paine for as we see (saith hee) there is no wickedness men will not attempt for pleasures, so wee try many to bee deterred from the study of vertue, onely for the feare of paine."[37] Wright sees the contest between pain and pleasure as bringing about fundamental changes in the body: "Vehement passions alter vehemently the temper and constitution of the body."[38]

One of the play's sources, Saxo Grammaticus's *Historiae Danicae*, gives Shakespeare a prototype for the representation of pleasure in *Hamlet.* With the help of his advisors, Feng, Amleth's uncle, devises a stratagem to expose his nephew's pretended lunacy: he employs a fair woman to accost and entice Amleth to the "temptations of love," which he would not be able to resist because all men are naturally "blindly amorous" and "impetuous"; therefore, under these conditions, Amleth's "wiliness" would be exposed.[39] Having been dispatched by Amleth's uncle, the young woman approaches Amleth in a dark, secluded place; and, as expected, the prince makes his move to "ravish" her but notices a straw stuck under the tail of a gadfly, which happened to fly nearby.[40] Interpreting this as a warning of danger, Amleth keeps his lust in check and leaves the woman alone. Likewise, *The Hystorie of Hamblet*, an analogue for Shakespeare's play, portrays a beautiful woman also dispatched to a secluded place in the woods to tempt Hamblet: "for the nature of all young men (especially such as are brought up wantonlie) is so transported with the desires of the flesh, and entreth so greedily into the pleasures thereof, that is almost impossible to cover the foul affection, neither yet to dissemble or hyde the same by art or industry, much lesse to shunne it."[41] In this instance, loyal courtiers warn him of the scheme; therefore, because of this knowledge, he escapes the entrapment and even persuades her to become his accomplice. Loving him "more than herselfe," she agrees to assist him, and therefore, as her reward, will enjoy "the pleasure of his body."[42] Unlike his prototypes, Hamlet seems more immune to temptations of pleasure, although the scheme from the source materials survives in the plan Polonius proposes to Claudius: "At such a time I'll loose my daughter to him. / Be you and I behind an arras then" (2.2.162–3). In his play, Shakespeare associates pleasure not with Hamlet, but with Claudius.

---

37 Thomas Wright, *The Passions of the Minde in General* (1604; London, 1620) 24; 75.

38 Wright, Passions of the Minde, 24; 75.

39 Geoffrey Bullough, *Narrative and Dramatic Sources of Shakespeare* (London: Routledge and Kegan Paul; New York: Columbia University Press, 1973) 7: 63. In the Arden edition, Ann Thompson and Neil Taylor think it unlikely that Shakespeare knew Saxo's story of Amleth, but he may have known Belleforest's narrative, although Shakespeare's play differs in significant ways from these sources and analogues (67–8).

40 Bullough 7: 64.

41 Bullough 7: 91.

42 Bullough 7: 92.

A split between the realms of pain and of pleasure becomes apparent in the first two scenes of the play. The thick darkness of the wintry night envelops disembodied voices on the battlements of a defamiliarized fortification.[43] To borrow the anthropologist James Clifford's words from another context, Shakespeare evokes a perspective that "values fragments, curious collections, unexpected juxtapositions—that works to provoke the manifestation of extraordinary realities drawn from the domains of the erotic, the exotic, and the unconscious."[44] From the edge of darkness, a sentinel's voice pierces the boundless surroundings: "Who's there?" (1.1.1). Within the first 20 lines, Horatio reintroduces Elsinore as a haunted place: "What, has this thing appeared again to-night?" (1.1.20). Bernardo, Francisco, and Horatio search for a term to describe the phenomenon they witnessed. They refer to the specter as the *thing*, "fantasy, "apparition," "figure," and "illusion." Though seemingly immaterial, the *thing* resembles "the king / That was and is the question of these wars" (1.1.110–11). Shakespeare collapses boundaries here to create not simply "indefinition," which, according to Stephen Booth, is the quintessential marker of Shakespearean tragedy,[45] but to demarcate the interstices of human experience and create competing perceptions of reality.[46]

The second scene takes place within Elsinore. Together, the first and the second scenes, in contrapuntal opposition, generate differently-textured perceptual landscapes. The *thing* of the first scene contrasts with the charismatic royal couple of the next. In his initial speech, Claudius addresses a bewildered, grief-stricken court and a country faced with the prospect of a foreign invasion. He offers himself as a bridge between mourning and celebration, emotional distress and intense pleasure. He justifies his marriage to Gertrude as a balancing act reconciling "an auspicious and a dropping eye," "mirth in funeral" and "dirge in marriage," and "delight and dole" (1.2.1–17). Likewise, he sends ambassadors to Norway to prevent war. Before long, Claudius outlines a plan to motivate his household, family, and country to leave behind the sorrows of the past and return to the pleasures of everyday life.

Claudius refers to his "dear brother's death" in a subordinate clause ("Though yet of Hamlet, our dear brother's death"); therefore, rhetorically avoiding the

---

[43] In *The Predicament of Culture: Twentieth-Century Ethnography, Literature, and Art* (Cambridge: Harvard University Press, 1988), James Clifford speaks of "a defamiliarized cultural reality" created by the ethnographies written by twentieth-century anthropologists (121). As I have argued elsewhere, I believe that Shakespeare tends to represent the cross-cultural experience in similar terms.

[44] Clifford 118.

[45] Stephen Booth, *"King Lear," "Macbeth," Indefinition and Tragedy* (New Haven: Yale University Press, 1983). Booth considers "indefinition" to be the benchmark of Shakespearean tragedy.

[46] In T*he Comic Matrix of Shakespeare's Tragedies: Romeo and Juliet, Hamlet, Othello, and King Lear* (Princeton: Princeton University Press, 1979), Susan Snyder demonstrates that Shakespeare uses a comic structure to create what she calls existential nightmare in competing perceptions of reality.

directness of the main clause, he relegates to grammatical, and by extension political, subordination a series of undesirables, including his brother's death, "hearts in grief," and "brow of woe." He foregrounds "discretion," implying personal and legal judgment and discernment, as a personal and political quality. In usage traceable to 1467, the *OED* defines discretion as "the power to decide, within the limits allowed by positive rules of law, as to punishments, remedies, or costs, and generally to regulate matters of procedure and administration." Through a clever grammatical sleight of hand, Claudius buries his brother and rises in his dead brother's stead, thereby transmuting "hearts in grief" into hearts in joy, dole into delight, a funeral into a wedding, and his dead brother's wife into his own. Astutely, he forges what I call a politics of pleasure.

The play's exposition makes clear that, shortly after his brother's death, Claudius moved quickly to seize the throne and restore stability by giving Denmark a complete royal family. Claudius, in his enthronement and marriage to the queen, offers royal rituals, grounded in ancient traditions, and puts royal pleasure on display, relying on personal charisma. Clifford Geertz defines "charisma," as "'a certain quality' that marks an individual as standing in a privileged relationship to the sources of being and a hypnotic power 'certain personalities' have to engage passions and dominate minds."[47] Geertz adds that royal charisma derives from "ceremonial forms by which kings take symbolic possession of their realm," rituals that "locate the society's center and affirm its connection with transcendent things by stamping a territory with ritual signs of dominance."[48] As the focus of the court's affection, Claudius and Gertrude, a beloved royal couple, together represent the foundation of monarchy. Although childless, the new king offers the country an heir and political stability, extending to Hamlet the love "which dearest father bears his son" (1.2.107–112). In public, he always refers to Hamlet as "our son," as for example when he tries to convince Hamlet not to leave for Wittenberg: "And we beseech you, bend you to remain / Here in the cheer and comfort of our eye, / Our chiefest courtier, cousin, and our son" (1.2.115–17). The past represents pain; the present and the future promise security, order, and tranquility. The play says nothing about Claudius's past, although it implies that he has remained unmarried and apparently childless, ready to assume the reins of power and marry his sister-in-law, when the occasion arises. Ironically, when Bernardo describes the ghost as

---

[47] Clifford Geertz, "Centers, Kings, and Charisma: Reflection on the Symbolics of Power," chapter 6 of *Local Knowledge: Further Essays in Interpretive Anthropology* (New York: Basic Books, 1983) 121.

[48] Geertz 125. In *Charismatic Authority in Early Modern English Tragedy* (Baltimore and London: The Johns Hopkins University Press, 2000), Raphael Falco argues that "tragedy is the preeminent discourse of the failure of charisma" (1): "emphasis on a group ideal tends to destroy the individuality of the human being at the group's core; and, conversely, emphasis on the autonomy of an individual charismatic leader destroys the group ideal" (1), suggesting that Hamlet himself has to resist being absorbed "into his father's charismatic sphere" (107). See also David M. Bergeron's review of Falco's book in *Shakespeare Quarterly* 53 (2002): 579–81.

"the same figure like the king that's dead" (1.1.41), he uncannily anticipates what seems to be Claudius' own goal in life—to be a figure "like the king that's dead."

Claudius marries Gertrude and takes the reins of power with the court's acquiescence: "Nor have we herein barred / Your better wisdoms, which have freely gone / With this affair along" (1.2.13–15). Claudius seeks consent, as a matter of course. In permitting Laertes to return to France, he first ascertains Polonius's approval (60). Facing a serious crisis brought about by Hamlet's killing of Polonius, he turns to his friends for advice: "Come, Gertrude, we'll call up our wisest friends / And let them know both what we mean to do / And what's untimely done" (4.1.38–40). Later, Claudius proposes that, before seeking revenge, Laertes choose "wisest friends" to "hear and judge 'twixt you and me" (4.5.202–3). Cautious, even-tempered, and calculating, Claudius takes steps to come across as reasonable, likable, stable, and public-spirited. In him, he assures the court, his subjects can find continuity and through him they remain allegiant to the throne.

To reassure his countrymen, Claudius restores the royal palace and the royal household as the center of Danish hospitality: king and queen dispense favor to a pleasure-seeking court. To this effect, he relies on images, words, and actions to establish and enforce a politics of pleasure through which he hopes to gain acceptance, while at the same time to isolate and expose his personal opponents and political enemies. I will discuss later Hamlet's alternative perspective, which I will link to a history of pain; for the time being, suffice it to say that Claudius sees Hamlet's inky cloak not just as a sign of personal grief or evidence of a quirky contrarian streak but also as political opposition and subversive intent. Subtly but forcefully, he characterizes mourning as "unmanly grief." In fact, he disallows Hamlet's request to return to Wittenberg because, as he states, "'tis most retrograde to our desire" (1.2.114). Claudius disapproves of anything "retrograde," contrary to his desire.[49]

In Claudius, pleasure and habit intermingle through public feasts in the great hall of Elsinore and private sexual pleasure with his brother's widow. He seeks pleasure and avoids pain; likewise, he certainly expects no sacrifice from his subjects or from himself. He does not miss an occasion to throw a party, as, for example, to rejoice in Hamlet's decision to remain in Denmark (1.2.122.28). In fact, as the flourish of trumpets and the shooting of canons in Act I, scene 4 make clear, Claudius follows up on his plan and hosts a lively banquet. To Hamlet, the feast seems indecorous or inappropriate: the carousing king "drains his

[49] In her characteristically didactic style, Lily B. Campbell, *Shakespeare's Tragic Heroes: Slaves of Passion* (New York: Barnes & Noble, 1930), argues that tragedy is primarily concerned with matters of evil in the world. She also suggests that "if *Hamlet* is read against a background of contemporary philosophy, it will come to life as a study in passion" (109); however, she narrowly focuses on how characters "of different temperaments" are placed "under the influence of the same passion, so that we may see the passion variously manifested" (109), a conclusion with which I do not agree. Nonetheless, I think that the book is of value as a source of information on cultural constructs of human interiority in Shakespeare's time.

draughts of Rhenish down," while "The kettledrum and trumpet thus bray out / The triumph of his pledge" (1.4.8–12). Hamlet thinks that the custom should be "more honored in the breach than the observance" (2.4.15–16) because it justifies others' perception of Denmark as a nation of drunkards. After Polonius announces that the ambassadors, Voltemand and Cornelius, "are joyfully returned" from Norway (2.2.40–41), Claudius calls his senior advisor the "father of good news" (42). Sensing Claudius' upbeat mood and seizing the opportunity to curry favor with the king, Polonius reveals that he has found "the very cause of Hamlet's lunacy" (49) and promises that "My news shall be the fruit of that great feast" (52), thus providing a double reason for celebration. Claudius misses no opportunity to drink and have fun; therefore, he sets a festive tone for his court. Such lavish feasting, according to Hamlet, undermines virtue and excessively "o'erleavens / The form of plausive manners" (29–30). As Mary Floyd-Wilson writes, "[Hamlet] implies that to behave like a Dane reduces all men and women—elite and base—to the level of corporeal appetite."[50] These events situate Claudius as the cultural insider, and Hamlet as the outsider, observing and commenting on the habits of his countrymen.

As the embodiment of pleasure, Claudius endorses two projects to tempt Hamlet to forget his father and embrace the pleasures of life. Ostensibly, these projects seek the cause of Hamlet's "transformation"—or as Claudius explains, "sith nor th'exterior nor the inward man / Resembles that it was" (2.2.6–7). Claudius entreats Rosencrantz and Guildenstern to "draw [Hamlet] on to pleasures" (2.2.10; 13–15). Simultaneously with this, he eagerly accepts Polonius's explanation that Ophelia's rejection of Hamlet's advances caused "Hamlet's lunacy" (2.2.49); in other words, denial of pleasure must surely harm one's mental health. He dismisses Gertrude's more sober assessment, "I doubt it is no other but the main, / His father's death and our o'erhasty marriage" (56–7), with a terse, "Well, we shall sift him" (58). However, faced with her husband's disapproval, she changes her mind. After Polonius analyzes Hamlet's progression into madness, Claudius poses a question to her, "Do you think 'tis this?" (2.2.151). She initially wavers but then offers a hedging statement: "It may be, very like" (2.2.152).

Eager to please, Polonius explains the dangers posed by the denial of the "ecstasy of love" and the madness that it can bring about. Although he knows,

---

50 Mary Floyd-Wilson, "English Mettle," in Gail Kern Paster, Katherine Rowe, and Mary Floyd-Wilson, (eds), *Reading the Early Modern Passions: Essays in the Cultural History of Emotion*" (Philadelphia: University of Pennsylvania Press, 2004) 142. See also Floyd-Wilson's discussion of "the ecologically embedded nature of early modern selfhood and ethnicity" (132) in "English Epicures and Scottish Witches," *Shakespeare Quarterly* 52.3 (2006): 131–61; the connection between diet and emotion in Michael C. Schoenfeldt, *Bodies and Selves in Early Modern England: Physiology and Inwardness in Spenser, Shakespeare, Herbert, and Milton* (Cambridge: Cambridge University Press, 1999) 17–19; Timothy J. Reiss, *Mirages of the Selfe: Patterns of Personhood in Ancient and Early Modern Europe* (Stanford: Stanford University Press, 2003); and Paster, *Humoring the Body*, 2.

or at least suspects, the true cause of Hamlet's perplexing demeanor, Claudius embraces Polonius' explanation, not simply to buy time and hide the murder, but also to avoid disrupting everyone's lives. In their second encounter, Claudius instructs Rosencrantz and Guildenstern to probe the cause of Hamlet's madness, but Gertrude insists on their initial project: "Did you assay him / To any pastime?" (3.1.14–15). Rosencrantz reports that at the news of the players' arrival at Elsinore, Hamlet seemed delighted: "Of these we told him, / And there did seem in him a kind of joy / To hear it" (3.1.17–19). Sensing that this might work, Claudius immediately reverts to his original plan: "Good gentlemen, give him a further edge / And drive his purpose into these delights" (3.1.26–7). Like their counterparts in the sources and analogues, Claudius, Gertrude, Polonius, Rosencrantz, Guildenstern, and others tempt Hamlet with pleasures, represented by Ophelia's body; in Shakespeare's play, they also promise the pleasures of theater. Sexual pleasure and theatrical entertainment may distract Hamlet and perchance even make him forget his suffering.

Pleasure, however, does not come without a price: it poses likely perils, and it comes to an end. In re-directing Laertes's revenge, Claudius challenges Laertes's filial obligation: "Laertes, was your father dear to you? / Or are you like the painting of a sorrow, / A face without a heart?" (4.7.106–8). Love—as well as the attendant feelings, emotions, and drives—resembles a flame, whose "spark and flame" time will extinguish (4.1.112), which seems the opposite of his response to Hamlet in Act I, scene 2. Claudius states:

> There lives within the very flame of love
> A kind of wick or snuff that will abate it,
> And nothing is at a like goodness still,
> For goodness, growing to a plurisy,
> Dies in his own too-much. That we would do
> We should do when we would, for this "would" changes,
> And hath abatements and delays as many
> As there are tongues, are hands, are accidents,
> And then this "should" is like a spendthrift sigh,
> That hurts by easing. (4.7.112–21)

Time lessens, qualifies, or changes the intensity of love, as it does the intensity of a flame. Ironically, to achieve his current leadership position and to become head of his family, Claudius had to count on the abatement of former loves for and allegiances to his deceased brother. In this case, time, working to his advantage, has snuffed out the flame of Gertrude's affection for her previous husband or of the country for its former king. When Claudius tries to guide Hamlet out of mourning, he argues that, although "mourning duties" and "obsequious sorrow" may be appropriate demonstrations of filial affection, "you must know your father lost a father / That father lost, lost his" (1.2.89–90) and that, in fact, "a common theme / Is death of fathers" (103–4). Substitute father for husband, "filial" for "wifely," and we could have an implied argument he may have used to gain Gertrude's affection. Certainly, the Player-King reminds his queen that her exaggerated protestations of love, though sincere, may not last: "What to ourselves in passion we propose, / The passion ending, doth the purpose lose" (3.2.186–7). Likewise, if Gertrude and the country can move on, Hamlet will, in due time, forget his father, for as the Player-King notes, "Purpose is but the slave to memory" (3.2.180).

Vestiges of that love must be astutely tapped and carefully channeled, or they may fuel personal betrayals or provide fodder for political causes. Public allegiance and personal commitment may prove fickle, tenuous, and temporary, as Laertes's second return from France illustrates. A band of insurgents, as the messenger reports, recognize the mild-mannered Laertes as their "riotous head": "The rabble call him lord, / And, as the world were now but to begin, / Antiquity forgot, custom not known, / The ratifiers and props of every word, / They cry, "'Choose we! Laertes shall be king!'" (4.5.102–6). His cry for justice gains him a pack of followers, whom Gertrude labels "Danish dogs." To Claudius's amazement, the rebels find little resistance, indicating that his own home offers little security: "The doors are broke" (4.5.111). In fact, Claudius points out to Laertes later that although he wishes he could rid himself of Hamlet, he has refrained from doing so for personal and political reasons. He states that Gertrude "Lives almost by [Hamlet's] looks" (4.7.12), adding that whether it be "my virtue or my plague," Gertrude is "so conjunctive to my life and soul" that he "could not but by her" (4.7.14; 16). Politically too, his hands are tied because of "the great love the general gender bear" Hamlet (18). He finds himself trapped between "affection" for Gertrude, public expediency, and desire to rid himself of an enemy. The flame of love brings about its own extinction—the country may accept another substitute leader, whether Claudius, Laertes, Hamlet, or Fortinbras. But that flame does not abate when one wishes it to do so; or, conversely, it may flicker on, when one wishes to extinguish it. Finally, pursuit of pleasure may prove a personal and political liability.

According to Hamlet, Claudius and Gertrude's "enseamèd bed"[51] encapsulates the corrupt nature of the pleasure-seeking king and of the court; it also poses political liabilities, which he draws on to undermine his uncle's political standing and reputation. Though kept out of sight, the royal bed, through numerous allusions, underscores a scandalous sexual, perhaps incestuous, relationship. Michael Neill argues that the "bed" in *Othello* symbolizes a preoccupation with a sensational, scandalous, bi-racial marriage; therefore, a "lurid vision of the bed" looms large in the audience's imagination as "the hidden object of the play's obsession," until finally revealed in Act V.[52] Since Barrymore's 1922 production of *Hamlet*, however, "modern productions have often included a bed," which implies oedipal

---

51 The *OED* defines *to enseam* as "To load with grease," adding: "The French word is now used only in sense of 'to grease (cloth)', whence perhaps the figurative use in Shakespeare."

52 Michael Neill, "Unproper Beds: Race, Adultery and the Hideous in *Othello*," in *Shakespeare's Middle Tragedies: A Collection of Critical Essays*, (ed.) David Young (Englewood Cliffs, NJ: Prentice Hall, 1993) 133.

desire.[53] George Hibbard notes that "the 2000 production at the Globe did not use a bed, though Hamlet dragged a sheet on from the discovery space when he talked of 'the rank sweat of an enseamèd bed'."[54] I suggest that, in the texts of *Hamlet*, however, Gertrude and Claudius's bed, though nearby, never makes an appearance onstage; consequently, it becomes, at least insofar as Hamlet himself is concerned, an object of no less lurid obsession than it does in *Othello*.

Opposite kinds of beds preoccupy the play's characters and the audience. The first reference underscores the ordinary bed. Bernardo relieves Francisco of the watch and comforts him: "Get thee to bed, Francisco" (1.1.07).[55] After the long, terrifying watch, Francisco needs to rest. The bed in *Hamlet* does not always symbolize rest, though; nor does it represent torment, restlessness and insomnia after Duncan's murder in *Macbeth* (2.2.34–5). Claudius does not suffer from insomnia; rather, in *Hamlet*, the murderer apparently sleeps undisturbed; and the murderer's wife, never tormented with regret or scruples, does not see phantoms. The murder victim, however, burns in Purgatory, escapes the "prison house" at night, spreads terror in his former abode, and haunts his beloved son. No wonder Hamlet perceives "sleep" and the "sleep of death" as interchangeable. For the ghost and for Hamlet, the bed may well represent not only Claudius's lust but also the incessant tossing and turning of a mind unwilling to let go of the waking hours. In his translation of Ovid's *Elegia 2*, Marlowe captures well this feeling: "What makes my bed seem hard seeing it is soft? / Or why slips downe the Coverlet so oft? / Although the nights be long, I sleepe not tho, / My sides are sore with tumbling to and fro."[56]

Lust and sordidness want to corrupt the "celestial bed," the symbol of virtue, as the Ghost instructs his son: "But virtue, as it never will be moved, / Though lewdness court it in a shape of heaven, / So lust, though to a radiant angel linked, / Will sate itself in a celestial bed / And prey on garbage" (1.5.53–7). Hamlet, however, believes that the celestial bed has already succumbed to lust's assault. Many references reinforce this point. In assuring her husband of her devotion, the Player-Queen, for example, ironically imagines her own bed becoming enseamèd: "A second time I will kill my husband dead / When second husband kisses me in bed" (3.2.176–7). Likewise, in the third act, as bedtime approaches, we become conscious that the characters, as they take care of late night business, will soon retire to their beds, some to sleep and others to engage in sinful, lustful, incestuous acts. Rosencrantz, for example, tells Hamlet that Gertrude "desires to speak with you in her closet ere you go to bed" (3.3.317–18). Lena Orlin argues that the early modern closet, not "always the object of desire we have assumed it to be," is also a place of privacy and solitude.[57] According to her, closets "capture privacy," giving

[53] Hibbard 334n.

[54] Hibbard 334n.

[55] Rosencrantz alludes to a bed put to similar uses (3.2.318), as discussed below.

[56] Christopher Marlowe, *The Complete Works*, (ed.) Fredson Bowers, second edition (Cambridge: Cambridge University Press, 1981) 2: 316.

[57] Orlin, *Locating Privacy*, 297. See also Orlin's essay, "Gertrude's Closet," *Shakespeare Jahrbuch* 134 (1998): 44–67, esp. 56–67.

it "a local habitation and a name," and serve as "convenient conceptual containers for the subjectivities, genderings, and sexualities in which we persistently interest ourselves."[58]

In *Hamlet*, Shakespeare contrasts closet and bedchamber: both are private spaces, but the bedchamber acquires sexual connotations. Charles Witham's watercolor in the 1870 promptbook for the Edwin Booth production depicts Gertrude's closet as a spacious room, "'extending 20 feet or so back from the footlights'—equipped with furniture."[59] The even more intimate bedchamber, however, remains hidden from view, although Polonius mentions it to Claudius: "I'll call upon you ere you go to bed / And tell you what I know" (3.3.34–5). A little later, Hamlet alludes to Claudius's bed, as he, mistaking penitent posture for contrition, spares his uncle's life: "When he is drunk asleep, or in his rage, / Or in th'incestuous pleasure of his bed" (3.3.89–90). His words echo the Ghost's earlier in the play: "Let not the royal bed of Denmark be / A couch for luxury and damnèd incest" (1.5.83–4). The Ghost has taken a position similar to that of Shakespeare and Fletcher's *Henry VIII*, when the Lord Chamberlain explains: "It seems the marriage with his brother's wife / Has crept too near his conscience" (2.2.15–16).[60] Interestingly, Quarto 1 does not locate either Gertrude or Ophelia in a closet; in Quarto 2, however, Hamlet visits Gertrude's closet, rather than the more shocking and scandalous bedchamber.

As the audience's attention shifts to Gertrude's closet, as it had done earlier with references to Ophelia's sewing closet, the vast spaces represented by Elsinore's long corridors, large halls, courtyards, and public areas seem to contract. In the closet scene, the Ghost reappears, now dressed according to Q1, "*in his nightgown*,"[61] as if ready to hop into bed with his former wife. A displaced lover, he does not linger

---

[58] Orlin, Locating Privacy, 297.

[59] Charles H. Shattuck, *The Hamlet of Edwin Booth* (Urbana: University of Illinois Press, 1969) 223. See Plate XIII.

[60] See *King Henry VIII*, (ed.) Gordon McMullan, Arden Shakespeare (London: Thomson Learning, 2000). McMullan notes that "*Conscience* begins here to acquire the sexual connotations that it bears in the rest of the play" (380n).

[61] See *Hamlet: The First Quarto 1603*, (ed.) Albert B. Weiner (Great Neck, NY: Barron's Educational Series, 1962) 137. Q1 reads, "*Enter the Ghost in his nightgown*." The *OED* defines "nightgown" as follows: "A loose gown specially used for putting on at (or during the) night in place of the ordinary clothes; a dressing-gown). Both Q2 and F1 read, "*Enter Ghost*." In *The Voice of Elizabethan Stage Directions: The Evolution of a Theatrical Code* (Newark: University of Delaware Press; London: Associated University Presses, 1999), Linda McJannet does a superb job of explaining and contextualizing the meaning of these and other stage directions. See especially McJannet's introduction and Chapter 6, "Action, Gesture and Special Effects" (15–32; 168–92). In Chapter 2, "Interpreting Stage Directions," in *Elizabethan Stage Conventions and Modern Interpreters* (Cambridge: Cambridge University Press, 1984) 19–52, Alan Dessen argues that the differences in stage directions among the three texts of *Hamlet* may indicate that the same scenes were staged differently in various productions by the same company (21).

around. Just as suddenly, he exits "out of the portal" (Q1); simultaneously, the private, intimate space of the closet expands and opens up through a mysterious passageway into an adjacent or parallel world into which her ghastly "pale" former husband, "in the habit as he lived," retires.[62] In *Hypnerotomachia: The Strife of Love in a Dreame* (1592), Francesco Colonna represents similar portals. The dreamer-lover enters strange buildings, passes through portals, and travels through adjoining valleys and mountains, which at first seem far away but move nearer as if "they had ioyned together with the building which was an inclosure or end of the valley betwixt mountaine and mountaine."[63]

After the ghost vanishes, the audience's attention refocuses on the adjoining royal bedchamber. Hamlet offers Gertrude an escape from the pleasurable habits of her bed; he cannot understand how she has chosen "but to live / In the rank sweat of an enseamèd bed, / Stewed in corruption, honeying and making love / Over the nasty sty" (3.4.91–4). Through olfactory imagery, Hamlet suggests that the bed reeks with bodily smells and fluids. Sweat mixes with grease and the "honey" of lovemaking: sweat, saliva, semen, and vaginal fluids are stewed together into a "nasty sty."[64] The pun on "stews" evokes "a brothel," a meaning that was derived from "stews" as "a heated room used for hot air or vapour baths," "on account of the frequent use of the public hot-air baths for immoral purposes" (*OED*). Tactile imagery, added to olfactory, transforms the royal bedroom into a chamber steaming with the heat of illicit, immoral, overpowering sexual activity.[65]

In *Pericles*, Gower notes that Antiochus seduced his own daughter; she, in turn, took "a liking" to her father: "By custom what they did begin / Was with long use accounted no sin" (I, Chorus, *ll.* 29–30). Anticipating Gower's words, Hamlet advises Gertrude not to go to "my uncle's bed" (3.4.160), to overcome or curb the power of addiction, with puns on repeated, customary action and virtue's suitable garments:

---

[62] Quarto 1, p. 138. The Folio text reads: "Why look you there: looke how it steals away: / My Father in his habit, as he liued, / Looke where he goes euen nowe out at the Portall." See Charlton Hinman, *The Norton Facsimile The First Folio of Shakespeare* (New York: W.W. Norton, 1968) 779. For a description of Edwin Booth's seminal staging of the scene, see Shattuck 231–4.

[63] Francesco Colonna, *Hypnerotomachia: The Strife of Love in a Dreame* (London, 1592), (ed.) Lucy Gent (Delmar, New York: Scholars' Facsimiles and Reprints, 1973) 18.

[64] "Stews," in usage dating back from the late Middle English period, meant a "brothel" (see *OED*).

[65] The revulsion here may be related to Julia Kristeva's discussion of the "erotization of the abject" in *Powers of Horror: An Essay on Abjection*, trans. Leon S. Roudiez (New York: Columbia University Press, 1982), especially "What flows from the other's 'innermost being', for the desirable and terrifying, nourishing and murderous, fascinating and abject inside of the maternal body" (54–5).

> That monster custom, who all sense doth eat,
> Of habits devil, is angel yet in this,
> That to the use of actions fair and good
> He likewise gives a frock or livery
> That aptly is put on. (3.4.162–6).[66]

Habits of mind and sexual desire intersect; addictive bodily pleasures corrode habits attendant on virtue. Hamlet advises her: "Refrain to-night, / And that shall lend a kind of easiness / To the next abstinence" (3.4.166–8). In fact, contrary habits may replace one another: "For use almost can change the stamp of nature" (3.4.169).[67]

As Peter Stallybrass and Ann Rosalind Jones write, "If Hamlet imagines habit or custom as a 'monster', it is because of its power to transform."[68] Hamlet imagines virtue as "a bodily practice," equating habit and the wearing of clothes: "Repeated wearing acts as an inscription upon the body."[69] Perhaps inadvertently, Hamlet vividly reminds Gertrude of the very things she will miss, if she avoids Claudius's bed: "Let the bloat king tempt you again to bed, / Pinch wanton on your cheek, call you his mouse, / And let him, for a pair of reechy kisses, / Or paddling in your neck with his damned fingers / Make you to ravel all this matter out" (3.4.183–9).[70] Clearly, to purge the royal bed, Hamlet battles a seemingly unbreakable alliance of the flesh, strengthened and reinforced by sexual habits, and, ironically, by the bonds of matrimony: "father and mother is man and wife, man and wife is one flesh" (4.3.50–51).

In Ophelia's experience, Shakespeare represents the tragedy that results when two opposite kinds of bed threaten to become one. In one of her songs, Ophelia relates a narrative of seduction and betrayal. The song speaks of a young man who seduced a young woman. After he made love to her, "Then up he rose and donned

---

[66] In his edition of the play, George R. Hibbard remarks, "Virtue is regarded as a garment which may, in time, exert an influence on its wearer's behaviour" (285n). One might also hear an echo of St John Chrysostom's second sermon on how to achieve a virtuous disposition: "For even if we do not seek virtue, but at least praise it, we shall perhaps be able to attain it; and even if we do not avoid evil, but at least censure it, we shall perhaps be able to escape it" (St John Crysostom, *On Wealth and Poverty*, trans. Catherine P. Roth [Crestwood, NY: St Vladimir's Seminary Press, 1999] 39).

[67] The wording here comes from Q2, although the conceptual frame remains constant in all three texts. In Q1, Hamlet tells her: "Forbear the adulterous bed tonight, / And win yourself by little, as you may; / In time it may be you will loath him quite" (see Weiner 138).

[68] Peter Stallybrass and Ann Rosalind Jones, "Fetishizing the Glove in Renaissance Europe," *Critical Inquiry* 28.1 (2001): 117.

[69] Stallybrass and Jones 117.

[70] The Folio reads "blunt king" (Hinman 779). "Bloat" suggests "soft, soft-bodied, flabby, pulpy; passing into 'puffy, puffed, swollen" (*OED* and Hibbard, p. 286, note 171); whereas, "blunt" evokes senses dulled by excessive pleasure (cf. *OED*: "Dull, insensitive, stupid, obtuse: said, it appears, originally of the sight, whence of the perceptions generally, and the intellect) as well as "rude, unpolished, rough, without refinement" (*OED*).

his clo'es / And dupped the chamber door, / Let in the maid, that out a maid / Never departed more" (4.5.52–5). Through multiple puns, the song refers to the sexual habits of young men, "Young men will do't if they come to't" because "By Cock, they are to blame" (4.5.60–61). When the young woman pointed out that her lover had promised to marry her, he retorted: "'So would I 'a' done, by yonder sun, / And thou hadst not come to my bed'" (65–6). In his quest to rid Denmark of another "couch of luxury," Hamlet has also contaminated Ophelia's bridal chamber, snuffed out her hopes and dreams, and hollowed out her own being into a madly, ghostly figure, teetering between the pain of her father's funeral and the "enseamèd," contaminated bed of a lover's betrayal. Claudius describes her as being "divided from herself and her fair judgment, / Without the which we are pictures or mere beasts" (4.5.85–6). Gertrude, however, poignantly describes what could have been: "I hoped thou shouldst have been my Hamlet's wife, / I thought thy bride-bed to have decked, sweet maid, / And not have strewed thy grave" (5.1.231–3). Ophelia becomes unhinged—teetering in a world caught between pleasure and unspeakable pain.

Claudius believes that mourning not only undermines his authority and political agenda but also implies treasonous allegiance to the deceased king. Claudius strives to isolate, hence contain, Hamlet. Hamlet, in turn, offers behind-the-scenes resistance, forcing Hamlet into the conundrum of how to wage a war against the enticing habits of pleasure. In his own way, each seeks to establish and maintain control over the deceased king's home.

House of Pain

In *Diatribai*, Epictetus argues that the remedy for a powerful habit is the contrary habit: "Listen to the contrary arguments … Oppose to one habit the contrary habit." He adds, "Against specious appearances we must have clear preconceptions, polished and ready to use."[71] Hamlet adopts a similar approach. To counter and combat his mother's unseemly sexual pleasure, Hamlet focuses on the pain he feels for the loss of his father. To do so, he aligns himself emotionally, hence politically, with his father, making mourning the center of his life.[72] Yet struggling

---

[71] Epictetus, *The Discourses: The Handbook, Fragments*, trans. Robin Hard and (ed.) Christopher Gill (London: Everyman/J.M. Dent, 1995) Book 1.4; 6. Epictetus's handbook was available in English translation: *The manuell of Epictetus, translated out of Greeke into French, and now into English, conferred with two Latine translations. Herevnto are annexed annotations, and also the apothegs of the same author* (London, 1567). STC 10423. See Chapter 1, "What things are in man, and what are not," and the definition of desire in chapter 5 of the 1567 edition. References to Epictetus crop up with some regularity in the period, as for example in Richard Barckley, *A Discourse of the Felicitie of Man* (London, 1603) 20.

[72] In *Shakespeare and Social Class* (Atlantic Highlands, NJ: Humanities Press International, 1988), Ralph Berry argues that "Hamlet," "the name of the father and the son, links identity to ancestry," but that the term "Prince is the rank at the center of the

to find the truest, most appropriate medium to express his allegiance to his father and his resistance to his uncle, he seemingly dooms himself to staging spectacles of pain, grief, and hurt.

As culturally determined phenomena, public or private expression of emotional suffering depends on degree of kinship, religious beliefs, and decorum; it also helps to define the boundaries of the permissible in a society.[73] In rural Brazil, for example, grieving families traditionally hired *Carpideiras*, or *choradeiras* to provide a loud, sorrowful accompaniment at wakes and at funerals. These mercenary or professional women chanted *incelências* or votive prayers for the deceased, and, most tellingly, served as precentors in loud, insistent, dramatic outbursts of moaning, weeping, and wailing, when the pallbearers moved the coffin from the house for the journey to the cemetery.[74] As Bronislaw Malinowski discovered, the Trobriand Islanders do not employ professional mourners but define in other ways who should participate

---

play," and that "*Prince* is not *King*, and most of the play is Hamlet's coming to terms with that fact" (95). This cogent analysis suggests that, although ancestry links Hamlet to his father, by becoming king, Claudius dooms Hamlet to the role of prince, thus opening a gulf in social status if not in social class between son and father. Bertram Joseph writes of "Hamlet's function of hurting to heal," similar to what a physician or surgeon might have to do (95), although he places this in the context of a fight between the forces of good and evil: "The more we contemplate the events of the play, the more they make us aware of the "mere hand" of providence destroying evil," *Conscience and the King* (London: Chatto & Windus, 1953) 130–37; reprinted as "The Theme," in David Bevington, (ed.), *Twentieth-Century Interpretations of "Hamlet"* (Englewood Cliffs, N.J.: Prentice-Hall, 1968) 103.

[73] This is not to deny that, like other human feelings and experiences, pain may find expression not only in culturally sanctioned, permitted ways but also in forbidden, taboo ways.

[74] "*Carpideira—Mulher mercenária que acompanhava os funerais pranteando os mortos*" [mercenary woman who used to accompany funerals, weeping and wailing for the dead]—See Aurélio Buarque de Hollanda Ferreira and José Baptista da Luz, (eds,) *Pequeno Dicionário Brasileiro da Língua Portuguesa* (São Paulo: Companhia Editora Nacional, 1972). According to the *Enciclopédia da Música Brasileira*, "the activity of the *carpideira*, in Brazil, may be spontaneous and non-remunerated, or rewarded with food, money, or clothes. It is generally performed by elderly women, whether blood relations or not, who provoke tears from the family with exalted phrases and dramatic gesticulation. The *carpideiras* initiate the singing of the *incelências*, intoned in a sinister and frightening voice. They are the repositories of votive prayers for the dead. These songs are sung and prayers are said before the beginning of the funeral procession" (translation mine). (http://cf2.uol.com.br/encmusical/listaverbete.asp?code=2248, January 3, 2003). Percy MacQuoid writes that England had its own version of paid mourners: "In 1575 Sir Thomas Gresham directed in his will that black gowns, of cloth at 6s. 8*d*. the yard, were to be given to a 100 poor men and a 100 poor women to bring him to his grave" (149). Similar arrangements were made for Sir Christopher Hatton's funeral in 1592. See Percy MacQuoid, "The Home: Furniture, Food and Drink, Christenings, Weddings, Funerals," in *Shakespeare's England: An Account of the Life & Manners of His Age* (Oxford: Clarendon Press, 1916) 2: 119–52.

in mourning rituals.[75] Because they fall under a taboo, the deceased's matrilineal kinsmen and children "must keep aloof from the corpse" and must not "display any outward sign of mourning in costume and ornamentation, though they need not conceal their grief and may show it by mourning."[76] The widow and the in-laws, not considered blood relations of the deceased, shave their heads, smear their bodies with soot, and howl "like demons in despair"; as Malinowski explains, "these are the non-kinsmen of the dead man, the people not actually bereaved."[77] Indeed, these rituals suggest how cultural practice and emotional displacement intertwine to produce distinctive languages of pain.

In her book, *The History of Pain*, Roselyne Rey argues that "pain involves a codified form of social behaviour which sets the parameters of allowable overt manifestations and regulates the expression of such innermost personal experiences, whether endured in the family bosom or alone in a solitary confrontation with the self."[78] She adds: "Pain always has a specific language, whether it is a cry, a sob, or a tensing of the features, and it is a language in itself as well."[79] Expressions of pain, demarcating "standards of permissiveness" and "notions of transgression" therefore intimately connect with a "dialectic concerning what must be concealed and what may be revealed."[80] The Trobriand ritual reminded Malinowski of Shakespeare's *Hamlet*: "And what makes the whole performance most disconcerting is the absence of the real protagonist—*Hamlet* without the Prince of Denmark."[81] Indeed, Malinowski's analogy may not be so far-fetched. In his emotional and political alliance to his father, Hamlet becomes the enemy of his uncle's pleasure and seeks an appropriate language to express his sorrow.[82]

---

75 Bronislaw Malinowski, *The Sexual Life of Savages in Northwestern Melanesia; An Ethnographic Account of Courtship, Marriage, and Family Life Among the Natives of the Trobriand Islands, British New Guinea* (1929; Boston: Beacon Press, 1987) 127.

76 Malinowski 128.

77 Malinowski, 129.

78 Roselyne Rey, *The History of Pain*, trans. Louise Elliott Wallance, J.A. Cadden, and S.W. Cadden (Cambridge, MA: Harvard University Press, 1995) 4. In a fascinating essay, "'Let me the curtains draw': The Dramatic and Symbolic Properties of the Bed in Shakespearean Tragedy," in Jonathan Gil Harris and Natasha Corda (eds), *Staged Properties in Early Modern English Drama* (Cambridge: Cambridge University Press, 2002), Sasha Roberts argues for "continuities between social practice and dramatic representations" in terms of the symbolic and dramatic uses of the bed on the stage, but makes generic distinctions regarding the use of properties in comedies and tragedies: "A materialist analysis of stage properties must not, then, lose sight of the contingencies of drama or the imperatives of fiction" (167).

79 Rey 4.

80 Rey 4.

81 Malinowski 148.

82 A.C. Bradley argues that Hamlet's melancholy is linked to Hamlet's "delay," and from a psychological perspective, "it is the center of the tragedy" (107). For a discussion of Hamlet's "delay" and connection to revenge, see also R.A. Foakes, *Shakespeare and Violence* (Cambridge: Cambridge University Press, 2003) 117–25. I am suggesting that, if

In perhaps the best-known and most influential study of pain, Elaine Scarry argues that "physical pain is exceptional in the whole fabric of psychic, somatic, and perceptual states for being the only one that has no object." She adds:

> Though the capacity to experience physical pain is as primal a fact about the human being as is the capacity to hear, to touch, to desire, to fear, to hunger, it differs from these events, and from every other bodily and psychic event, by not having an object in the external world … This objectlessness, the complete absence of referential content, almost prevents it from being rendered in language: objectless, it cannot easily be objectified in any form, material or verbal.[83]

Scarry finds it "appropriate to think of pain as the imagination's intentional state, and to identify the imagination as pain's intentional object."[84] Framed this way, the connection between pain and imagination explains Hamlet's search for the means to represent his father's pain and the realization that customary signs fail to seize the essence of pain. Eric P. Levy writes, "in *Hamlet,* thought or interior apprehension not only engenders inward pain," it also triggers "the need to terminate the pain."[85] Repeatedly, Hamlet resorts to the imagination and deploys imaginative devices to grasp his father's pain and to externalize his most inward pain for the loss of his father and the betrayal of his mother.

Throughout the play, Shakespeare creates reflection chambers to parallel Hamlet's plight and echo chambers to reverberate the anguished, painful cries, not only of the ghost but also of Hamlet. Like the wintry darkness of the opening scene, an atmosphere of pain manifests itself at crucial occasions. At first meteorological phenomena and allusions become central thematic conduits used to convey representations of pain. The pervasive darkness in the opening scene has an immediate effect on bodies and minds. Francisco introduces this when he indicates that "'Tis bitter cold / And I am sick at heart" (1.1.8–9). Bernardo notices a change in Horatio: "You tremble and look pale" (1.1.53). What Horatio describes as "a guilty thing," the ghost is chastened away by "the morn in russet mantle clad" (1.1.166). This anticipates Claudius' statement about "hearts in grief" (1.2.3), as well as Hamlet's dominant mood, felt in both mind and "sullied flesh": "How weary, stale, flat, and unprofitable / Seem to me all the uses of this world" (1.2.133–4). Horatio describes the ghost to Hamlet: "A countenance more in sorrow than in anger" (1.2.232). The ghost makes "the night hideous" (1.4.54).

---

there is anything one might call "delay," this is Hamlet's attempt to find a space to stage a history of pain through which he hopes to garner sufficient emotional and political support to overcome the inducements to pleasure staged by his uncle and by his mother.

[83] Elaine Scarry, *The Body in Pain: The Making and Unmaking of the World* (New York and Oxford: Oxford University Press, 1985) 161–2.

[84] Scarry 162.

[85] Eric P. Levy, *Hamlet and the Rethinking of Man* (Madison: Farleigh Dickinson University Press, 2008) 143.

Derived from old French, *hidos* (eleventh century *hisdos*, from *hisde*, *hide*, horror, fear), "hideous" originally meant frightful, dreadful, and horrible, but gradually evolved into "revolting to the senses or feelings."[86] Indeed, the ghost assumes "some other horrible form" (1.4.72), being linked to a decaying body, "rank and gross in nature," and rotten flesh that melts, thaws, and resolves itself into a dew. Marcellus concludes: "Something is rotten in the state of Denmark" (1.4.89). Later in the play, in Ophelia's description of the scene in her sewing closet, Hamlet resembles a ghost: "Pale as his shirt, his knees knocking each other, / And with a look so piteous in purport / As if he had been loosed out of hell / To speak of horrors" (2.1.81–4). One can hardly come into contact with the corpse without contamination, whether in body or mind.

When we first meet Hamlet, before he has met the ghost, we already sense that Hamlet struggles with how best to express his innermost pain. Hamlet sets himself apart—in dress as well as demeanor—from the rest of the court. Degrees of kinship have already been blurred, not only in what Claudius refers to as "our sometime sister, now our queen," but most significant in Claudius' reference to Hamlet as both "cousin" and "son." Hamlet counters this with an aside, focusing on the blurred, foggy degrees of kinship Claudius embodies, "A little more than kin, and less than kind" (1.2.65). Claudius is the first to call attention to Hamlet's difference, "How is it that the clouds still hang on you?" (1.2.66), which Hamlet counters by saying that he has been overexposed to the sun. The meteorological metaphors connect the present clouds hanging over Hamlet to the darkness that enveloped the stage in the previous scene.[87] Gertrude goes even further, developing the metaphorical cluster:

> Good Hamlet, cast thy nighted color off,
> And let thine eye look like a friend on Denmark.
> Do not for ever with thy vailèd [lowered; drooped][88] lids
> Seek for thy noble father in the dust.
> Thou know'st 'tis common. All that lives must die,
> Passing through nature to eternity. (1.2.68–73)

---

86 Cf. *OED*. In usage dating from 1330, "hideous" means "terrible, distressing, or revolting to the moral sense; abominable, detestable; odious." Modern French "*hideux*" means hideous, horrible, frightful, appalling, shocking. In "The World of *Hamlet*," in Alfred Harbage, (ed.), *Shakespeare: The Tragedies: A Collection of Critical Essays* (Englewood Cliff: Prentice-Hall, 1964), Maynard Mack writes of the atmosphere created in the play: "The ghost's injunction to act becomes so inextricably bound up for Hamlet with the character of the world in which the action must be taken—its mysteriousness, its baffling appearances, its deep consciousness of infection, frailty, and loss—that he cannot come to terms with either without coming to terms with both" (59).

87 Interestingly, Q1 does not mention meteorological phenomena; rather, it focuses on psychological ones: "And now princely son Hamlet, / What means these sad and melancholy moods?" (73).

88 *OED* definitions.

Dressed in discordant night-colored clothes, Hamlet, suggests Gertrude, looks for a father in the wrong place—in the dust—rather than in a new "Denmark"; namely, Claudius. If, as Hamlet agrees, death is a common occurrence in nature, she wonders why he doesn't accept that and move on: "If it be, / Why seems it so particular with thee?" (1.2.74–5). Therefore, as Gail Paster writes, "If Hamlet's refusal—presumably in defiance of a royal edict from Claudius—to cast off this external coloration expresses his desire not to blend in, it also signals his lack of influence on the courtiers."[89] The word "seems" opens a gap between "is" and "as-if," which as Paster notes, Hamlet perceives as a disconnection between the inner experience and the exterior physical sign of mourning.[90]

Hamlet confronts these fundamental contradictions, when he objects to the gap that Gertrude's use of the word "seems" opens, a gap between the exterior indicators of mourning—"inky cloak," "customary suits of melancholy black," sighs, tears, dejected countenance—and the inner realm of emotions (1.2.76–86). Hamlet relies on traditional Western European trappings of mourning to express his innermost grief; yet he realizes that these cannot "denote me truly." Katherine Eisaman Maus observes that authors coming from varying traditions of religious belief as "the Puritan Perkins, the Anglican Foxe, the Jesuit Wright, and the heterodox Ralegh all yearn for techniques of penetration, excavation, exposure," while they still voice "their mistrust of those techniques."[91] She suggests that these writers reflect upon "a universal insight into the irreducible mysteriousness of human beings to one another": "The difference between knowing oneself 'from the inside' and knowing other people 'from the outside' may seem so fundamental to social life that it cannot be the property of a particular historical moment."[92] Maus argues that, if not perforce cultural universals, "distinctions between a socially visible exterior and an invisible personal interior" have a long philosophical history.[93] Of particular concern in the Renaissance, she adds, is "a discrepancy" between "inward disposition" and "outward appearance"—an "unexpressed interior" and "a theatricalized exterior."[94] Maus concludes: "the dramatic techniques favored by English Renaissance dramatists further aggravate the relationship between spectacle and truth."[95] Hamlet confronts, yet cannot resolve, the seeming contractions between exterior theatricality and interior emotion.

In his first soliloquy, Hamlet compares Gertrude and Niobe, both capable of apparently similar yet truly opposite expressions of pain and sorrow. Niobe,

---

89 Gail Kern Paster, *Humoring the Body: Emotions and the Shakespearean Stage* (Chicago: University of Chicago Press, 2004) 36.

90 Paster 36.

91 Katherine Eisaman Maus, *Inwardness and the Theater in the English Renaissance* (Chicago: University of Chicago Press, 1995) 12.

92 Maus 12; 2.

93 Maus 12.

94 Maus 13.

95 Maus 31.

daughter of Tantalus and extremely proud mythical queen of Thebes, boasted of having been blessed with more children than Leto, who had only the twins, Apollo and Artemis, and therefore "the abundance of my blessings is my safeguard. I am beyond the reach of Fortune's blows, for though she may take much away from me, still she will leave me much more than she takes."[96] To add insult to injury, she boasted that her family was superior to Leto's: "Suppose some of my children could be taken from me: though bereaved, still I should not be reduced to a mere two, such as Leto's family consists of—one might as well have no children at all!"[97] To placate their mother's fury and avenge the injury, Apollo and Artermis slaughtered all of Niobe's children. To end his life and heartache, Niobe's husband, Amphion, falls on his sword. Grief-stricken and shedding copious tears, Niobe was instantly transformed by Zeus into a continually weeping stone on Mount Sypylus in Lydia.[98]

In Hamlet's imagination, Gertrude becomes associated with Niobe. He is amazed that the Niobe that his mother used to be has been transformed into her stony double within a period of a month (1.2.143–9). But unlike Niobe's, Gertrude's prodigious metamorphosis results not from grief but from the speed with which she forgets her first husband and the voracious desire with which she embraces his brother: "Within a month, / Ere yet the salt of most unrighteous tears / Had left the flushing in her galled eyes, / She married" (1.2.153–6). As the ghost puts it, she allowed Claudius to seduce her and bend to his lust "the will of my most seeming-virtuous queen" (1.5.46). In hindsight, Hamlet imagines his mother's former affectionate gestures, protestations of love, and expressions of grief as shallow and insincere, her nature being governed not by "discourse of reason" but habits of mind, shaped by a body enfettered to "increase of appetite."

Equally puzzling to Hamlet is the actor's ability to play a part, so true to life that it seems to surpass life. At Hamlet's request, the actor recites Aeneas' tale to Dido about the sacking of Troy, the killing of Priam, and the state of despair that Hecuba fell into, as she watched "Pyrrhus make malicious sport / In mincing with his sword her husband's limbs" (2.2.453–4). In *Dido, Queen of Carthage*, Marlowe has Aeneas describe Pyrrhus as follows: "At last came Pyrrhus, fell and full of ire, / His harness dropping blood, and on his spear / The mangled head of Priam's youngest son" (2.2.213–15).[99] In *The Aeneid*, the source used by Marlowe and Shakespeare, Virgil depicts Dido as being obsessed with the fall of Troy; she demands "to hear once more / In her wild need the throes of Ilium, / And once more hung on the narrator's words."[100] As Polonius observes, the player seems

---

96 Ovid, *Metamorphoses*, trans. Mary M. Innes (London and New York: Penguin Books, 1955) 139.

97 Ovid 139.

98 Ovid 142.

99 Christopher Marlowe, *The Complete Plays*, (ed.) J.B. Steane (London and New York: Penguin Books, 1986).

100 *The Aeneid of Virgil*, trans. Robert Fitzgerald (New York: Vintage Books, 1990) 4: 108–11.

moved by his performance: "Look, where he has not turned his color, and has tears in's eyes" (2.2.459–60). Hamlet, when left alone onstage, ponders in a soliloquy the "monstrous" phenomenon of an exaggerated outpouring of emotions of an actor impersonating Hecuba: "And all for nothing, / For Hecuba!" (2.2.495–6). Hamlet adds: "What's Hecuba to him, or he to Hecuba, / That he should weep for her?" (2.2.497–8).

A fault line becomes apparent between pain and its referent. Pain seems to be a floating sign, which though carrying meaning, lacks a point of reference. Caught between life and the fiction of theater, Hamlet wonders at the capacity of a true *carpideira* like the actor to display what seems to be genuine emotion, although the referent, Hecuba, the object for which he cries, means nothing to him personally. Hamlet connects two kinds of performance or spectacle: the pain and grief of a theatrical make-believe and the suffering in life, with a source in the heart: "What would he do / Had he the motive and the cue for passion / That I have? He would drown the stage with tears" (2.2.498–500). Paradoxically, the actor, who has no motive, can represent Hecuba's grief so true to life; yet Hecuba means nothing to him. Contrarily, Hamlet, who has abundant reason to move the world with his pain and suffering, cannot even bring himself to cry. If he could, he wonders, the spectacle would amaze the audience. Ironically, Niobe and Gertrude should be doubles of each other; yet Gertrude resembles the *carpideira*-actor, who can perform pain, yet feels none. Hamlet, on the other hand, feels pain, yet cannot properly embody it in a performance. Thus Hamlet searches for the appropriate media—clothes, gestures, language, and actions—that best express a history of pain and yet finds none. He senses a profound disconnect between the experience and the language of pain.

In the play, the characters try to identify an appropriate way to express the inward experience of pain, suffering, and mourning; yet, repeatedly, the theater can only offer spectacles or representations of pain, with Hamlet, either as observer or participant.[101] The spectacles provide the foundation for a history of pain. As the center of what Michel de Certeau might call a "historiographical operation,"

---

[101] In "The Spectacle of Suffering in Spanish Streets," in *City and Spectacle in Medieval Europe*, Medieval Studies at Minnesota, Vol. 6, (eds) Barbara A. Hanawalt and Kathryn L. Reyerson, (Minneapolis and London: University of Minnesota Press, 1994), Maureen Flynn studies the annual expressions of grief through reenactment of Christ's passion on the eve of Holy Thursday in medieval Castile: "the *disciplinantes*, barefoot penitents, walked the cobblestone streets, flailing long knotted and waxed-tipped ropes across their backs until blood drenched their linen tunics and spilled over onto darkened pavements" (154). She adds that "the public wanted to see the spirit of contrition and repentance in excess, a tragedy of tremendous potential that left no intellectual doubt about the transcendent value of corporal pain … The key to the whole spectacle was to be seen in the bodies of the actors. With their heads covered in hoods as tokens of modesty, their knees bent in humility, their moist flesh streaked with blood, they were the consummate image of passion. The orchestrated movements of their bodies, like masks worn in a tragedy, were designed to amplify the suffering of man" (163).

Hamlet revisits his father's sites of pain and in the process creates some of his own. Certeau argues that historiography and death are, in fact, intertwined endeavors: "On the one hand, writing plays the role of a burial rite, in the ethnological and quasi-religious meaning of the term; it exorcises death by inserting it into discourse. On the other hand, it possesses a symbolizing function; it allows a society to situate itself by giving itself a past through language, and it thus opens to the present a space of its own."[102] Although unable to bring his father back to life and restore him to his home, Hamlet nonetheless imagines, internalizes, and reconstructs his father's suffering, including the agony of death. Sites of physical pain and mental anguish, associated with Hamlet's father, are, however, kept off stage, although the ghost describes them in vivid detail. I will therefore examine first the orchard scene and then the "prison house."

In his narrative in Act I, scene 5, the ghost represents and thus provides a link between two primordial sites of pain: the orchard and the prison house. Through vivid description, the ghost takes Hamlet to the scene where Claudius poisoned his brother, and to the prison house where Hamlet's father has been kept since his death. In the king's orchard, Claudius commits the almost perfect murder and also conducts an experiment: the almost perfect substitution of one brother for another. In describing his death, the ghost emphasizes the excruciating pain he felt as he lay dying. The poison, like a "leperous distillment," coursed through his veins, and curdled his blood. His body, as if overtaken by leprosy, began to rot and decay: "And a most instant tetter[103] barked about / Most lazarlike with vile and loathsome crust / All my smooth body" (1.5.59–73). Tellingly, his "ears" become "porches"; and his veins and arteries, the "natural gates and alleys." He equates body and citadel, the king's person and the king's castle.

Claudius took advantage of his brother's daily habits on that fatal afternoon. Through the labyrinth of his brother's ears, he poured the juice of hebona, the leperous distillment, and filled his brother's body with poison. From being healthy and smooth, the king's body turned into something loathsome and crusty, the blood from thin and wholesome into something thick and curdled. Thereby, Claudius caught his brother physically and spiritually off guard and deprived him "of life, of crown, of queen" (1.5.75). The ghost describes the scene in the orchard as "O, horrible! O, horrible! most horrible!" (1.5.80), his dying experience making the afternoon hideous, as his ghastly figure as a specter now renders the night.

The ghost also refers to a prison house, a torture chamber, where he is kept during daylight hours, a place enveloped in sulphurous and tormenting flames, where "the foul crimes done in my days of nature / Are burnt and purged away" (1.5.12–13). The Ghost adds:

---

[102] Michel de Certeau, *The Writing of History*, trans. Tom Conley (New York: Columbia University Press, 1988) 100.

[103] The *OED* defines "tetter" as "a general name for any pustular herpiform eruption of the skin, as eczema, herpes, impetigo, ringworm, etc." The word also occurs as a noun in *Troilus and Cressida* (5.1.27) and as a verb in *Coriolanus* (3.1.78).

But that I am forbid
To tell the secrets of my prison house,
I could a tale unfold whose lightest word
Would harrow up thy soul, freeze thy young blood,
Make thy two eyes like stars start from their spheres,
Thy knotted and combined locks to part,
And each particular hair to stand an [on] end
Like quills upon the fretful porcupine. (1.5.13–20).

Though the victim of a crime, the ghost, sentenced to Purgatory, must "walk the night" and then spend the daylight hours confined in "fast flames," being burnt and purged. This "eternal blazon" is not, however, for "ears of flesh and blood" (22). Ironically, like the royal bed, the quintessential emblem of pleasure, the prison house remains hidden, kept off stage. Shut out of both places, Hamlet can only imagine what goes on in that prison. In a sense, the ghost makes it possible, as Greenblatt writes, for Hamlet "to encounter within carefully demarcated boundaries what might otherwise spiral out of control; to know states of extreme suffering and exaltation that are normally inaccessible."[104] As a forbidden, hidden place, the "prison house," through the imagination, becomes lurid, mysterious, and lugubrious. In addition, as Greenblatt aptly concludes, "Narrative is the principal means of doing what painting does: creating and populating a space."[105] We cannot underestimate the impact of the ghost's ambiguous, broken narrative on Hamlet's imagination.

The Argentine writer Alejandra Pizarnik creates a most memorable surrealistic representation of pain, torture, and pleasure in her short story, "The Bloody Countess," which imagines the sexual perversions and madness of Erzsebet Bathory (1560–1614), a female murderess during the Turkish occupation of Hungary, 1526–1699, who would attract and then torture to death young aristocratic maidens.[106] Pizarnik based her story on Valentine Penrose's book, *Erzsebet Bathory, la Comtesse Sanglante*.[107] In the evil, diabolical secret chambers of the dungeon of Erzsebet's castle, the maidens meet slow and excruciating death through machines and instruments of torture, including "the iron maiden," water tanks, the lethal cage, whipping, red-hot pokers, scissors or shears, and knives. Pizarnik concludes that Countess Bathory, who "reached beyond all limits the uttermost pit of unfettered passions," "is yet another proof that the absolute freedom of the human creature is

---

[104] Greenblatt, *Hamlet in Purgatory*, 82. Greenblatt discusses extensively the status of Purgatory in Protestant England.

[105] Greenblatt, *Hamlet in Purgatory*, 88.

[106] See Valentine Penrose, *Erzsebet Bathory, la Comtesse Sanglante* [*The Bloody Countess*], trans. Alexander Trocchi (1970; rpt. London: Creation Books, 1996), and Alejandra Pizarnik, "The Bloody Countess," in *Other Fires: Short Fiction by Latin American Women*, (ed.) Alberto Manguel (New York: Clarkson N. Potter & Crown Publishers, 1986) 70–87.

[107] Pizarnik 71.

horrible."[108] Indeed, the ghost's prison house, like the countess' torture chambers, has a desensitizing effect. Hamlet attempts to recreate his own versions of torture chambers through which he hopes to punish others.

When Hamlet decides to rewrite *The Mousetrap* and present the murder of Gonzago as an allegory of his family's history of pain, he is obviously "speaking daggers," using metaphors and theatrical representation to make Claudius face his crime, envision the pain he has caused to others, and perhaps confess. In many contemporary revenge tragedies, the avenger uses a theatrical occasion, such as Hieronimo's "Tragedy of Soliman and Perseda" in *The Spanish Tragedy* or Vindice's carefully staged masque in *The Revenger's Tragedy*, to carry out his revenge plot. In *Hamlet*, however, the play-within-the-play serves no other purpose but to "catch the conscience" of Claudius, although it opens a window into sites of pleasure and of pain, as Hamlet imagines them. In the dumb show, the embrace, the gestures—"*He takes her up, and declines his head upon her neck*" (3.2.133–4)—the bucolic surroundings ("*He lies him down upon a bank of flowers*")—all seem to point to a loving relationship between the king and queen. Yet when "*another man*" comes in, kisses the crown, and "*pours poison in the sleeper's ears*," another side of this relationship emerges: "*The poisoner, with some three or four, come in again, seem to condole with her. The dead body is carried away. The poisoner woos the Queen with gifts; she seems harsh awhile, but in the end accepts love*" (3.2.126–9). When Ophelia asks for an explanation of the meaning of the show, Hamlet indicates that the prologue will explain it, "Ay, or any show that you will show him." Hamlet seems to indicate that the show is nothing but show; yet he makes it reflect the burden of his pain.

The play-within-the play also focuses on a language of pain. A long marriage of 30 years approaches its end, for the Player-Queen laments, "But woe is me, you are so sick of late, / So far from cheer and from your former state" (3.2.158–9), which the player-king confirms, "Faith, I must leave thee, love, and shortly too" (169). The player-king thinks it likely that she will remarry, but she promises: "A second time I kill my husband dead / When second husband kisses me in bed" (175–6). In short sequence, the play-within-the play unfolds, resembling the plot of the larger play: the player-queen exits, the player-king falls asleep in his garden. Lucianus, the king's nephew, creeps into the garden, pours poison in Gonzago's ear, and courts Gonzago's widow, Baptista, and wins her love. When Claudius, upset with the performance, "rises," as Ophelia points out, Hamlet wonders in the Folio text, "What, frighted with false fire?" Claudius cries out, "Give me some light. Away!" (260). Hamlet assumes that the performance has had its intended effect: "let the stricken deer go weep, / The hart ungallèd play." When Guildenstern asks to have a word with Hamlet, Hamlet responds, "a whole history." Guildenstern notes that the king is "in his retirement marvellous distempered … with choler" (295; 298). Gertrude herself is "in most great affliction of spirit" (305–306), and Hamlet speaks of drinking "hot blood" (383). A theater of metaphors unsettles the world of experience.

---

[108] Pizarnik 87.

In Gertrude's closet, experience unsettles a theater of metaphors. When Hamlet makes a pass with his sword through the arras and stabs Polonius to death, he creates real pain for himself, Ophelia, and Laertes. Hamlet realizes that his act has now put him on a level with Claudius and Gertrude: "A bloody deed—almost as bad, good mother, / As kill a king, and marry with his brother" (3.4.28–30). The loss of Polonius is felt throughout Elsinore. Ophelia goes mad, and Laertes seeing her gives voice to his pain: "O heat, dry up my brains; tears seven times salt / Burn out the sense and virtue of mine eye!" (4.5.154–5).

Charles and Elaine Hallett argue that revenge tragedy taps into "a volcano of smoldering rage" at the "core of human nature."[109] They name the motifs—the ghost, madness, the delay, the play-within-the-play, and death of the avenger—that define the genre. The ghost's entreaties to revenge unleash the hero's madness—"Passion must consume his entire being" (9). The avenger "hardens himself to carry out the entreaties of the ghost," whereby he must reshape his world: "the delay might be defined as the pause necessitated by the revenger's need to construct his world-within-a-world, that private, self-justifying world which will foster the act the external world would never sanction."[110] Finally, the avenger enters the "self-created illusory world" of the play-within-the play to carry out the act of revenge: "By acting within the framework of the mock play, the avenger is symbolically confusing the real world with a world created out of his own psyche which he has projected upon it."[111] I know of no revenge tragedy that fits this mold, although some or all of these elements may be found in several revenge tragedies of the Renaissance. In his study of charisma in tragedy, Raphael Falco argues: "Throughout *Hamlet*, revenge encourages conduct inimical both to charismatic authority and to the collective dynamic."[112] He adds that both Hamlet and Laertes "neutralize" their "charismatic claim[s] by abandoning irrational revolutionary conduct for the dispassion and calculation of personal revenge."[113] From a certain perspective these two arguments seem mutually exclusive: for the Halletts, the avenger gets himself lost in a world of madness and theatrical events; whereas, for Falco, the avenger fails to maintain a charismatic and hence political appeal for the sake of personal revenge. Ironically, both interpretations cannot account for a politics of pleasure, deployed and staged by Claudius and Gertrude, or the history of pain that Hamlet embodies and stages in spectacular ways.

Competing emotions vie for control of Hamlet's father's former abode and attempt to displace each other. The royal bed remains hidden in a chamber of "unfettered passions"; likewise, the prison house, the horrible chamber of torture, remains off stage. Hamlet must imagine both the unseemly pleasure taking place

---

109 Charles A. Hallett and Elaine S. Hallett, *The Revenger's Madness: A Study of Revenge Tragedy Motifs* (Lincoln, NE: University of Nebraska Press, 1980) 7.

110 Hallett and Hallett 10.

111 Hallett and Hallett 10.

112 Falco 114.

113 Falco 114.

in his mother's bed and unspeakable horrors of his father's torture chamber. Pleasure and pain engender spectacles; yet the sites to which they refer and on which they center, remain out of sight as if they were unreal, a theatrical illusion. Hamlet's struggle becomes urgent. He has to confront, as Greenblatt suggests, "the fading of remembrance," a feeling that "other thoughts and emotions" might bring about "some interruption or diminution of mourning and remembrance."[114] As the light and warmth of the morning approach, the ghost must return to his hidden torture chamber: "The glowworm shows the matin to be near / And gins to pale his uneffectual fire" (1.5.89–90). Hamlet, at times, surely must feel like the glowworm in the darkness, struggling to counter the dazzling fire of his uncle's seductive politics of pleasure.

In *Diatribai*, Epictetus teaches: "Impressions [appearances] come to us in four ways. Things are, and appear so to us; or they are not, and do not appear to be: or they are, and do not appear to be: or they are not, and yet appear to be."[115] The challenge for the educated person, he adds, is "to form a right judgment in all these cases."[116] In *The Tempest,* Ferdinand believes, as Ariel's song intimates, that his father's body, buried "full fathom five," has changed, not rotted, his bones turning into coral and his eyes into pearls; after all, the song underscores: "Nothing of him that doth fade / But doth suffer a sea change / Into something rich and strange" (1.2.397–402). Obviously, Alonso has not died, and he and Ferdinand eventually reunite. Yet, while believing his father has died, Ferdinand falls in love, proclaims himself king, and betroths Miranda. As in the song, Ferdinand can recycle his father's body, adjust himself to loss, mourn but briefly, and then get on with his life. Once his dead father returns as an apparition, Hamlet does not have the benefit of such an ecological solution; rather, Hamlet cannot discard his father's legacy and the broken fragments of a life cut short by murder and betrayal. In *Hamlet*, home provides no escape, even when mysterious portals open onto worlds unknown. To be "at home" in *Hamlet* implies an intense battle for control of public and intimate space. Hamlet seeks to erect boundaries in his father's former house, yet seemingly unable to rebuild and restore walls his uncle and his mother have taken down.

---

[114] Greenblatt, *Hamlet in Purgatory*, 221–2.

[115] Epictetus, Book 1.27.

[116] Epictetus, Book 1.27.

Chapter 4
Boundaries of Home in *Macbeth*

> If one were to give an account of all the doors one has closed and opened, of all the doors one would like to re-open, one would have to tell the story of one's entire life
>
> —Gaston Bachelard.[1]

Architecture serves many purposes: it arranges and partitions spaces, covers voids, and erects barriers. Walls, floors, and ceiling envelop and enclose, setting limits and defining boundaries.[2] If architecture is "literally bricks and mortar, house and home, shelter and enclosure," then, Peter Eisenman argues, the "paradox of architecture" is "to dislocate that which it locates."[3] I take this to mean that architecture also connects: corridors, stairways, and doors bridge adjoining spaces; doors allow passage to other spaces; and windows afford a view of other places, even as we remain stationary. Architecture inspired the central question of Bachelard's dialectics of inside and outside: "Where can one flee, where find refuge?"[4] Therefore, in this chapter, I will focus on the boundaries of home in *Macbeth*, and explore the house as a place of refuge. In *Macbeth*, I will argue, however, that Shakespeare addresses the seeming failure of architecture to provide shelter, establish boundaries, and separate inside from outside. In *Macbeth*, as in *Hamlet*, the emplacement of the body in architectural space becomes crucial to the representation of home life. In *Macbeth*, the house creates adjacency, juxtaposition, and contiguity. In this ambiguous boundary, domestic life abuts a fantastical, wild world.

The Wilds of Scotland

The Scotland of the play is an imagined place. Shakespeare taps into and combines a complex array of popular images, beliefs, and as A.C. Bradley notes, spaces associated with "obscurer regions" of life, "secret forces," and "mysterious phenomena."[5] The play establishes a divide between the outdoors, associated

---

[1] Bachelard, *Poetics of Space*, 224.

[2] Architecture requires symmetry and equilibrium, and even asymmetrical design requires symmetry to define its parameters. See Herman Weyl, *Symmetry* (Princeton: Princeton University Press, 1952) 16, 13.

[3] Peter Eisenman, "Blue-Line Text + Outline from the 'Edge of Between,'" *Architectural Design* 58.7–8 (1988): 6–9.

[4] Bachelard, *Poetics of Space*, 218.

[5] Bradley 269; 270.

with the witches, and the indoors, associated with the Macbeths, through which Shakespeare contrasts and combines radically different modes of dwelling, associated with the outdoors and with the indoors. Shakespeare turns the outdoors over to the three Weird Sisters, and the indoors to the Macbeths; yet outdoors and indoors remain contiguous, invading and pervading each other's domain. Neither house nor the sturdiest of castles can keep these realms apart. I will therefore discuss the outdoors first and then the dwelling places represented in the play.

The Scots were known to be notoriously quarrelsome, as Portia suggests in *The Merchant of Venice* (1.2.73–8); and as Don Pedro de Ayala comments in 1498: "They spend all their time in wars, and when there is no war they fight with one another."[6] Having adapted well to their country's topography and environment, the Scots also learned to turn the rugged topography into military advantage. Medieval and early modern travelers describe Scotland as a starkly rugged country and deem the living conditions, especially of the general population, miserable. Jean Froissart, who was in Scotland in the fourteenth century, notes that, when traveling or waging war, the Scots use no carriages, because of the mountainous terrain; carry no provisions of bread and wine; drink river water rather than water mixed with wine; have no need for pots because they do not prepare meals, presumably because they eat raw meat of cattle, which are slaughtered as needed for food. Although they often eat "sodden flesh," they have a remedy: they eat oatmeal baked into "cracknel or biscuit" in order to "warm their stomachs"; therefore, he adds, they can "perform a longer day's march than other soldiers."[7] According to Froissart, the French barons and knights, being used to the comforts of their homeland, such as "handsome hotels, ornamented apartments, and castles with good soft beds to repose on," were shocked at the poverty and hard life in Scotland.[8] In the fifteenth century, Aeneas Sylvius described Scotland as "nothing but a rugged wilderness, unvisited by the genial sun."[9] He was also struck by the poor, who "in a state of nakedness" beg at the church doors.[10] In the early seventeenth century, John Taylor, the Water Poet, found the Scottish roads exceedingly precarious: "the way so uneven, stonie, and full of bogges, quagmires, and long heath, that a dogge with three legs will outrunne a horse with foure."[11] At another point, he writes that he traveled in Scotland for 12 days "before I saw either house, corne field, or habitation of any creature, but deere, wilde horses, wolves, and such like creatures."[12]

---

6 P. Hume Brown, *Early Travellers in Scotland* (Edinburgh: David Douglas, 1891) 1: 43.

7 Brown, *Early Travellers*, 1: 8–9. "Sodden" has a range of meanings: boiled, rotten, spoiled, or improperly cooked.

8 Brown, *Early Travellers*, 1: 11.

9 Brown, *Early Travellers*, 1: 29.

10 Brown, *Early Travellers*, 1: 29.

11 John Taylor, *Travels through Stuart Britain: The Adventures of John Taylor, the Water Poet*, (ed.) John Chandler (Stroud, Gloucestershire: Sutton Publishing, 1999) 39.

12 Taylor, *Travels*, 39.

Travelers emphasize the absence of houses, inns, and other comforts, associated with life in England or on the Continent. Froissart describes the Scots' disdain for or nonchalant attitude about the destruction of their houses, quoting the comments he heard: "'If the English burn our houses, what consequence is it to us? We can rebuild them cheap enough, for we only require three days to do so, provided we have five or six poles and boughs to cover them.'"[13] According to Aeneas Sylvius, in the towns "the houses are for the most part constructed without lime"; in the country, the roofs of the houses are made of "turf" and "the doors of the humbler dwellings are made of the hide of oxen."[14]

In 1598, Fynes Moryson found that the living conditions had improved, houses being made of "unpolished stone" and some of "freestone."[15] He remarks on the absence of inns everywhere, and the need for travelers to seek lodging in private residences, where living conditions varied considerably. Odd customs, especially those regarding sleeping arrangements, catch his attention: the bedsteads are "cubbards in the wall, with doores to be opened and shut at pleasure, so as we climbed up to our beds." The Scots use doubled sheets, sewn at the bottom but open at the top and side; likewise Moryson thinks it odd that the Scots give their guests a cup of wine at bedtime.[16] Even in a bedchamber of a private residence, one cannot escape the wilds. In the early seventeenth century, John Taylor writes that, having sought shelter for the night at Huntly Castle, built around 1450, in Aberdeenshire, he woke up with the "hideous noyse" made by a wild Scottish "deafe and dumbe" "wench," who having crept into his chamber, tried to hop into his bed. Startled by the noise, Taylor jumped out of bed and promptly "thrust my dumbe beast out of my chamber; and for want of a locke or latch, I staked up my doore with a great chaire."[17]

Unlike the woman in John Taylor's bedroom, the witches in Shakespeare's play never physically enter the bedchamber of the Macbeths; yet, they too disturb the domestic in other ways. Macbeth's insomnia and Lady Macbeth's sleep-walking later in the play reveal the disruption that the witches initiated or brought about. The witches in the play thrive in the ambiguous "hurly-burly" and chaos of the war, "when the battle's lost and won" (1.1.3–4). They become the quintessential enemy of domestic space, and by extension undermine architecture's function of providing shelter and containing space. Naturally, they do what witches were believed to do. When the Weird Sisters appear in Act I, scene 3, they summarize their intervening activities. One has been "killing swine"; another tried to steal chestnuts from a sailor's wife, whose husband is off to Aleppo, "master o'th'Tiger," to where the Witch proposes to sail in a sieve. All three collude to derail the sailor's journey. Then in the First Witch's words, what they plan for the sailor may

13 Brown, *Early Travellers*, 1: 10.

14 Brown, *Early Travellers*, 1: 26–7.

15 Brown, *Early Travellers*, 1: 84.

16 Brown, *Early Travellers* 1: 89–90.

17 Taylor, *Travels*, 45.

also apply to Macbeth: they plan to keep him awake for "sev'n nights, nine times nine" and make him "dwindle, peak, and pine," although not destroy his "tempest-tossed" boat (1.3.19–25). To underscore her malignant intent, she even produces "a pilot's thumb / Wrecked as homeward he did come" (1.3.28–9). In this context, the witches bring together the domestic world of the sailor's wife, who is cracking and sorting her chestnuts, and forces of nature, represented by the turbulent sea, where many sailors meet their fate. In Shakespeare's Scotland, even domesticated animals threaten to revert to a wild state. Ross and the Old Man report that on the night of Duncan's assassination the king's horses "Turned wild in nature, broke their stalls, flung out," and more tellingly, "they ate each other" (2.4.15–16, 18). Shakespeare's Weird Sisters disturb those homeward bound. They do so because they can affect the lives of voyagers who traverse their domain and come under their influence.

In his representation of the witches, Shakespeare combines materials from folklore, popular beliefs, and classical literature. For example, Mary Floyd-Wilson argues that in *Macbeth,* "Shakespeare depicts Scotland's environment as paradoxically fair and foul—climatologically temperate and authentically demonic."[18] She notes, as well, that the play also presents "a correspondence between witchcraft and weather."[19] At the beginning of the play, the witches enter, preceded by thunder and lightning; they plan their next meeting to take place "in thunder, lightning, or in rain" (1.1.1–2). Indeed, *Macbeth* underscores the wild nature of the wind-swept Scottish landscapes, a topsy-turvy world, where "Fair is foul, and foul is fair" (1.1.12), a perception echoed in Macbeth's first line: "So foul and fair a day I have not seen" (1.2.38). Peter Stallybrass notes that the witches represent "disorder in nature," have the customary evil "familiars," and can foresee the future.[20] He adds that they bear "features typical of the English village 'witch,'" yet remain mysterious and supernatural.[21] Frederick Kiefer raises the question of whether the witches are nymphs or fairies. He remarks that the old, lean, sexually

[18] Mary Floyd-Wilton, "English Epicures and Scottish Witches," 142. For the purposes of my discussion, I am not interested in her argument that Shakespeare, drawing on "geohumoralism and Neostoicism," interrogates popular notions of Scottish temperance (142). Based in part on a statement in Levinus Lemnius's *The Secret Miracles of Nature* (London, 1658), she argues that evil spirits can mingle with food, humors, and air (144). This point seems quite relevant to my argument. Although Lemnius's book was published in 1658, long after *Macbeth*, some of these connections can be traced to an earlier period.

[19] Floyd-Wilson, "English Epicures and Scottish Witches," 143. I do not, however, find her argument that Shakespeare presents the witches' "powers as indigenous to Scotland in particular" (143) entirely persuasive; nor do I find a preponderance of evidence to support her conclusion that "Macbeth recognizes, in other words, that his passions are ecological" (151).

[20] Peter Stallybrass, "*Macbeth* and Witchcraft," in *Focus on Macbeth*, (ed.) John Russell Brown (London and Boston: Routledge & Kegan Paul, 1982) 195; and Deborah Willis, *Malevolent Nurture: Witch-Hunting and Maternal Power in Early Modern England* (Ithaca and London: Cornell University Press, 1995) 213.

[21] Stallybrass, "*Macbeth* and Witchcraft," 195.

ambiguous witches have "the kind of bodies shaped by a hard life outdoors"; the witches "manipulate, contaminate, and traverse" the air, with which they are especially associated.[22] They wear "wild attire" and are "shape-shifters."[23]

The witches occupy a supernatural world and a human one of household, family, and community, with Lady Macbeth providing a bridge between them.[24] Frances Dolan argues that Lady Macbeth embodies "the witch as a dangerous familiar and her witchcraft as 'malice domestic'"; therefore, through Lady Macbeth the witches invade "the household and its daily life."[25] Wendy Wall goes further by suggesting that *Macbeth* offers a "crossover between heath and hearth," whereby the Weird Sisters "make household tasks into the uncanny" and invert everyday life; their "grotesque brew" exaggerates and distorts "the sinister nature" of contemporary medical remedies.[26] Indeed, the witches boil almost anything in their cauldron of "hellbroth," including toads, snakes, mummy, "ravined salt-sea shark," "gall of goat," "finger of birth-strangled babe," "nose of Turk, and Tartar's lip," "baboon's blood," and so forth (4.1.1–87). The witches' cauldron may have had its genesis in Medea's brew from John Studley's 1566 translation of Seneca's play;[27] or perhaps in misunderstandings of the Scottish diet, dependent on cauldrons of boiled food. Fynes Moryson reports that the Scots eat "red Colewort and cabbage, but little fresh meate." He writes that "The Gentlemen recken their revenewes, not by rents of monie, but by chauldrons of victuals," but feed their servants and family on "Corne and Rootes, not spending any great quantity on flesh."[28] He writes of his experience as a dinner guest in a knight's house, where the knight's servants brought to the table "great platters of porredge, each having a little peece of sodden meate."[29] "Sodden meate"[30] seems to be a recurring theme in foreign accounts of Scottish eating habits. In his overall assessment, Moryson writes: "And I observed no Art of Cookery, or furniture of Houshold stuffe, but rather rude neglect of both."[31]

---

22 Frederick Kiefer, *Shakespeare's Visual Theatre: Staging the Personified Characters* (Cambridge: Cambridge University Press, 2003) 111.

23 Kiefer 112. In *Shakespeare's Speaking Pictures: Studies in Iconic Imagery* (Albuquerque: University of New Mexico Press, 1974), John Doebler argues that the witches serve as "iconic images uniting the opposites of destiny and freely tempted evil" (120).

24 Frances Dolan, *Dangerous Familiars*, 225.

25 Dolan, *Dangerous Familiars*, 226.

26 Wendy Wall, *Staging Domesticity*, 199.

27 See Bullough, *Narrative and Dramatic Sources*, 7:521–2; and for an insightful discussion of Seneca's influence on the play, see Miola, *Shakespeare and Classical Tragedy*, 92–121, and the introduction to his edition of the play: *Macbeth*, a Norton Critical Edition (New York and London: W.W. Norton, 2004) vii–xxi.

28 Brown, *Early Travellers*, 1: 88.

29 Brown, *Early Travellers*, 1: 88.

30 In this context, I take "sodden" to mean "boiled."

31 Brown, *Early Travellers*, 1: 89.

The Weird Sisters connect with home in another way. They appear, as Macbeth and Banquo journey to Forres and from thence to Macbeth's home at Inverness. The journey home traverses a wild world (1.3.39–47). The hybrid, sexually ambiguous figures (1.3.39–47)—withered and wild, not like humans yet treading upon the earth, female and yet bearded like males—greet Macbeth with his familiar title, Thane of Glamis, and yet also with other titles that do not seem to belong to him: "Thane of Cawdor" and king. Banquo tries to calm the startled Macbeth, to whom he now refers as "noble partner"; yet he must recognize that the apparition seems indeed "fantastical." The Weird Sisters vanish, as Macbeth describes, "Into the air, and what seemed corporal melted / As breath into the wind. Would they had stayed!" (81–2). The wheels of Macbeth's mind turn, as in a vortex of what he refers to as "the imperial theme," which depends on a fantastical murder plan, yet in a realm where "nothing is / But what it is not" (1.3.129; 139;141–2). The strange figures, mirroring the scraggy, desiccated, wind-swept surroundings, provide inspiration for the crime that Macbeth imagines and soon plans to carry out in the inner sanctum of his home. Shakespeare's witches, women without a home, seek to wreck the homes of others.

In *Macbeth*, the unknown is not an empty space, on the edges of which stands the central character; but rather it permeates and empties out the realm of domestic life. Therefore, my argument differs from Janet Adelman's: she suggests that "Lady Macbeth brings the witches' power home: they get the cosmic apparatus, she gets the psychic force."[32] Rather, I submit, Macbeth himself contaminates and empties out his home. Indeed, the play illustrates what Catherine Belsey calls "the increasing perception of the loving family as a place of danger" in the early modern period.[33] Throughout the play, domestic space borders the unknown "on every side," as Arthur Conan Doyle's character remarks about another mysterious world.[34]

Macbeth's Houses

Scholars have ascertained the basic facts about the historical Macbeth, although everyday life in Scotland of the time remains sketchy. Macbeth took over as king of Moray in 1032; married Gruoch, the widow of Gille Comgáin, whom Macbeth had killed; killed Duncan I, king of Scots, in battle; ascended the Scottish throne

---

32 Adelman, *Suffocating Mothers*, 137.

33 Catherine Belsey, *Shakespeare and the Loss of Eden: The Construction of Family Values in Early Modern Culture* (New Brunswick: Rutgers University Press, 2000) 23.

34 I am paraphrasing the words of Lord John Roxton, a character in Arthur Conan Doyle, *The Lost World* (New York: Hodder & Sloughton, 1912) 94. Lord Roxton's comments come as the expedition treks its way to a fantastical, fictional prehistoric world that has survived unchanged in the highlands on the edges of the Amazon.

in 1034; went on a pilgrimage to Rome in 1050, and so forth.[35] Duncan's son, Malcolm III, leading a Northumbrian army, defeated Macbeth on July 27, 1057 at Dunsinane; then on August 15, 1057, Malcolm killed Macbeth in battle at Lumphanan in Mar. Upon Macbeth's death, Lulach (d. 1058), Macbeth's stepson with Gruoch, became king; but he too was killed less than a year later and was, according to tradition, buried on Iona.[36] According to Richard Fletcher, "Macbeth used marriage to exploit his enemies' divisions."[37] Gruoch "belonged to a branch of the Scots' dynasty" involved in blood feuds with Kenneth II (d. 995) and his grandson Malcolm II (d. 1034); no contemporary evidence supports later claims that she had committed "a treacherous breach of the rites of hospitality."[38] We also know little about the residences of Macbeth and Gruoch. However, later writers connect them to Inverness, Forres, and Dunsinane. Andrew Wyntoun's *Chronicle* (c. 1420) describes Macbeth's building of the castle at Dunsinane:

> And in till Scotland þan as king
> This Makbeth maid gret stering,
> And set him for his gret powere
> Ane hous of fenss to mak of weire
> Apone þe hycht of Dunsynnane (*ll.* 1999–2003)[39]

Wyntoun explains that Macbeth employed "mony oxin" to transport timber and stone from Fife and Angus for the great castle that he was building in Dunsinane (*ll.* 2005–2007).

Raphael Holinshed, in *Chronicles of England, Scotlande, and Irelande* (1587), refers to various dwellings such as those related to the rebellion against Natholocus, King of Scotland (c. 242–280): a privy chamber, the Castle at Forres, and "Enverns," where the king is slaughtered. Further, Holinshed mentions Macbeth's attempt to keep the Castle at Forres uncontaminated by murder. Macbeth instructs the murderers to kill Banquo and Banquo's son somewhere "without the palace," because "he would not have his house slandered, but that in time to come he

35 Dauvit Broun, "Macbeth (*d.* 1057)," *Oxford Dictionary of National Biography*, Oxford University Press, 2004 [http://www.oxforddnb.com.www2.lib.ku.edu:2048/view/article/17356, accessed April 29, 2009]. See G.W.S. Barrow, *Scotland and Its Neighbours in the Middle Ages*. (New York: Continuum, 1992) 51. One of the thorough studies of the historical Macbeth is Nick Aitchison, *Mabeth: Man and Myth* (Stroud: Sutton Publishing, 1999).

36 Broun, "Macbeth," *Oxford Dictionary of National Biography.*

37 Richard Fletcher, *Bloodfeud: Murder and Revenge in Anglo-Saxon England* (London: Penguin, 2002) 136.

38 Fletcher, *Bloodfeud*, 136.

39 Andrew, of Wyntoun, *The Original Chronicle of Andrew of Wyntoun*, (ed.) François J. Amours (Edinburgh and London: W. Blackwood, 1903–14) 4: 254–301, especially p. 280. See also Bullough, *Narrative and Dramatic Sources*, 7: 434–5.

might cleare himselfe."[40] Likewise, Holinshed refers to Macduff's Castle at Fife: "[Macbeth] besieged the castell where Makduffe dwelled"; and, although those who were in the castle opened the gates and allowed Macbeth and his troops to enter, "neverthelesse Makbeth most cruellie caused the wife and children of Makduffe, with all other whom he fouond in that castlel, to be slaine."[41]

The Scottish monarchs shared some of the habits of their English counterparts. Numerous travel narratives, ranging from the fourteenth to the early seventeenth centuries, document foreign visitors' impressions of and experiences in Scotland.[42] According to Don Pedro de Ayala, the Scottish kings spent little time in the cities; rather, the king, the court, and their officers used to find lodging in castles and abbeys: "They do not remain long in one place,"[43] visiting and policing their subjects, administering justice, and collecting rents. Simon Thurley estimates, for example, that Henry VIII made "some 1,150 moves between houses with his court," 830 of which to his own houses, and "the rest to ecclesiastical or courtier houses."[44] After 1530, when the number of royal houses increased dramatically, Henry and his court stayed primarily in royal houses.[45] He adds that the generally smaller, less comfortable courtier houses could not provide accommodation for the entire court, which had to be lodged elsewhere. The greater royal houses, such as Hampton Court, could accommodate as many as 1,500 people; whereas the "lesser houses," designed in part "to feed the King's riding household," did not "provide a large number of courtier lodgings."[46] Thurley notes that in July 1545, for example, "a great encampment of tents," with furnishings brought from Whitehall, had to be set up to accommodate all the courtiers who had come to see the opening of Nonsuch.[47] At the beginning of *Macbeth*, Duncan, for example, announces his intention to visit the Macbeths at Inverness; likewise, Macbeth and Lady Macbeth live in three separate royal houses. In contrast to Henry VIII, however, Duncan and the Macbeths seem to have small entourages.

In 1598, Fynes Moryson traveled 10 miles from the village of King-horn to Falkland in Scotland to visit "the Kings House for hunting, but of old belonging to the Earles of Fife, where I did gladly see James the sixth King of the Scots, at the time lying there to follow the pastimes of hunting and hawking."[48] Unlike Henry VIII's hunting lodges, however, James VI's house was "of old building

---

40 Bullough, *Narrative and Dramatic Sources*, 7: 498.

41 Bullough, *Narrative and Dramatic Sources*, 7: 500.

42 Information about Scotland must have been readily available from other sources, especially from numerous Scots who settled down in London after King James ascended the English throne.

43 Brown, *Early Travellers*, 1: 46.

44 Thurley, *Royal Palaces of Tudor England*, 73.

45 Thurley, *Royal Palaces of Tudor England*, 73.

46 Thurley, *Royal Palaces of Tudor England*, 63.

47 Thurley, *Royal Palaces of Tudor England*, 63.

48 Brown, *Early Travellers*, 1: 85.

and almost, having nothing in it remarkable."[49] Likewise, John Taylor saw the ruins of Kindrochet Castle, built by Malcolm III (1031–93) as a hunting lodge.[50] Apparently, as in England, the Scottish kings had an array of castles and hunting lodges at their disposal. Shakespeare uses this information to underscore the restlessness of the Macbeths.

In *King Lear*, Lear plans to move from the house of one daughter to that of the next. In the meantime, however, his castle seemingly vanishes in Act I, not to be mentioned again in the play, as noted in Chapter One. In *Macbeth*, Shakespeare represents mobility in a much more sinister way. After the murder of Duncan, the Macbeths abandon the stability represented by their home at Inverness and adopt the restlessness and mobility of the Scottish kings. Their tragedy occurs in three home spaces, representing different domestic arrangements at Inverness, Forres, and Dunsinane—the first two of which they seemingly abandon. Each castle represents a stage in their domestic life. Inverness symbolizes a marital partnership dominated by Lady Macbeth, leading to a violation of rules of hospitality and a domestic space transformed into a murder scene. At Forres, Macbeth asserts his independence. Although Lady Macbeth remains involved in domestic life and management of the house (she oversees the banquet and looks after Macbeth's wellbeing), she becomes increasingly displaced. Macbeth, however, asserts his dominance as king and commissions the murder of Banquo. Dunsinane reveals nothing but the specter of their former domestic life. In different ways, the Macbeths ruin three places of residence. The Macbeths contaminate or pollute Inverness; they leave Forres haunted; and they empty out Dunsinane. Ironically, as they move from castle to castle, they find themselves more and more confined.

Inverness

In her discussion of *King Lear*, as mentioned in Chapter 1, Linda Woodbridge argues that "the domestic interiors of *King Lear* cannot be called homey," concluding that "the absence of details conjuring domestic coziness fits perfectly a play where 'home' is a myth to be exploded."[51] In contrast, *Macbeth* does bring to mind images of "domestic coziness." The play supports Lena Orlin's argument about the "domestication of great houses" in the early modern period: "domestic arrangements" became "less communal," households increasingly centered on "nuclear families," and "persons of all classes" sought a greater degree of "personal comfort."[52] Shakespeare goes to great lengths to domesticate the Macbeths' Castle at Inverness, by emphasizing concepts of home and home life. Early in the play,

[49] Brown, *Early Travellers*, 1: 85.

[50] Taylor, *Travels*, 41.

[51] Woodbridge, *Vagrancy*, 206.

[52] Lena Cowen Orlin, "Spaces of Treason in Tudor England," in *Center or Margin: Revisions of the English Renaissance in Honor of Leeds Barroll*, ed. Lena Cowen Orlin (Selinsgrove: Susquehanna University Press, 2006) 159.

the Macbeths seem to share a loving, affectionate relationship, which, I think, contrasts with what was known about the less intimate conjugal arrangements of the historical St. Edward the Confessor (c. 1003–1066), king of England, and his wife Edith (d. 1075). Unlike the Macbeths, Edward and Edith, as was widely known, never consummated their marriage because Edward had taken a secret vow of chastity.[53] In addition, Shakespeare turns Inverness into a place dominated and controlled by a woman. One wonders if Shakespeare was aware of accounts, such as that of Don Pedro de Ayala, who describes Scottish women as "courteous in the extreme" and "really honest, though very bold"; but, more tellingly, "They are absolute mistresses of their houses, and even of their husbands in all things concerning the administration of their property, income as well as expenditure."[54] Together, however, Macbeth and his wife initially come across as a charismatic but dangerous couple, with Lady Macbeth as the dominant, controlling partner.

Suddenly and unexpectedly, the castle at Inverness enters the audience's consciousness as the Macbeths' home and the center of their domestic life. Immediately after making Malcolm Prince of Cumberland, Duncan first mentions Macbeth's home when he announces that he wishes to visit Macbeth's castle at Inverness and therefore "bind us further to you" (1.4.442–3). These two announcements, one naming an heir and the other an intention to honor Macbeth for his bravery on the battlefield against Cawdor and the Norwegian forces, intertwine. In a frenzied state, Macbeth volunteers to serve as royal harbinger, gallop home, and inform his wife of the king's visit. He will purvey lodgings for the king, as well as apprise his wife of the king's approach. The offices of harbinger and purveyor anticipate his role as host to his royal guest; but he also wants to rush home so that he and Lady Macbeth can make preparations for the assassination of the king, as he mutters in an aside (1.4.48–53). The scene concludes with Duncan's praise of Macbeth: "he is full so valiant, / And in his commendations I am fed; / It is a banquet to me" (54–6).

The next two scenes (Scenes 5 and 6) provide a double view of the inside and of the outside of the Macbeths' home. Macbeth's frenzied hurry to send word to his wife becomes apparent in Scene 5, which opens with Lady Macbeth reading his letter. The letter describes his frenzy:

---

53 On Edward's marriage in general and the cult of St Edward, see Frank Barlow, (ed.), *The Life of King Edward*, second edition (Oxford: Clarendon, 1992) 22–4, and Appendix D (150–63). Presumably, to compensate for the English royal couple's lack of intimacy, the anonymous *Life* suggests that "Edith, from the very beginning of her marriage, clad him [Edward] in raiments, either embroidered by herself or of her choice" (25). In *The Middle English Verse Life of Edward the Confessor* (Philadelphia: University of Pennsylvania, 1942), Grace Edna Moore discusses the question of Edward and Edith's virginity throughout their marriage (xiii–xviii). In *The lyfe of Saynt Edwarde confessour and kynge of Englande* (London, 1533), Edward fears that "his vowe of chastite sholde be openly knowen," when the royal council initiates the marriage arrangements (Sig. B^{v}).

54 Brown, *Early Travellers*, 1: 47.

> When I burned in desire to question them [the Weird Sisters] further, they made themselves air, into which they vanished. Whiles I stood rapt in the wonder of it, came missives from the king, who all-hailed me Thane of Cawdor, by which title, before, these weïrd sisters saluted me, and referred me to the coming on of time with "Hail, king that shalt be!" (1.5.3–10)

Macbeth refers to her as his "dearest partner of greatness"; he also wants to share the news with her, so "that thou mightst not lose the dues of rejoicing by being ignorant of what greatness is promised thee" (10–13). Before he arrives, however, she has already confided in a soliloquy that she deems his nature to be "too full o' th' milk of human kindness" (1.5.16), therefore ill prepared for committing murder.

The letter was obviously dispatched before Duncan announced his intention to visit the Macbeths at Inverness. A messenger, who enters at line 29, brings tidings that "The king comes here tonight" (30); to which she responds incredulously: "Thou'rt mad to say it! / Is not thy master with him? who, were't so, / Would have informed for preparation" (30–2). Yet, as the Messenger exits, she realizes that an opportunity arises: "The raven himself is hoarse / That croaks the fatal entrance of Duncan / Under my battlements" (37–9). Her home has become her battlements, and she gets ready at her battle station, invoking metaphysical aid to "unsex" her and fill her from head to foot with "direst cruelty." Her female body must metamorphose into that of a murderess, her blood thickened and remorse deadened. Evil spirits, witches' familiars, must possess her body: "Come to my woman's breasts / And take my milk for gall, you murd'ring ministers" (46–7). Like her husband earlier, she wants to hide the deed from heaven: "Come, thick night, / And pall thee in the dunnest smoke of hell, / That my keen knife see not the wound it makes" (49–51). By the time Macbeth arrives, she already greets him as Glamis, Cawdor, and "Greater than both," and she indicates that the future has already arrived. In preparation for "This night's great business" and her "dispatch," she encourages him to dissemble, disguising his murderous intent behind the appearance of a loving host: he needs to bear signs of welcome in his eye, hand, and tongue, while his mind fixates on killing. Although she trusts him to carry out the murder, her words suggest that she manages the house and exercises control over their domestic space: "Leave all the rest to me" (72).

When viewed from the outside, the castle appears placid and beautiful, but appearances deceive. As the royal party approaches the palace gates, Duncan notes that "This castle hath a pleasant seat. The air / Nimbly and sweetly recommends itself / Upon our gentle senses" (1.6.1–3). According to Banquo, the martlet, the "guest of summer," makes Macbeth's castle its "loved mansionry," which all agree represents a good omen. The martlet inhabits everywhere around this house—"No jutty, frieze, / Buttress, nor coign of vantage, but this bird / Hath made his pendent and procreant cradle" (1.6.6–8), adding "The air is delicate" (10). When Lady Macbeth appears at the gate, she offers her hospitality and service, for as she puts it, the king "loads our house" (19); and Duncan himself refers to this castle as Macbeth's "home," exchanging further niceties and asking to be conducted to his host. This warm personal touch—the Lady of the Castle coming to the castle gate to welcome a guest—goes hand in hand with the seemingly scaled-down household. Arthur Kinney writes that "In 1600, James's servants numbered in the thousands. By stark contrast, the grand castle at Inverness has only a stage complement of servants."[55] Kinney sees the "hollowness of Macbeth's household" in relation to the "inadequacy of his hospitality," the failure of servants to perform their duties, and the prevailing dysfunctional nature of the house.[56] I think, however, that Shakespeare may be suggesting something about the cozy, warm, intimate yet deceiving atmosphere of the Macbeths' home. For themselves, the Macbeths perceive their house as a place of shelter, sanctuary, and hiding. In reality, however, the house becomes a deadly trap for unsuspecting guests, as this dialogue reveals:

> MACBETH. My dearest love,
> Duncan comes here tonight.
> LADY MACBETH. And when goes hence?
> MACBETH. Tomorrow, as he purposes. (1.5.57–60).

The affectionate tone cannot hide their sinister double intent as hosts and as killers: "He that's coming / Must be provided for" (1.5.65–6). As hosts, they will give Duncan a warm reception and ensure his comfort under their roof; but as murderers, they will make sure that their guest will never emerge alive from their house.[57] In the sanctuary of their home, the Macbeths feel that they can act as they please, cover the foulest crime, and remain in an accountability-free zone. In a sense, the Macbeths go against the prevailing notion that the outdoors, not the indoors, provide more privacy for and protection from discovery of embarrassing, illegal, or criminal activity.[58]

But even within the castle, a dichotomy between the public space of the banquet and the private space of bedchambers becomes apparent. Both are, however, kept hidden from the audience's eyes. References to the banquet occur here and there as in Lady Macbeth's comment that Duncan has almost finished

---

55 Arthur F. Kinney, *Lies Like Truth: Shakespeare, Macbeth, and the Cultural Moment* (Detroit: Wayne State University, 2001) 174.

56 Kinney, *Lies Like Truth*, 176–7.

57 In *Scenic Form in Shakespeare* (Oxford: Clarendon, 1971), Emrys Jones draws a parallel here to the scene in Seneca's *Thyestes*, in which Atreus, "a host with murderous intentions, hypocritically welcomes his victims to his home" (211).

58 In "Illicit Privacy and Outdoor Spaces in Early Modern England," *Journal for Early Modern Cultural Studies* 9.1 (2009), Mary Thomas Crane argues that "because of servants among the wealthy, and because of space constraints among the poor," privacy was to be found not in closets and bedchambers but outdoors (4). The Macbeths, however, believe that they can find true privacy to commit murder and hide the crime in the inner sanctum of their home. Obviously, later in the play, Macbeth can also find privacy in the outdoors, where he goes for a private consultation with the witches.

Fig. 4.1 Banquet Scene. Bartolomeo Scappi, *Opera* (Venice, 1570). Typ 525.70.773. Houghton Library, Harvard University.

eating, and her surprise that Macbeth left the dining hall. Imagery associated with travel and hospitality abounds. Weariness from the long day's hard journey and wine drugged with sleep-inducing, mind-altering concoctions will create the appropriate conditions for "the great quell," as Lady Macbeth points out to her husband:

> When in swinish sleep
> Their drenched natures lies as in a death,
> What cannot you and I perform upon
> Th' unguarded Duncan? (1.7.62–71)

She does not indicate where the supposedly numerous household servants might be, or whether she has drugged their drinks as well. Perhaps, the household servants and functionaries retreat to their bedchambers for the night. Neither husband nor wife refers to these servants, but they draw attention to various bedchambers, including their own (2.2.63) and those where Duncan and his entourage sleep.

Hosts must lock and unlock doors, watchfully guarding the privacy and security of their houses, households, and guests. In fact, the first reference to doors occurs when Macbeth considers his duty as host: "Then, as his host, / [I] should against his murder shut the door / Not bear the knife myself" (1.7.15–17). Later, pacing outside of Duncan's chamber, she says, "The doors are open" (2.3.5), the doors to Duncan's bedchamber and to the second chamber, where the grooms sleep, blissfully unaware that they will be blamed for the murder. Kept out of the audience's view, these chambers symbolize the horrors of murder and hideous crime. Yet everyone who enters these chambers emerges transformed. Although earlier in the play Lady Macbeth chastised her husband for lack of courage, "When thou durst do it, then you were a man" (1.7.49), when she lays the daggers at the appointed place for Macbeth's use, she has second thoughts: "Had [Duncan] not resembled / My father as he slept, I had done't" (2.2.12–13). When Macbeth announces that he has "done the deed," the screeching owls and crying crickets frighten him. He complains about the "sorry sight" inside the chamber, having found himself unable to say "amen" to the prayers of those "two lodged together" in the adjacent chamber. He also hears a voice in the darkness, pronouncing a sentence: "'Sleep no more! / Macbeth does murder sleep'" (2.2.38–9). The plans begin to come unraveled. Macbeth carries the bloody daggers in his hands, instead of planting them in the appointed place. Regaining her courage, Lady Macbeth returns the daggers to the grooms' bedchamber, as she chastises her husband: "The sleeping and the dead / Are but as pictures. 'Tis the eye of childhood / That fears a painted devil" (2.2.56–8).

Many scholars associate Macbeth's castle, especially at this moment in the play, with a medieval hell-castle. Upon hearing Macduff and Lennox knock at the gate, the Porter rouses himself out of bed. Feeling put out, the Porter refers to "hell gate," Beelzebub, equivocator, and other images associated with hell (2.3.15). John Doebler, for example, writes that "From inside hellcastle, however, the passageway to the outside world is the other side of hellmouth, hellgate, guarded by its traditional porter."[59] The image of hell-castle also brings to mind, as Anne Lancashire points out that "in the dungeon of the traditional hell-castle stands a boiling cauldron for the torture of damned souls."[60] For a while, various images coalesce to reinforce the transformation of the Macbeths' home into hell-castle. Macbeth shows Macduff the door to Duncan's chamber (48); and as Macduff exits the stage to rouse Duncan out of bed, Lennox reports the events of the unruly night: chimneys blown down, strange screams of death heard, and voices prophesying with accents terrible. As Macduff emerges from the crime scene, he utters the words, "O horror, horror, horror—" (2.3–62), at first unable to describe what he has seen; but then he summons a description: "Most sacrilegious murder hath broke ope / The Lord's anointed temple and stole thence / The life o' th' building!" (2.3.65–8). Indeed, the metaphor seems appropriate. If the king's body is God's temple, then the death of the body also deprives the building of life. Seemingly in shock, Lady Macbeth underscores the implications for her own home: "Woe, alas— / What, in our house?" (2.3.85–6). Shakespeare does not, however, sustain these images of hell-castle beyond this point in the play. Rather, he focuses on the illusion of impenetrability of walls.

In many ways, the Macbeths trust walls too much. They assume that the walls of their castle will create a barrier between inside and out, between great hall and private chamber, between the bedchamber as site of repose and site of murder.[61] But "Something there is that doesn't love a wall."[62] The castle does not provide enclosure. The home no longer offers security from the terrors of the outside. Rather, as Inverness becomes dangerous, the characters depart for other places. Donalbain and Malcolm, the king's sons, fearing for their own lives, flee, respectively to Ireland and to the court of Edward the Confessor in England. Macbeth kills and blames the sleeping grooms for the regicide. Duncan's body, carried to Colmekill, will rest in "the sacred storehouse" of his ancestors. Horrified and haunted by the bloody crime they have committed, Macbeth and Lady Macbeth make a hasty journey to Scone to be crowned king and queen of Scotland, never again to return to Inverness. As in *King Lear*, the Castle at Inverness has been abandoned at the end of Act II, when the scene moves on to the Royal Castle of Forres. In a sense, Macbeth and Lady Macbeth unhouse themselves and others. An apparently friendly, homey place ceases to exist, as they seek refuge somewhere else. The safety of domestic enclosure proves but an illusion.

---

59 Doebler 132.

60 Lancashire, "The Emblematic Castle," 231.

61 My analysis of *Macbeth* draws inspiration from Karen Chase and Michael Levenson's fascinating discussion of the function of walls in Victorian novels, especially Dickens's *Our Mutual Friend.* See Chase and Levenson, *The Spectacle of Intimacy: A Public Life for the Victorian Family* (Princeton: Princeton University Press, 2000) 143. Chase and Levenson do not discuss Shakespeare.

62 I am quoting, of course, Robert Frost's poem, "Mending Wall."

Forres

Like Othello and Desdemona's dislocation to Cyprus, the Macbeths' move to the royal house at Forres offers new opportunities for a fresh start, but it also leaves behind a gruesome crime scene and an emptied-out castle, which had served as their home. Shakespeare's sources in fact suggest that Macbeth and Lady Macbeth lived quite happily for many years between the time Macbeth killed Duncan in battle and the time Malcolm organized a rebellion challenging the legitimacy of Macbeth's rule. Located 160 miles North of Edinburgh, this castle, the ruins of which remain visible to this day, served as the occasional residence of early Scottish kings."[63] In *Macbeth*, Forres contrasts with Inverness in significant ways. Until contaminated by the regicide, Inverness conveys a sense of intimacy, especially emphasized with references to bedchambers and areas out of public view. Even the more public great hall, where the Macbeths host a banquet for their royal guest and his entourage, remains offstage; therefore, the action of the play emphasizes behind-the-scenes conversations and secret preparations for the assassination of Duncan. Forres, however, affords a more public setting, the action revolving around the banquet hall, where Macbeth and Lady Macbeth discharge their duties as royal hosts at a banquet. But even here, Macbeth finds time to privately confer with the murderers of Banquo. The scenes set in Forres, which span over much of Act III, intertwine the royal banquet and Banquo's murder. I will argue that in Act III, Macbeth takes the lead as protector of the new home; in the process, he keeps Lady Macbeth largely in the dark about his plan for the murder of Banquo and later of Macduff.

Inverness started out as an intimate place of dwelling; Forres, however, affords little intimacy or privacy between husband and wife. The more intimate areas of the royal house, such as bedchambers and closets, remain secluded or inaccessible. The characters do not mention activities related to these areas, except at the end of Act III, scene 4, when Lady Macbeth mentions bedtime and draws attention to Macbeth's insomnia. Instead, attention focuses on the banquet. Banquo begs leave to absent himself and Fleance until dinner time; to which Macbeth sinisterly responds, "Fail not our feast" (3.4.28), anticipating never to see Banquo or Fleance again. Macbeth cannot concentrate exclusively on either the banquet or the murder, which, as he instructs the hired murderers, "must be done tonight / And something from the palace" (3.1.131–2).[64] The banquet provides a cover, an alibi, or "clearness" with "no rubs nor botches in the work" (133–4). Lady Macbeth reminds her husband that, although obviously distracted, he "Be bright and jovial among our guests tonight" (3.2.28–9).

As in the preparations for Duncan's assassination, Macbeth divides his attention between his impending duties as royal host and his plan for the murder, between

---

63 Edward Sugden 199.

64 We recall that in *Titus Andronicus* Aaron and Tamora plan to use the forest outside of Rome for similar purposes.

the bright banquet hall and the treacherous forest some distance from the palace. Unlike the murder of Duncan, an enterprise conceived and carried out jointly by husband and wife, the murder of Banquo engages Macbeth alone and does not bring the royal couple together. Rather, unaware of Macbeth's precise plans, Lady Macbeth wonders why he "keep[s] alone," and even advises him pointedly: "'Tis safer to be that which we destroy / Than by destruction dwell in doubtful joy" (3.2.7–8). Nonetheless, the royal couple eagerly anticipate nightfall, imagining the bat's flight, "black Hecate's summons," the "shard-born beetle" ringing "night's yawning peal," "seeling night," the crow's flight to the "rooky wood," and "night's black agents" wreaking havoc on their unsuspecting prey (3.2.40–57). During the banquet, they discharge their ceremonial roles as king and queen; the scene, still retaining some tenderness between them, downplays the more intimate conjugal relationship, characteristic of Inverness. J.P. Dyson remarks that Macbeth attempts "to pass himself off as an inhabitant of the 'martlet' world, the ordered and harmonious world of the banquet, while his real habitat is the 'raven' world, the world of the First Murderer."[65]

As Lady Macbeth recedes into the background, "Macbeth seems to grow stronger and bolder;"[66] or in Rebecca Bushnell's words, he becomes "most 'manly'—and most depleted—in his full tyranny."[67] If he was a "prisoner of gender" in Inverness, in Forres, he comes into his own.[68] For a while, he grows in confidence, assuming that Forres can offer "harbor" for himself, "his murderous ways, and his brittle deluded hopes."[69] Yet he fails miserably to protect his new home and to discharge his domestic duties. He cannot control the course of events. Hearing the news of Fleance's escape, Macbeth feels "cabined, cribbed, confined, bound in / To saucy doubts and fears" (3.4.24–5). Lady Macbeth chastises her husband for his failure to propose the expected "cheer," reminding him that the banquet entails more than consumption of food: "To feed were best at home; / From thence, the sauce to meat is ceremony: / Meeting were bare without it" (3.4.33, 35–6). Macbeth himself cannot forget Banquo, indicating that he misses his former friend and wishes that "he were here." Ironically wishing he had "roofed" Banquo, Macbeth finds himself displaced from the banquet table, as Banquo's ghost enters and takes his "stool." Macbeth discovers that "The table's full" (46). Further, Banquo's ghost derails any attempt to keep his new home safe from contamination.

As Thomas Cartelli writes, the appearance of Banquo's ghost may imply "embodied hallucination," as various scholars suggest, but more interestingly, the

---

65 J.P. Dyson, "The Structural Function of the Banquet Scene in *Macbeth*," *Shakespeare Quarterly* 14.4 (1963): 372.

66 Floyd-Wilson, "English Epicures and Scottish Witches," 156.

67 Rebecca Bushnell, *Tragedies of Tyrants: Political Thought and Theater in the English Renaissance* (Ithaca: Cornell University Press, 1990) 63–9; and Perry, *Making of Jacobean Culture*, 145.

68 See Robert Kimbrough, "Macbeth: The Prisoner of Gender" *Shakespeare Studies* 16 (1983): 175–90.

69 Ross, *Custom of the Castle*, 124.

scene "make[s] the audience perceptually intimate with Macbeth at the precise moment when he becomes perceptually estranged from his only confidante, Lady Macbeth," who remains "unaware of the immediate occasion of Macbeth's distraction, his murder of Banquo."[70] The ghost interrupts Macbeth's repeated attempts to carry on, as Lady Macbeth attempts to cover for him and explain away her husband's strange behavior as a momentary "fit" or as "a thing of custom" (3.4.56, 98). Macbeth fails to establish boundaries between bloody murder and inviting home. At the conclusion of this scene, the play disposes of the Castle at Forres—the second castle to disappear. No other scene in the play will be set at Forres.

Further, Banquo's ghost unsettles but also helps Macbeth focus his attention on the dead Banquo and on the living Macduff. Keeping a spy, "a servant fee'd," in Macduff's house (3.4.133), Macbeth receives intelligence about his former ally's treason. The second consultation of the witches seeks to address these two concerns and find answers for his troubling questions:

> Though castles topple on their warders' heads,
> Though palaces and pyramids do slope
> Their heads to their foundations, though the treasure
> Of Nature's germens tumble all together
> Even till destruction sicken, answer me
> To what I ask you. (4.1.78–83)

The sequence of apparitions—armed head, a bloody child, a crowned child carrying a tree, eight kings, Banquo's ghost, and a king with a mirror—seems like emblems bearing a disturbing message: Banquo's heirs will constitute a long line of kings. Yet they also bring the apparent comfort of no harm from anyone born of woman, and not until "Great Birnam Wood to high Dunsinane Hill / Shall come against him" (4.1.115–16). The consultation with the witches also inspires Macbeth to destroy Macduff's family, as he states: "The castle of Macduff I will surprise," and kill "his wife, his babes, and all unfortunate souls / That trace him in his line" (4.1.172–5). Macduff himself inexplicably abandons his wife and son, and his household servants (4.2) to the slaughter that Macbeth has planned for them. Macbeth finds security not in the safety of the royal house at Forres, but rather in the wilds of Scotland, where he finds inspiration to destroy Macduff's household and also to abandon Forres and move to Dunsinane.

Dunsinane

Repeatedly, Macbeth proves himself the destroyer rather than protector of domestic space. In comparison to his previous residences, Macbeth uses Dunsinane more like a watchtower in a fortification than a home. In fact, located on one of the

---

[70] Thomas Cartelli, "Banquo's Ghost: The Shared Vision," *Theatre Journal* 5.3 (1983): 390, 392.

Sidlaw Hills over 1,000 feet high, some seven miles Northeast of Perth, Dunsinane "commands an impressive view."[71] Insomnia and watchfulness characterize the Macbeths' residence at this castle, whose circumvallation marks where a castle once stood.[72] As Charles Ross puts it best, "Dunsinane shelters a man who lives in constant fear."[73] Although Dunsinane seemingly provides security and safety from the outside world, it cannot function as a normal home. Domestic activities have been significantly scaled down or oddly displaced: the castle takes on the spectral qualities of its few disquieted, disturbed ghostly inhabitants.

Many moral treatises from the period offer advice on achieving tranquility of mind, a prerequisite for happiness. Joseph Hall says that "tranquilitie of the mind is, as of the Sea and weather, when no winde stirreth, when the waues doe not tumultuously rise and fall upon each other."[74] To achieve such a state, one must master the passions, "as not sometimes to over-joy his griefe, or over-grieve his joy," but achieving a "balance."[75] Macbeth certainly fits Hall's description of the "franticke man" who cannot become "settled in an habitual rest."[76] He becomes frantic, indeed in his own words, "blanched with fear" (3.4.117) at the sight of the "horrible shadow" of Banquo. I suggest that a turning point in Macbeth's life occurs when he looks the ghost of his former friend in the eye and says: "Thou hast no speculation in those eyes / Which thou dost glare with" (3.4.96–7). Editors usually gloss "speculation" as vision, the first meaning recorded for the word in the *OED*; however, the word also means "an observer or watcher," or a "spy," as Shakespeare uses it in *King Lear* to refer to servants, "Which are to France the spies and speculations / Intelligent of our state" (3.1.24–5).[77] "Speculum" is also a looking glass, a mirror. All these meanings derive from Latin "*speculari*, to spy out, watch, examine, observe, etc.; *specula* a look-out, watch-tower" (*OED*). I propose that "speculation" carries all of these meanings. Banquo's ghost stares but cannot see; Macbeth stares into Banquo's spectral eyes and finds no reflection. The ghostly eyes are mirrors that do not reflect, through which one cannot see. Lombarda, one of the best-known trobairitz, refers to "*lo mirailz e no veser descorda*," a "mirror with no image" that disturbs the sense of self.[78] As a result

---

71 Sugden 160, and photograph of Dunsinane Hill in Aitchison, *Macbeth: Man and Myth*, 90.

72 Sugden 160.

73 Ross, *Custom of the Castle*, 125.

74 Joseph Hall, *Heaven upon earth, or of true peace, and Tranquilitie of minde* (London, 1606) 7. See also George Webbe, *The Practice of Quietness* (London, 1617), esp. 10–12.

75 Hall, *Heaven upon earth*, 8.

76 Hall, *Heaven upon earth*, 11. Webbe, *Practice of Quietness*, describes the frantic man as one who is "too suspicious," "too furious," "injurious," or "litigious" (13).

77 See *OED*.

78 Magda Bogin, *The Women Troubadours* (New York: Paddington Press, 1976; rpt. New York: Norton, 1980) 116–17, as quoted in Robert Bayliss, *The Discourse of Courtly Love in Seventeenth-Century Spanish Theater* (Lewisburg: Bucknell University Press, 2008) 42. For a study of mirrors in the period, see Debora Shuger, "The 'I' of the Beholder:

of the encounter with such a mirror, Macbeth seeks to see as far as he can, which eventually situates him at Dunsinane.[79]

Towers and turrets serve many purposes in literature. In Chrétien de Troyes' *Le Chevalier de la Charrette* [*The Knight of the Cart*], Meleagant takes Lancelot prisoner and locks him in a tower, especially built for the purpose. Lancelot, "given some paltry morsels of food through" a window, would waste away.[80] In Gottfried von Strassburg's "Tristan and Isolt," Tristan, injured in the thigh with a poisoned spear, ends up in his castle's tower, waiting for his beloved Isolt of the White Hand to return and nurse him back to health. A white sail signals Isolt's approach; a black sail indicates that she is not to come. From the tower of the castle, Tristan's current wife, the Isolt of the Black Hand, lies to him about the color of the approaching sail; and he dies, having lost all hope of ever seeing his beloved Isolt again.[81] In his *Complaint*, Thomas Hoccleve (c. 1368–1426) describes recovery from a bout of mental illness, a walk through streets where he imagines everyone is talking about him, and his return to his chamber at home alone to look himself in a mirror, "I streighte vnto my mirour / and my glas / To looke how þat me," seeking to see what others might have seen in his face; yet finding but his "troublid spirit," unable to rest.[82] Although the precise location of the chamber cannot be determined, Hoccleve "return[s] home to the protected and private space of his chamber."[83] Like Hoccleve, Macbeth retreats to his chamber. On the one hand, he feels secure, ordering his servants to hang "banners on the outward walls," so that if his enemies come, they will discover that "Our castle's strength / Will laugh a siege to scorn" (5.5.1–3). But also like Lancelot and Tristan, Macbeth languishes in despair.

Renaissance Mirrors and the Reflexive Mind," in *Renaissance Culture and the Everyday*, (eds) Patricia Fumerton and Simon Hunt (Philadelphia: University of Pennsylvania Press, 1999) 21–41. She argues that "Before the mid-seventeenth century, most people seem rather to have encountered their image reflected in another—for us, a deeply unfamiliar sort of mirroring," as illustrated in *Troilus and Cressida* (3.3.47), where the word "speculation" occurs in the sense of "vision" (39). However, "speculation," she adds, "is not reflexive": "Unlike its glass counterpart, the mirror of the other does not reflect on compulsion; to see oneself, another person must return the salute, must choose to respond, and by responding, give back one's image" (39). Although she does not discuss *Macbeth*, I think that her analysis supports my argument about the eyes of Banquo's ghost. See also Scipion Dupleix, *The resoluer; or Curiosities of nature* (London, 1635) 284–7.

[79] Ironically, the ghost of the eighth king in Act IV, scene 1, carries a mirror that shows what Macbeth does not wish to see; namely, a long line of Banquo's descendants.

[80] Chrétien de Troyes, *The Complete Romances of Chrétien de Troyes*, trans. David Staines (Bloomington: Indiana University Press, 1990) 244.

[81] Roger Sherman Loomis and Laura Hibbard Loomis, (eds), *Medieval Romances* (New York: Random House, 1957) 225–32.

[82] Thomas Hoccleve, *Thomas Hoccleve's Complaint and Dialogue*, (ed.) J.A. Barrow, The Early English Text Society (Oxford: Oxford University Press, 1999) 13–15. I am grateful to Misty Schieberle, University of Kansas, for bringing this example to my attention.

[83] Ethan Knapp, *The Bureaucratic Muse: Thomas Hoccleve and the Literature of Late Medieval England* (State College: Penn State University, 2001) 169.

Watchfulness dominates the last act of the play, which opens with the Doctor and Gentleman describing how Lady Macbeth has become an automaton. For two nights, she has risen from bed and walked, as if awake but in fact sound asleep. Since Macbeth went to the battlefield, she has been getting out of bed, putting on her nightgown, unlocking her closet, writing and sealing a letter, and then returning to bed—all of these actions performed "while in a most fast sleep" (5.1.8). The doctor offers his diagnosis: "A great perturbation in nature, to receive at once the benefit of sleep and do the effects of watching" (9–10). Lady Macbeth appears: she bears a light, rubs her hands as if trying to wash them—"Out, damned spot! Out, I say" (35)—smells blood, chastises Macbeth, hears a knocking at the gate, speaks of how "hell is murky," and proceeds as if reliving the fateful night of Duncan's murder at Inverness: "To bed, to bed; there's knocking at the gate. Come, come, come, come, give me your hand. What's done cannot be undone. To bed, to bed, to bed" (5.2.65–7).

Despite the apparent busy preparations for war, a sense of emptiness prevails at Dunsinane. The fortress takes on the ghostly, spectral quality of its inhabitants. Caithness reports that Macbeth is "mad" and his cause "distempered"; and, and according to Angus, those Macbeth "commands move only in command, / Nothing in love" (19–20). Macbeth's interior seems disordered, as Menteith observes: "Who then shall blame / His pestered senses to recoil and start, / When all that is within him does condemn / Itself for being there?" (24–7). When Macbeth appears in Act V, scene 3, he seems profoundly isolated, not wanting to hear any more reports from the field, confident in the Weird Sisters' prophecy: "'Fear not, Macbeth. No man that's born of woman / Shall e'er have power upon thee'" (6–7). He recognizes that he has killed and gained power for nothing; as he summons Seyton, he feels sick at heart. He says that he has "lived long enough," for his "way of life / Is fall'n into the sere, the yellow leaf"; yet he will never enjoy what accompanies old age, such as "honor, love, obedience, troops of friends" (5.3.21–30).

In Scene 5, he hears women's cries from some inner chamber, and he considers how his senses have become numb. As he says, he has almost forgotten "the taste of fears;" his senses would have been on edge to hear "a night-shriek" and his hair would stand on end: "I have supped full with horrors. / Direness, familiar to my slaughterous thoughts, / Cannot once start me" (13–15). When Seyton brings word of Lady Macbeth's death, Macbeth gives his most famous speech about the creeping pace of tomorrows into "dusty death," and his observation about the meaning of life:

> Life's but a walking shadow, a poor player
> That struts and frets his hour upon the stage
> And then is heard no more. It is a tale
> Told by an idiot, full of sound and fury,
> Signifying nothing. (5.5.17–28)

As predicted by the Weird Sisters, he has never been able to produce an heir. Earlier, he felt that the future promised great accomplishments; and on the night of Duncan's assassination, he had contemplated his position: "But here upon

135

In Reges desides.

EMBLEMA XVIII.

Rex agit in Scena frontem Diademate vinctus,
Et clamyde insignis Sceptra superba gerit:
Nil iubet, aut loquitur Tragici tenet inde Cothurni
Primas sed partes nuntius, aut famulus.
Regibus aptantur tot priscæ ludicra Scenæ,
Qui nisi res agitent, nomen inane ferunt.

COMMENTARIVS.

1 CVM ergò, docente Seneca, *Officium sit imperare, non Regnum*; Regesque à Regendo dicantur, & unusquisque secundùm etymologiam sui nominis vivere debeat, ut ex Sacris Canonibus Nicolaus Cusanus admonuit, meritò post Ausonium, & Horatium Divus Isidorus scriptum reliquit, tamdiu quemlibet Regis nomen tenere, quamdiu rectè fecerit, & concreditum sibi à Deo munus impleverit. Quod idem valet, atque illud Divi Pauli: *Qui præsunt in solitudine præsint*. Hoc est, ut pro commissis sibi populis eos labores, curas, vigiliasque suscipiant, de quibus adeò latè in superioribus diximus, Sciantque magnam, qua se pollere credunt Fortunam, non in licentiam, sed in patientiam vertere, & Nomen Numenvè suum, non tam honoris, quàm oneris esse, non fœlicissimi, sed vigilantissi-

Senec. epist. 90.
Nicol. de Cusa lib. 5. exc. pag. 412.
Auson. in Monos. Horat. lib. 1. epis. 1. Isidor. de sum. bono, cap. 98.
D. Paul. in epist. ad Rom. cap. 18. v. 8.

I 4 mi,

Fig. 4.2 Emblem of a King Onstage. Juan de Solórzano Pereyra, *Emblemata Centum*. Matriti, 1653. Summerfield D523. Courtesy of Special Collections, Spencer Research Library, University of Kansas Libraries.

this bank and shoal of time, / We'd jump the life to come" (1.7.6–7). He faces meaningless, empty tomorrows, without his partner of greatness, without a son, without hope.[84]

Dunsinane simultaneously serves as refuge and prison.[85] Macbeth finds a strange sense of security in the palace. Unable or unwilling to leave the fortress, he cannot rest or enjoy comfort therein. The interior space of his mind and heart reflects his surroundings. When Malcolm orders that each soldier cut down a bough from Birnam Wood and bear the branch in his hand, he not only makes the second prophecy come true; he also symbolically returns life to the desiccated, hollowed out, and withered world that the Macbeths have created for themselves. Malcolm, who lived in exile in Edward the Confessor's court, a world of miracles and healing, returns still a virgin, to rid his homeland of the "dead butcher and his fiendlike queen."[86] He easily gains admittance to Macbeth's castle. Siward reports that "The castle's gently rendered: / The tyrant's people on both sides do fight"; in fact, Siward opens the gates and invites him in: "Enter, sir, the castle" (5.8.29). Macbeth himself at first refuses to fight Macduff, but decides not to yield, and therefore, "To kiss the ground before young Malcolm's feet" (5.8.28).

As Gaston Bachelard in *Poetics of Space* writes, "Outside and inside form a dialectic of division, the obvious geometry of which binds us as soon as we bring it into play in metaphorical domains. … "[87] The geometry of this metaphysics "confers spatiality upon thought," upon concepts of "open and closed," which inform every system.[88] Indeed, as Lady Macbeth observed, the Weird Sisters promised them "metaphysical aid"; what she and Macbeth did not realize then was that this metaphysical aid split their world into a fearful geometry. It opened a door into a wild world, which crept into their lives. As Bachelard points out, "If one were to give an account of all the doors one has closed and opened, of all the doors one would like to reopen, one would have to tell the story of one's entire life."[89] But, we also need to remember his profound question: "And then, onto what, toward what, do doors open? Do they open for the world of men, or for the world of solitude?"[90]

---

[84] Ross, in *The Custom of the Castle*, sees this emptying of Dunsinane as preparation for new residents ("He [Macbeth] empties his castle to allow its reinscription by others") and as a kind of exorcism by removing "foul accretions to provide a glimpse of a proper future, a more civil society" (125, 129).

[85] Ross recognizes part of the phenomenon I am describing, when he writes that "Dunsinane appears to Macbeth as a refuge" (127).

[86] In "The Theatre of the Mind: An Essay on *Macbeth*," *ELH* 42.3 (1975), Richard S. Ide points out that Macbeth views himself as "a ranting tyrant on an absurd world stage" (358).

[87] Bachelard, *Poetics of Space*, 211–12.

[88] Bachelard, *Poetics of Space*, 211–12.

[89] Bachelard, *Poetics of Space*, 224.

[90] Bachelard, *Poetics of Space*, 224.

Shakespeare suggests a commerce between body and architecture. In fact, in the early modern period, architecture often served as a metaphor for the structure of the human body, as for example in Cyril Tourneur's *The Atheist's Tragedy* and in Shakespeare's *Two Gentlemen of Verona*. In Tourneur's play, D'Amville, compares the body of his dying elder son, Rousard, to the collapse of a great building: "His gasping sighs are like the falling noise / Of some great building when the groundwork breaks. / On these two pillars stood the stately frame / And architecture of my lofty house" (5.1.75–8).[91] Likewise, in *The Gentlemen of Verona*, Valentine, wandering in a forest on the outskirts of Mantua, connects the interior space of his heart to the surrounding forest (5.4.1–3). The shadowy forest, devoid of human presence, reminds him of the void left in his heart by the absence of his beloved Silvia. The extended metaphor transforms his breast into an abandoned house:

> O thou that dost inhabit in my breast,
> Leave not the mansion so long tenantless,
> Lest, growing ruinous the building fall
> And have no memory of what it was. (5.4.7–10).

The tenant has moved out of the lofty mansion of his breast, leaving behind an uninhabited, unoccupied, empty building. Architectural emptiness threatens to bring down the entire structure and even erase the memory of what the mansion used to be. Dwelling presence and material structure reinforce and support each other. Architecture intermixes materiality and habits of everyday life.

Macbeth and Lady Macbeth do not drain "all sense of home" out of their country, as Linda Woodbridge writes of *King Lear*.[92] Their castles do not vanish or rend; nor do the Macbeths become wanderers in the vast mysterious empty spaces of their kingdom; rather, they retreat deeper into the materiality of their domestic spaces. In "Of Building," Francis Bacon argues that one should seek a house with the best possible features; since one rarely finds the ideal house to suit all of one's needs, one may settle for something less. However, he adds, if one has several dwellings to choose from, then "what he wanteth in one, he may find in the other."[93] The Macbeths, like other sovereigns, have different homes to choose from; yet, as they move from house to house, seeking security and refuge, they find none, for each home seems to hem them in like prison walls.[94] The house as the

91 Cyril Tourneur, *The Atheist's Tragedy; Or, The Honest Man's Revenge*, in *Four Revenge Tragedies*, (ed.) Katherine Eisaman Maus (Oxford and New York: Oxford University Press, 1995).

92 Woodbridge, *Vagrancy*, 208.

93 Francis Bacon, "Of Building," in *The Essays or Counsels, Civill and Morall* (London, 1625), sig. Ll1–Ll2, as quoted in Orlin, *Elizabethan Households*, 10.

94 I am paraphrasing the words of William Azel Cook, *By Horse, Canoe and Float through the Wilderness of Brazil* (Akron, OH: The Werner Company, 1909) 11. He writes: "What was in this great, mysterious world, only the edges of which we could see, and which seemed to conceal itself from us behind insurmountable barriers that hemmed us in like prison walls?"

center of domestic life in *Macbeth* does not contain, even as it becomes weighted down by what the residents gather, collect, and accumulate. Ironically, Malcolm summarizes what the Macbeths irrevocably lost when they killed Duncan. In preparation for the final assault on Dunsinane, Malcolm predicts what Scotland desperately needs: “Cousins, I hope the days are near at hand / That chambers will be safe” (5.4.1–2). At the end of the play, he can accomplish what the Macbeths had destroyed: he will restore bedchambers to their proper use and once again try to safeguard the boundaries of home.

Conclusion

In *A Booke of Christian Praiers* (1608), Richard Day offers two prayers, one for going "abroad" into the dangerous snares of the world and the other for returning home safely; or, as he puts it, "out of storms into a haven."[1] Day sees the house as a refuge "from the annoyance of the weather, from the cruelty of beasts, and from the waves and turmoils of this troublous world."[2] By contrast, in *A Warning for Fair Women*, "Tragedie," with knife and whip in hand, walks onstage, demanding "Roome, roome for God's sake" (Ind., 11).[3] Tragedie wants room to represent "passions that must move the soule" (Ind., 44).[4] "Auditors preparde for *Tragedie*" (Ind., 83) expect a stage "hung with black curtains, "ebon tapers" lit, and a "deadly banquet" prepared. Under these conditions, along with appropriate sound effects, the playhouse becomes a "fatal house":

> To leade blacke murther to this damned deed,
> The ugly Screechowle, and the night Raven,
> With flaggy wings and hideous croking noise,
> Do beate the casements of this fatal house,
> Whilst I do bring my dreadful Furies forth (Dumb Show I, 771–86).[5]

Shakespeare mentions such conventions, as for example, in references to "Black stage for tragedies and murders fell" (*Rape of Lucrece*, 766); "woeful tragedy" in *1 Henry VI* (1.4.77); and the "tragic loading" of the bed in *Othello*. Even Buckingham in *Richard III* boasts of being able to "counterfeit the deep tragedian" (3.5.5). In Shakespeare's major tragedies, houses never constitute immutable safe havens; rather, such houses all become "fatal." The tragic experience hinges on the emplacement of embodied tragic subjects in houses and home spaces.

---

1 Richard Day, *A Booke of Christian Praiers* (London, 1608), sig. C1, excerpted in Orlin, *Elizabethan Households*, 29.

2 Day, *Christian Praiers* (London, 1608), sig. C1, excerpted in Orlin, *Elizabethan Households*, 29.

3 *A Warning for Fair Women: A Critical Edition*, ed. Charles Dale Cannon (The Hague: Moulton, 1975). The play was entered in the Stationers' Register on November 17, 1599. All references from this play will be to this edition and are hereafter cited parenthetically.

4 Her allegorical counterparts, Comedie and Historie, however, mock tragic conventions, even offering a satire of "a filthie whining ghost, / Lapt in some fowle sheete, or a leather pelch,"crying out "Vindicta, revenge, revenge" (Ind., 54–5, 57), presumably an allusion to Shakespeare's *Hamlet*.

5 In other words, the stage is ready for Seneca's Thyestean feast: "The table was set with black candles, drink set out in skulls and the Furies served it up." Cannon adds: "The tradition of these diabolical suppers might be behind the cauldron scene in *Macbeth*" (182n).

Throughout this book, I have examined places of residence and questions of dwelling. The four tragedies represent specific dwelling places, to which the inhabitants allude, and specific locations they traverse on the tragic journey. As Lear disposes of his property, his castle also disappears in a literary tour-de-force. The castle, clearly connected to a patriarchal system in transition, leaves voids to be filled. Lear spends much of the rest of the play searching for a suitable dwelling place to replace the one that vanished. Throughout *King Lear*, the home becomes a highly contested place, as the characters engage in a spirited debate about orderly household governance. Goneril and Regan see Lear's abdication as a great opportunity to seize the moment, undo their father's policies, shape new policy, and eventually even reexamine the foundation of their marriage and assert their own sexual desire. Together with Edmund, they advance a new vision of family, based not on patriarchal traditions but rather on self-interest. Initially, Goneril relies on established gender roles in the management of her house; yet she also subverts the roles, as she expels her father from her house, and later challenges her husband's authority. Regan and Cornwall band together in a conjugal and criminal partnership, not unlike that of the Macbeths later. Anticipating Lear's unwelcome visit, they abandon their house and seek shelter in Gloucester's house. Here they take over the house and violate the boundaries between guest and host. In Gloucester's home, Edmund, Regan, and Cornwall re-imagine fundamental social and cultural relations, symbolized by the cruel and harsh treatment of Lear in Act II and of Gloucester in Act III.

Early modern writers saw the household as a prototype and microcosm for a perfect commonwealth. Echoing such writers, Shakespeare dramatizes the collapse of the social order as a housing crisis and a fierce contest for control of domestic space. The disappearance of Lear's castle and the dismantling of his home, Edmund's ascendancy, and the collapse of patriarchal control empower Goneril and Regan, who feel sexually liberated from the former legal, moral, and domestic constraints. In this reshuffling, houses and castles recede into the background. Questions of survival loom large as the characters traverse vast expanses of Lear's kingdom. The play unsettles notions of inside and outside—leaving, closing doors, exile, not belonging.

Othello weaves together cross-cultural issues and the story of a marriage caught between two radically different modes of dwelling. The play dramatizes its central characters' unhousing as a clash between a sedentary, urban, home-centered way of life and a mobile, non-permanent form of dwelling. Brabantio's house in Venice and Othello's home in Cyprus offer but an illusion of stability. Othello's travels and military history reinforce his uprooted identity as a wandering, wheeling stranger, with no fixed place of residence. Iago's strategy centers on having Othello revisit and re-imagine his marriage and his life. In Cyprus, physical space seems to shrink, the bedchamber eventually becoming the central focus of attention; yet the ancestral landscapes of Othello's childhood and travels haunt him and undermine his desire for security and stability. Like Caravaggio, Shakespeare manipulates lighting effects to accentuate a thick darkness that reduces the field of vision. In the source materials, the Moor and the Ensign literally bring down the ceiling over Desdemona's bed; in *Othello*, Shakespeare symbolizes the destruction of the household through the thick darkness that envelops, penetrates, and transforms the house into something mysterious, exotic, and dangerous.

In the opening scene of *Hamlet*, Kronborg Castle already bears the emotions and experiences of its residents; and throughout the play, Hamlet and Claudius compete to re-imagine, inscribe, and control the domestic space of the castle. Claudius seeks to erase the reminders of his brother's ownership and presence; Hamlet wants to reassert his father's claim to the house, wife, throne, and family. Shakespeare intertwines house and body. Claudius offers to transform Elsinore into a house of pleasure and a center of festivity; whereas Hamlet, deeply hurt by his father's death and his mother's betrayal, seeks to inscribe Elsinore as a house of pain, a tragic stage to represent his sense of suffering and emotional distress. Claudius forges political, personal, and even sexual alliances, as needed, to solidify his grasp of the throne; Hamlet, however, aligns himself emotionally with the ghost of his father, as he seeks to counter his uncle's politics of pleasure. To be "at home" in *Hamlet* entails a battle for control of domestic and intimate space.

Macbeth and Lady Macbeth, like Lear, do not reside long in one place. Deeming their home at Inverness a safe haven, they choose it as a site for the murder of their royal guest; yet they discover that their home abuts a wild world. Outdoors and indoors remain contiguous, invading and pervading each other's domain. The Macbeths trust walls too much: to keep the external world out, to separate bedchambers as site of repose and as a site of murder, to protect them from the consequences of their crime. They ruin each of their houses. As they move from royal house to royal house, they feel more and more confined, retreating deeper into the materiality of their haunted domestic space. They end up isolated, haunted by their crimes, in Dunsinane, a fortress, which ironically cannot safeguard them from themselves.

Sebastian Serlio argued that tragic action must always happen in "the houses of great Lords, Dukes, Princes, and kings."[6] His stage design, however, based on unchangeable standard scenes for comedy, tragedy, and satire could never accommodate or reflect, for example, the fluid sense of scenery envisioned in the great tragedies. I have argued that Shakespeare requires that we imagine subtle or radical changes of scenery through language, props, and special effects. To this purpose, the bare platform stage, serving as a tabula rasa, becomes a flexible, vibrant canvas or screen upon which imagined places appear or can be projected. This virtual space accommodates localized and unlocalized action. As the action requires, space expands or contracts; action represented may shift from indoors to outdoors and back again. Public locations morph into intimate areas. In all four plays, Shakespeare takes full advantage of the Elizabethan theater's continuous staging of place. In this kind of theater, the stage functions as an unreal background that can be summoned to represent specific locations. Shakespeare creates imagined homes and domestic spaces for his characters, regardless of

6 Sebastian Serlio, *The First Booke of Architecture* (London, 1611), Fol. 25^{v}.

whether the Globe or other playhouses had the technical resources to render physical surroundings in a realistic way.

In fact, a theater producer needs relatively little to transform any space. In 1994, I had my undergraduate students in a senior seminar on Modern Drama conduct such a theatrical experiment at Xavier University, Cincinnati. As part of a major assignment in the course, we undertook a full-scale production of Oscar Wilde's *Salomé*.[7] After studying possible spaces on campus for our production, we chose the former Jesuit chapel, which some 25 years earlier, had been converted into a non-descript pit-shaped faculty lounge. Our first challenge was to adapt the faculty lounge as a small amphitheatre for an audience of about 80 persons to be seated on raised platforms built on two sides of our improvised stage. To recreate Herod's palace, we draped stage furniture and the performance area with a black cloth, which in turn would contribute to the palace's somber and nightmarish atmosphere. We positioned six ensconced lighting instruments on the floor pointing upwards to generate columns of light reminiscent of the slender, graceful columns of the imagined palace. Electricians from Xavier's Physical Plant installed spotlights outside the room to illuminate the stunning stained glass windows of the former chapel. The simple stage design helped locate the dramatic action on the borders of the profane and the sacred, the sacrilegious and the worshipful, reinforced with music, sound effects, and the lascivious, frenetic dance of the seven veils, choreographed to Sephardic music.

Significant markers of houses and domestic spaces underscore the centrality of such spaces to the tragic experience in Shakespeare. Michael Goldman suggests that the early modern printed play texts do not simply represent "a single and final authorial version of the text"; rather, as working scripts from busy repertory companies, they reflect "many varied performance occasions."[8] In this context, the scripts encode markers of stage design, although we cannot link these markers to specific performances. As I have suggested, stage design here stems from and becomes a function of dramatic narratives, created by props, stage directions, and characters' comments about and responses to their perceived physical surroundings. When a location becomes significant to the dramatic narrative, Shakespeare encodes markers of place and therefore invites the audience to imagine the required location where the action unfolds. In other words, he encodes an imagined, virtual dramatic reality. Body and house become entangled in phenomena of perception, which recovers fragmentary, unstable, contingent images of domestic spaces, where Shakespeare situates embodied subjectivity. Houses become part of the tragic journey and reflect the effects of the tragic experience as a dislocation of habits of mind, disruption of households, and destruction of home.

---

[7] Oscar Wilde, *Salomé*, Theatrical production at Xavier University, November 18–20, 1994. Full-scale production of the play was done in conjunction with and as a class project for my Senior Seminar (ENGL-499). We were fortunate to count on the help of several Cincinnati-based theater professionals, including Gary Goldhoff, Christina Schnock, and Salli LoveLarkin, who generously volunteered time and resources to make the production possible.

[8] Michael Goldman, "*Hamlet*: Entering the Text," *Theatre Journal* 44.4 (1972): 456.

Bibliography

Manuscripts

British Library. Add. MS. 9810. A *Large Chart of the Coasts of Europe, with the Black Sea, the Mediterranean, and Western Coast of Africa*. By Giacopo Veschonte. Genoa, October 10, 1562.

British Library. MS Harleian 4425. Fol. 39.

Primary Sources

Africanus, John Leo. *A Geographical Historie of Africa*. Trans. John Pory. London, 1600; *The History and Description of Africa*. Ed. Robert Brown. London: Hakluyt Society, 1896.

Alberti, Leon Battista. *The Ten Books of Architecture: The 1755 Leoni Edition*. New York: Dover Publications, 1986.

———. *Della Famiglia*. Trans. Renée Neu Watkins. *The Family in Renaissance Florence*. Columbia: University of South Carolina Press, 1969.

Andrew of Wyntoun. *The Original Chronicle of Andrew of Wyntoun*. Ed. François J. Amours. 6 vols. Edinburgh and London: W. Blackwood, 1903–14.

Anonymous. *A very proper treatise, wherein is breefely set forth the art of limming*. London, 1583. STC 24254.

———. *A Warning for Fair Women: A Critical Edition*. Ed. Charles Dale Cannon. The Hague: Mouton, 1975.

———. *The lyfe of Saynt Edwarde confessour and kynge of Englande*. London, 1533. STC 7500.

Aristotle. *The Complete Works of Aristotle*. 2 vols. Ed. Jonathan Barnes. Princeton: Princeton University Press, 1984.

Bacon, Roger. *The Opus Majus of Roger Bacon*. Trans. Robert Belle Burke. New York: Russell & Russell, 1962.

Barckley, Richard. *A Discourse of the Felicitie of Man*. London, 1603.

Barlow, Frank, ed., *The Life of King Edward*. Second Edition. Oxford: Clarendon Press, 1992.

Bate, John. *The mysteries of Nature, and Art*. 1577; London, 1634. STC 1577.

Bertelli, Pietro. *Diuersarū nationum habitus*. Patauij, 1594, 96.

Bible. The Authorized King James Version. Iowa Falls: World Bible Publishers, n.d.

Bishop, Elizabeth. *The Complete Poems, 1927–1979*. New York: Farrar, Straus and Giroux, 1979.

Bloody Banquet, The. By T.D. London, 1639. Rpt. Malone Society Reprints. Oxford: Malone Society, 1962.

Boaistuau, Pierre. *Certaine secrete wonders of nature*. Trans. Edward Fenton. London, 1569. STC 3164.5.

Bourne, William. *Inventions or Devices*. London: Thomas Woodcock, 1578.

Braun, Georg, and Abraham Hogenberg. *Civitates orbis terrarum*. 6 vols. Brussels, 1574–1618.

Brown, P. Hume. *Early Travellers in Scotland*. 2 vols. Edinburgh: David Douglas, 1981.

Bullough, Geoffrey, ed. *Narrative and Dramatic Sources of Shakespeare*. 8 vols. London: Routledge and Kegan Paul; New York: Columbia University Press, 1957–1975.

Bülow, Gottfried von, and Wilfred Powell. *Diary of the Journey of Philip Julius, Duke of Stettin-Pomerania, through England in the Year 1602*. *Transactions of the Royal Historical Society*, New Series, 6 (1892): 1–67.

Camden, William. *Remaines concerning Brittaine*. London, 1629. STC 4525.

Carr, Ralph. *The Mahumetane or Turkish historie*. London, 1600. STC 17997.

Caus, Salomon de. *La perspectiue, auec la raison des ombres et miroirs*. London, 1611. STC 4868.7.

Chaucer, Geoffrey. *The Canterbury Tales*. Ed. A.C. Cawley. London: J.M. Dent; New York: E.P. Dutton, 1958.

Chrétien de Troyes. *The Complete Romances of Chrétien de Troyes*. Trans. David Staines. Bloomington: Indiana University Press, 1990.

Cleaver, Robert. *A goodlie forme of householde gouernment*. London, 1598. STC 5383.

Colonna, Francesco. *Hypnerotomachia: The Strife of Love in a Dreame*. London, 1592. Ed. Lucy Gent. Delmar, New York: Scholars' Facsimiles and Reprints, 1973.

Contarini, Gasparo. *The Commonwealth and Government of Venice*. Trans. Lewes Lewknor. London, 1599. STC 5642.

Coryat, Thomas. *Coryats crudities*. London, 1611. STC 5808.

Crysostom, St John. *On Wealth and Poverty*. Trans. Catherine P. Roth. Crestwood: St. Vladimir's Seminary Press, 1999.

Cunliffe, John W., ed. *Early English Classical Tragedies*. Oxford: Clarendon Press, 1912.

Cunningham, William. *The Cosmographical Glass*. London, 1559. STC 6119.

Dekker, Thomas. *The pleasant comedie of old Fortunatus*. London, 1600. STC 6517.

———. *The Dramatic Works of Thomas Dekker*. Ed. Fredson Bowers. Vol. 4. Cambridge: Cambridge University Press, 1961.

Du Moulin, Pierre. *The Elements of logick*. London, 1624. STC 7323.

Dupleix, Scipion. *The resoluer; or Curiosities of nature*. London, 1635. STC 7362.

Edelman, Charles, ed. *The Stukeley Plays*. Manchester: Manchester University Press, 2005.

Elviden, Edmund. *The closet of counsells*. London, 1569. STC 7622.

Epictetus. *The Discourses: The Handbook, Fragments*. Trans. Robin Hard. Ed. Christopher Gill. London: Longman/J.M. Dent, 1995.

———. *The manuell of Epictetus*. London, 1567. STC 10423.

Euripides. *The Bacchae and Other Plays*. Trans. Philip Vellacott. Harmondsworth and Baltimore: Penguin Books, 1954.

Fonte, Moderata. *The Worth of Women: Wherein Is Clearly Revealed Their Nobility and Their Superiority to Men*. Ed. and trans. Virginia Cox. Chicago: University of Chicago Press, 1997.

Fougasses, Thomas de. *The General historie of Venice*. Trans. W. Shute. London, 1612. STC 11207.

Gascoigne, George. *Noble Arte of Venerie or Hunting*. London, 1576. STC 24328.

———. *Noble Arte of Venerie or Hunting*. London, 1611. STC 24329.

Greene, Robert. *Greenes Mourning Garment: Given Him by Repentance at the Funerals of Love*. London, 1616. STC12251.

Gross, G.W., ed. and trans. *The Diary of Baron Waldstein*. London: Thames and Hudson, 1981.

Guest, Charlotte, trans. *The Mabinogion, Mediaeval Welsh Romances*. Third Edition. London: D. Nutt, 1910.

Hakluyt, Richard. *The principal navigations, voyages, traffiques & discoveries of the English nation*. 12 vols. Glasgow: J. MacLehose and Sons, 1903–1905.

Hall, Joseph. *Heaven upon earth, or of true peace, and Tranquilitie of minde*. London, 1606.

Hardison, O.B., Jr, ed. *English Literary Criticism: The Renaissance*. New York: Appleton-Century-Crofts, 1963.

Hawes, Stephen. *The historie of graunde Amoure and la bell Pucel, called the Pastime of plesure*. 1509: London, 1554. STC 12950.

Herbert, George. *The Works of George Herbert*. Ed. F.E. Hutchinson. Oxford: Clarendon Press, 1959.

Hervet, G. *Xenophons treatise of householde*. London, 1532. STC 26073.

Hewitt, Barnard, ed. *The Renaissance Stage: Documents of Serlio, Sabbatini and Furttenbach*. Trans. Allardyce Nicholl, John H. McDowell, and George R. Kernodle. Coral Gables: University of Miami Press, 1958.

Heywood, Thomas. *The Dramatic Works*. 6 vols. New York: Russell & Russell, 1964.

Heylyn, Peter. *Cosmographie in four booke: containing the chorographie and historie of the whole world, and all the principall kingdomes, provinces, seas and isles thereof*. London, 1652. WING H1689.

Hinman, Charlton, ed., *The Norton Facsimile: The First Folio of Shakespeare*. New York: W.W. Norton, 1968.

Hoccleve, Thomas. *Thomas Hoccleve's Complaint and Dialogue*. Ed. J.A. Burrow. The Early English Text Society. Oxford: Oxford University Press, 1999.

Jodelle, Ėtienne. *Cléopâtre captive*. Ed. Kathleen M. Hall. Exeter: University of Exeter, 1979.

———. *Œuvre Complètes*. Ed. Enea Balmas. Vol. 2 Paris: Gallimard, 1965.

Johnson, Richard. *The pilgrimage of man*. London, 1612. STC 14691.5.

Karwill, Victor von. *Queen Elizabeth and Some Foreigners ... Unpublished Letters from the Archives of the Hapsburg Family*. Trans. T.H. Nash. London: John Lane, 1928.

Knolles, Richard. *The generall historie of the Turkes*. London, 1603. STC 15051.

———. *The generall historie of the Turkes*. London, 1610. STC 15052.

La Serre, M. de. *The mirrour which flatters not*. Trans. T. Cary. London, 1639. STC 20490.

Le Fanu, Sheridan. "Carmilla." In *A Glass Darkly*. Ed. Robert Tracy. Oxford: Oxford University Press, 1993.

Le Roy, Louis. *Of the interchangeable course, or variety of things in the whole world*. London, 1594. STC 15488.

Longinus. *On the Sublime. Classical Literary Criticism*. Trans. T.S. Dorsch. Harmondsworth and Baltimore: Penguin Books, 1965.

Loomis, Roger Sherman, and Laura Hibbard Loomis, eds. *Medieval Romances*. New York: Random House, 1957.

Mawe, John. *Travels in the Interior of Brazil; Particularly in The Gold and Diamond Districts of That Country*. London, 1816.

Mexía, Pedro. "Of Sumptuous Buildings." In *[Archaio-ploutos] containing, ten following bookes to the former Treasurie of auncient and moderne times*. London, 1619. STC 17936.5.

Milton, John. *John Milton*. Eds, Stephen Orgel and Jonathan Goldberg. Oxford: Oxford University Press, 1990.

Moore, Grace Edna. *The Middle English Verse Life of Edward the Confessor*. Philadelphia: University of Pennsylvania, 1942.

Moryson, Fynes. *An Itinerary*. 1617; Glasgow: James MacLehose and Sons, 1907. STC 18205.

Nichols, John, ed., *Progresses, Processions, and Festivities of James I*. 4 vols. London, 1828.

Ovid. *Metamorphoses*. Trans. Mary M. Innes. London and New York: Penguin, 1955.

Parker, Kenneth, ed., *Early Modern Tales of Orient: A Critical Anthology*. London and New York: Routledge, 1999.

Peacham, Henry. *The Art of Living in London*. London, 1642.

———. *Minerva Britanna, or a garden of theatrical devices*. London, 1612. STC 19511.

Pizarnik, Alejandra. "The Bloody Countess." In *Other Fires: Short Fiction by Latin American Women*. Ed. Alberto Manguel. New York: Clarkson N. Potter & Crown Publishers, 1986. 70–87.

Platter, Thomas. *Thomas Platter's Travels in England 1599*. London: Jonathan Cape, 1937.

———, and Horatio Busino. *The Journals of Two Travellers in Elizabethan and Early Stuart England*. London: Caliban Books, 1995.

Pliny, the Elder. *Natural History: A Selection*. Trans. John F. Healy. Harmondsworth and New York: Penguin, 1991.

———. *The Historie of the World*. Trans. Philemon Holland. London, 1601. STC 20029.

Plutarch. *The Lives of the Noble Grecians and Romans*. Trans. Thomas North. 2 vols. 1579; New York: The Heritage Press, 1941.

———. *The philosophie, commonlie called, the morals*. Trans. Philemon Holland. London, 1603. STC 20063.

Poe, Edgar Allan. *The Complete Works of Edgar Allan Poe*. Ed. James A. Harrison. Vol. 12. New York: George D. Sproul, 1902.

Purchas, Samuel. *Hakluytus posthumus, or, Purchas his Pilgrimes: contayning a history of the world in sea voyages and lande travells by Englishmen and others*. 20 vols. Glasgow: J. MacLehose and Sons, 1905–1907.

Rankins, William. *A mirrour of monsters*. London, 1587. STC 20699.

São Bernardino, Frei Gaspar de. *Itinerário da India por Terra até este Reino de Portugal*. Lisbon, 1611.

Scappi, Bartolomeo. *Opera de Bartolomeo Scappi, cvoco secreto di Papa Pio V*. Venice, 1570.

Seneca. *Seneca His Tenne Tragedies*. Trans. Thomas Newton. London, 1581.

Serlio, Sebastian. *The First Booke of Architecture*. London, 1611. STC 22235.

———. *The Five Books of Architecture: An Unabridged Reprint of the English Edition of 1611*. New York: Dover Publications, 1982.

Shakespeare, William. *The Complete Pelican Shakespeare*. Eds, Stephen Orgel and A.R. Braunmuller. New York, Harmondsworth, & London: Penguin, 2002.

———. *The First Quarto of* Othello. Ed. Scott McMillin. Cambridge: Cambridge University Press, 2001.

———. *Hamlet*. Ed. Ann Thompson and Neil Taylor. *The Arden Shakespeare*. London: Cengage Learning, 2006.

———. *Hamlet*. Ed. George Hibbard. Oxford: Oxford University Press, 1987.

———. *Hamlet: The First Quarto of 1603*. Ed. Albert B. Weiner. Great Neck: Barron's Educational Series, 1962.

———. *King Henry VIII*. Arden Shakespeare. Ed. Gordon McMullan. London: Thomson Learning, 2000.

———. *King Lear*. Ed. Kenneth Muir. The Arden Shakespeare. New York: Random House, 1952.

———. *King Lear*. Ed. R.A. Foakes. The Arden Shakespeare. Third Series. London: Thomas Nelson and Sons, 1997.

———. *Macbeth*. Ed. Nicholas Brooke. Oxford: Oxford University Press, 1990.

———. *Macbeth*. Ed. Robert S. Miola. A Norton Critical Anthology. New York: W.W. Norton, 2004.

———. *Macbeth*. A New Variorum Edition of Shakespeare. Ed. Horace Howard Furness, Jr. New York: Dover Publications, 1963.

———. *Othello*. Ed. Edward Pechter. A Norton Critical Edition. New York and London: W.W. Norton, 2004.

———. *Othello*. Ed. E.A.J. Honigmann. *The Arden Shakespeare*. Third Edition. Walton-on-Thames: Thomas Nelson & Sons, 1996.

———. *Othello*. Ed. Russ McDonald. *The Pelican Shakespeare*. Eds, Stephen Orgel and A.R. Braunmuller. Harmondsworth, and New York: Penguin, 2002.

———. *Othello*. Ed. Michael Neill. *Oxford Shakespeare*. Oxford: Oxford University Press, 2006.

Sherley, Anthony. *A True Report of Sir Anthony Shierlies Iourney Ouerland to Venice fro[m] thence by Sea to Antioch, Aleppo, and Babilon, and soe to Casbine in Persia*. London, 1600. STC 22425.

Spenser, Edmund. *The Faerie Queene*. Ed. Thomas P. Roche. London: Penguin, 1987.

———. *A View of the State of Ireland*. Eds, Andrew Hadfield & Willy Maley. Oxford: Blackwell, 1997.

Taylor, John. *Travels through Stuart Britain: The Adventures of John Taylor, the Water Poet*. Ed. John Chandler. Stroud, Gloucestershire: Sutton Publishing, 1999.

Tomkis, Thomas. *Lingua: or The combat of the tongue, and the fiue senses for superiority*. London, 1607. STC 24104.

Troyes, Chrétien de. *The Complete Romances of Chrétien de Troyes*. Trans. David Staines. Bloomington: Indiana University Press, 1990.

Turberville, George. *Tragicall Tales*. London, 1587. STC 24330.

Webbe, George. *The Practice of Quietness*. London, 1617.

Weinberg, Bernard, ed. *Critical Prefaces of the French Renaissance*. Evanston: Northwestern University Press, 1950.

Weyden, Rogier van der. *Middelburg Altarpiece, Three Magi,* detail, c.1445–1448, oil on panel, Gemaldegalerie, Berlin. http://www.abcgallery.com/W/weyden/weyden25.html, August 16, 2005.

Wotton, Henry. *The Elements of Architecture*. London, 1624. Rpt. Charlottesville: University Press of Virginia, 1968.

Wright, Thomas. *The Passions of the Minde in General*. 1604; London, 1620.

Xenophon. "On Hunting." In *Xenophon in Seven Volumes*. Trans. Sir John Sandys. Rev. T.K. Hubbard. http://www.perseus.tufts.edu.

Secondary Sources

Aalst, V.D. van, and Krijna Nelly Ciggaar. *Byzantium and the Low Countries in the Tenth Century: Aspects of Art and History in the Ottonian Era*. Hernen: A.A. Brediusstichting, 1985.

Abate, Corinne S., ed. *Privacy, Domesticity, and Women in Early Modern England*. Aldershot and Burlington: Ashgate, 2003.

Abrams, M.H., and Stephen Greenblatt, eds. *The Norton Anthology of English Literature*. Seventh Edition. New York: W.W. Norton, 2000.

Adelman, Janet. "'Born of Woman': Fantasies of Maternal Power in *Macbeth*." In Garber, ed. *Cannibals, Witches, and Divorce*. 90–121

———. *Suffocating Mothers: Fantasies of Maternal Origin in Shakespeare's Plays*. New York and London: Routledge, 1991.

Ågren, Maria, and Amy Louise Erickson, eds. *The Marital Economy in Scandinavia and Britain 1400–1900*. Burlington: Ashgate, 2005.

Aitchison, Nick. *Macbeth: Man and Myth*. Stroud: Sutton, 2000.

Ajmar-Wollheim, Marta, and Flora Dennis, eds. *At Home in Renaissance Italy*. London: Victoria and Albert Museum, 2006.

Akbari, Susanne Conklin. *Seeing through the Veil: Optical Theory and Medieval Allegory*. Toronto, Buffalo, and London: University of Toronto Press, 2004.

Araújo, Maria Marta Lobo de. "The Archbishops of Braga and their Assistance to the Poor in Early Modern Portugal." *Mediterranean Studies: Journal of the Mediterranean Studies Association* 17 (2008): 97–117.

Ariès, Philip, and Georges Duby, eds. *A History of Private Life: Revelations of the Medieval World*. Trans. Arthur Goldhammer. Cambridge and London: Belknap Press of Harvard University Press, 1988.

Arnheim, Rudolf. *The Power of the Center: A Study of Composition in the Visual Arts*. Revised edition. Berkeley: University of California Press, 1988.

Art Gallery of South Wales, and National Gallery of Victoria. *Caravaggio & His World: Darkness & Light*. Sidney, Australia: Art Gallery of New South Wales; Melbourne: National Gallery of Victoria, 2003.

Assmann, Aleida. "Spirits, Ghosts, Demons in Shakespeare and Milton." In Höfele and Koppenfels, eds. *Renaissance Go-Betweens*. 200–213.

Babcock, Barbara A., ed. *The Reversible World: Symbolic Inversion in Art and Society*. Ithaca: Cornell University Press, 1991.

Bachelard, Gaston. *Poetics of Space*. Trans. Maria Jolas. Boston: Beacon Press, 1994.

Barker, Deborah and Ivo Kamps, eds. *Shakespeare and Gender: A History*. London and New York: Verso, 1995.

Barrett, L.L. "The Inner Recess of the Public Stage in Renaissance Spain." *Research Opportunities in Renaissance Drama* 10 (1967): 25–48.

Barrow, G.W.S. *Scotland and Its Neighbours in the Middle Ages*. New York: Continuum, 1992.

Barry, Boubacar. *Senegambia and the Atlantic Slave Trade*. Cambridge: Cambridge University Press, 1998.

Bartels, Emily C. "Shakespeare's 'Other' Worlds: The Critical Trek." *Literature Compass* 5/6 (2008): 1111–38.

———. *Speaking of the Moor: From Alcazar to Othello*. Philadelphia: University of Pennsylvania Press, 2008.

Basterra, Gabriela. *Seductions of Fate: Tragic Subjectivity, Ethics, Politics*. Houndsmill: Palgrave Macmillan, 2004.

Battistini, Matilde. *Symbols and Allegories in Art*. Trans. Stephen Sartarelli. Los Angeles: J. Paul Getty Museum, 2002.

Bayley, John. *Shakespeare and Tragedy*. London: Routledge & Kegan Paul, 1981.

Bayliss, Robert. *The Discourse of Courtly Love in Seventeenth-Century Spanish Theater*. Lewisburg: Bucknell University Press, 2008.

Beckerman, Bernard. *Shakespeare at the Globe 1599–1609*. New York: Macmillan, 1962.

Beckwith, John. *Early Medieval Art*. New York: Praeger, 1964.

Beer, E.S. de. "The Early History of London Street-Lighting." *History* 25.100 (1941): 311–24.

Belsey, Catherine. *Shakespeare and the Loss of Eden: The Construction of Family Values in Early Modern Culture*. New Brunswick: Rutgers University Press, 2000.

Berger, Thomas L. "The Petrarchan Fortress of *The Changeling*." *Renaissance Papers* (1969): 37–46.

———, William C. Bradford, and Sidney L. Sondergard. *An Index of Characters in Early Modern English Drama: Printed Plays, 1500–1660*. Cambridge; New York: Cambridge University Press, 1998.

Bergeron, David Moore. *English Civic Pageantry 1558–1642*. Revised edition. Tempe: Arizona State University Medieval and Renaissance Center, 2003.

———. "King James's Civic Pageant and Parliamentary Speech in March 1604." *Albion* 34 (2002): 213–31.

———. "*King Lear* and John Hall's Casebook." *Shakespeare Quarterly* 23 (1972): 206–7.

———. "Representation in Renaissance English Civic Pageants." *Theatre Journal* 40 (1988): 319–31.

———. Review of *Charismatic Authority in Early Modern English Tragedy* by Raphael Falco. *Shakespeare Quarterly* 53 (2002): 579–81.

———. "Symbolic Landscape in English Civic Pageantry." *Renaissance Quarterly* 22.1 (1969): 32–7.

Bergman, Gösta M. *Lighting in the Theatre*. Stockholm: Almqvist & Wiksell International, 1977.

Berry, Edward. "Othello's Alienation." *SEL* 30.2 (1990): 315–33.

Berry, Ralph. *Shakespeare and Social Class*. Atlantic Highlands: Humanities Press International, 1988.

Bevington, David M. *Action Is Eloquence: Shakespeare's Language of Gestures*. Cambridge: Harvard University Press, 1984.

Black, James. "Hamlet Hears Marlowe; Shakespeare Reads Virgil." *Renaissance and Reformation* 18.4 (1994): 17–28.

Blackmore, Josiah. *Moorings: Portuguese Expansion and the Writing of Africa*. Minneapolis: University of Minnesota Press, 2009.

Bogin, Meg. *The Women Troubadours*. New York: Paddington Press, 1976; rpt. New York: Norton, 1980.

Booth, Stephen. *King Lear, Macbeth, Indefinition and Tragedy*. New Haven: Yale University Press, 1983.

Borri, Francesco. "'Neighbors and Relatives': The Plea of Rižana as a Source for Northern Adriatic Elites." *Mediterranean Studies* 17 (2008): 1–26.

Bovill, E.W. *The Golden Trade of the Moors*. Oxford, and New York: Oxford University Press, 1958.

Bradbrook, Muriel C. *Themes and Conventions of Elizabethan Tragedies*. Cambridge: Cambridge University Press, 1964.

Bradley, A.C. *Shakespearean Tragedy*. 1904; Cleveland and New York: Meridian Books, 1963.

Brandt, Michael, and Arne Eggebrecht. *Bernward von Hildesheim und das Zeitalter der Ottonen: Katalog der Ausstellung, Hildesheim 1993*. Hildesheim: Bernward Verlag; Mainz am Rhein: von Zabern, 1993.

Braudel, Ferdinand. *Capitalism and Material Life 1400–1800*. Trans. Miriam Kochan. New York: Harper & Row, 1973.

Brook, Peter. *The Empty Space*. New York: Simon & Schuster, 1968.

———. *The Open Door: Thoughts on Acting and Theatre*. New York: Theatre Communications Group, 1995.

Brotton, Jerry. “Tragedy and Geography.” Dutton and Howard, *Companion*. Vol. 1. 219–40.

Broun, Dauvit. “Macbeth (*d.* 1057).” Oxford Dictionary of National Biography. Eds, H.C.G. Matthew and Brian Harrison. Oxford: OUP, 2004. April 29, 2009. <http://www.oxforddnb.com.www2.lib.ku.edu:2048/view/article/17356>.

Brown, John Russell, ed. *Focus on Macbeth*. London and Boston: Routledge, 1982.

Brown, Patricia Fortini. *Private Lives in Renaissance Venice: Art, Architecture, and The Family*. New Haven and London: Yale University Press, 2004.

Burlinson, Christopher. *Allegory, Space and The Material World in the Writings of Edmund Spenser.* Woodbridge; New York: Boydell & Brewer, 2006.

Bushnell, Rebecca. *Tragedies of Tyrants: Political Thought and Theater in the English Renaissance*. Ithaca: Cornell University Press, 1990.

Butterworth, Philip. *Magic on the Early English Stage*. Cambridge: Cambridge University Press, 2005.

———. *Theatre of Fire: Special Effects in Early English and Scottish Theatre*. London: The Society for Theatre Research, 1998.

Cahill, Patricia A. *Unto the Breach: Martial Formations, Historical Drama, and the Early Modern Stage*. Oxford: Oxford University Press, 2009.

Callaghan, Dympna. *Shakespeare Without Women: Representing Gender and Race on the Renaissance Stage*. London and New York: Routledge, 2000.

Campbell, Erin, ed. *Growing Old in Early Modern Europe: Cultural Representations*. Aldershot, and Burlington: Ashgate, 2006.

Campbell, Lily B. *Scenes and Machines on the English Stage during the Renaissance: A Classical Revival*. Cambridge: Cambridge University Press, 1923.

———. *Shakespeare's Tragic Heroes: Slaves of Passion*. New York: Barnes & Noble, 1930.

Carpenter, Thomas H., and Christopher A. Faraone, eds. *Masks of Dionysus*. Ithaca: Cornell University Press, 1993.

Carroll, William C. *Fat King, Lean Beggar: Representations of Poverty in the Age of Shakespeare*. Ithaca: Cornell University Press, 1996.

Carson, Neil. "Shakespeare and the Dramatic Image." In *Mirror up to Shakespeare: Essays in Honour of G.R. Hibbard.* Ed. J.C. Gray. Toronto: University of Toronto Press, 1984. 34–43.

Cartelli, Thomas. "Banquo's Ghost: The Shared Vision." *Theatre Journal* 5.3 (1983): 389–405.

Casey, Edward S. *The Fate of Place: A Philosophical History.* Berkeley, Los Angeles and London: University of California Press, 1998.

———. *Imagining: A Phenomenological Study.* Bloomington and London: Indiana University Press, 1976.

Caspall, John. *Fire & Light in the Home Pre-1820.* Woodbridge: Antique Collectors' Club, 1987.

Certeau, Michel de. "Spatial Stories." In *The Practice of Everyday Life.* Vol. 2. Eds, Michel de Certeau, Luce Giard, and Pierre Mayol. Trans. Steven Rendall. Berkeley: University of California Press, 1984. 115–30.

———. *The Writing of History.* Trans. Tom Conley. New York: Columbia University Press, 1988.

Chambers, E.K. *The Elizabethan Stage.* 4 vols. Oxford: Clarendon Press, 1951.

Chase, Karen and Michael Levenson. *Spectacle of Intimacy: A Public Life for the Victorian Family.* Princeton: Princeton University Press, 2000.

Chojnacki, Stanley. "Social Identity in Renaissance Venice: The Second *Serrata.*" *Renaissance Studies* 8.4 (1994): 341–58.

Christianson, John Robert. *On Tycho's Island: Tycho Brahe and His Assistants, 1570–1601.* Cambridge: Cambridge University Press, 2000.

Cieraad, Irene, ed. *At Home: An Anthropology of Domestic Space.* Syracuse: Syracuse University Press, 1999.

Clark, Donald Lemen. "Rhetoric and English Renaissance Literature." *Shakespeare Quarterly* 2.3 (1951): 195–204.

Clifford, James. *The Predicament of Culture: Twentieth-Century Ethnography, Literature, and Art.* Cambridge: Harvard University Press, 1988.

———. "Traveling Cultures." *Routes: Travel and Translation in the Late Twentieth Century.* Cambridge: Harvard University Press, 1997. 17–46.

Cohen, William A. *Embodied: Victorian Literature and the Senses.* Minneapolis: University of Minnesota Press, 2009.

Collington, Philip D. "Othello the Liar." In *The Mysterious and the Foreign in Early Modern England.* Eds, Helen Ostovich, Mary V. Silcox, and Graham Roebuck. Newark: University of Delaware Press, 2008. 187–205.

———. "Sans Wife: Sexual Anxiety and the Old Man in Shakespeare." In *Growing Old in Early Modern Europe: Cultural Representations.* Ed. Erin Campbell. Aldershot and Burlington: Ashgate, 2006. 185–207.

Comensoli, Viviana. *'Household Business': Domestic Plays of Early Modern England.* Toronto: University of Toronto Press, 1999.

Condee, William Faricy. *Theatrical Space: A Guide for Directors and Designers.* Lanham: Scarecrow, 1995.

Cook, Katherine. *A.C. Bradley and His Influence in Twentieth-Century Criticism.* Oxford: Clarendon Press, 1972.

Cook, Olive. *The English House Through Seven Centuries*. New York: Overlook Press, 1983.

Crane, Mary Thomas. *Framing Authority: Sayings, Self, and Society in Sixteenth-Century England*. Princeton, NJ: Princeton University Press, 1993.

———. "Illicit Privacy and Outdoor Spaces in Early Modern England." *Journal for Early Modern Cultural Studies* 9.1 (2009): 4–22.

———. "Marvell's Amazing Garden." In Floyd-Wilson and Sullivan, Jr, eds. *Environment and Embodiment*, 35–54.

———. "No Space Like Home: *The Comedy of Errors*." In *Shakespeare's Brain: Reading with Cognitive Theory*. Princeton: Princeton University Press, 2001. 36–66.

———. "'Players in your huswifery, and huswives in your beds': Conflicting Identities of Early Modern Women." In *Maternal Measures: Figuring Caregiving in the Early Modern Period.* Eds, Naomi J. Miller and Naomi Yavneh. Burlington: Ashgate, 2000. 212–17.

Csikszentmihalyi, Mihaly, and Eugene Rochberg-Halton. *The Meaning of Things: Domestic Symbols and the Self.* Cambridge: Cambridge University Press, 1981. Esp. Chapter 5, "The Home as Symbolic Environment." 121–45.

Daileader, Celia. *Eroticism on the Renaissance Stage: Transcendence, Desire, and the Limits of the Visible*. Cambridge: Cambridge University Press, 1998.

Debrunner, Hans Werner. *Presence and Prestige: Africans in Europe. A History of Africans in Europe before 1918.* Basel: Basler Afrika Bibliographien, 1979.

Deleuze, Gilles. *The Fold: Leibniz and the Baroque*. Trans. Tom Conley. Minneapolis: University of Minnesota Press, 1993.

Dessen, Alan C. *Elizabethan Stage Conventions and Modern Interpreters*. Cambridge: Cambridge University Press, 1984.

———. *Recovering Shakespeare's Theatrical Vocabulary*. Cambridge: Cambridge University Press, 1995.

Di Biase, Carmine G., ed. *Travel and Translation in the Early Modern Period.* Amsterdam and New York: Editions Rodopi B.V., 2006.

Dillon, Janette. *The Cambridge Introduction to Early English Theatre*. Cambridge: Cambridge University Press, 2006.

———. *Theatre, Court and City, 1595–1610*. Cambridge: Cambridge University Press, 2000.

Doebler, John. *Shakespeare's Speaking Pictures: Studies in Iconic Imagery*. Albuquerque: University of New Mexico Press, 1974.

Dolan, Frances. *Dangerous Familiars: Representation of Domestic Crime in England, 1550–1700*. Ithaca: Cornell University Press, 1994.

Donaldson, Ian. *Jonson's Magic Houses: Essays in Interpretation*. Oxford: Clarendon, 1997.

Drakakis, John. "Shakespeare and Venice," in Michele Marrapodi, ed. *Italian Culture*, 169–86.

———, and Dale Townshend, ed. *Gothic Shakespeares*. Oxford: Routledge, 2008.

Dreher, Diane Elizabeth. *Domination & Defiance: Fathers and Daughters in Shakespeare*. Lexington: University Press of Kentucky, 1986.

Dubrow, Heather. *Shakespeare and Domestic Loss: Forms of Deprivation, Mourning, and Recuperation.* Cambridge: Cambridge University Press, 1999.

Duby, Georges. *France in the Middle Ages*. 1987; Oxford: Blackwell, 1991.

Dutton, Richard and Jean E. Howard. *A Companion to Shakespeare's Works: The Tragedies*. Vol. 1. Oxford: Blackwell, 2003.

Dyson, J.P. "The Structural Function of the Banquet Scene in *Macbeth*." *Shakespeare Quarterly* 14.4 (1963): 369–78.

Earle, T.F., and K.J.P. Lowe, eds, *Black Africans in Renaissance Europe*. Cambridge: Cambridge University Press, 2005.

Eisenman, Peter. "Blue-Line Text + Outline from the 'Edge of Between'." *Architectural Design* 58.7–8 (1988): 6–9.

Erickson, Amy Louise. *Women and Property in Early Modern England.* London: Routledge, 1993.

Everleigh, David J. *Candle Lighting*. Aylesbury: Shire Publications, 1985.

Faegre, Torvald. *Tents: Architecture of the Nomads*. New York: Anchor Books, 1979.

Fairchild, Arthur H.R. *Shakespeare and the Arts of Design*. University of Missouri Studies. Columbia, MO: University of Missouri, 1937.

Falco, Raphael. *Charismatic Authority in Early Modern English Tragedy*. Baltimore and London: The Johns Hopkins University Press, 2000.

Fletcher, Richard. *Bloodfeud: Murder and Revenge in Anglo-Saxon England.* London: Penguin, 2002.

Floyd-Wilson, Mary. "English Epicures and Scottish Witches," *Shakespeare Quarterly* 52.3 (2006): 131–61.

———. *English Ethnicity and Race in Early Modern Drama*. Cambridge: Cambridge University Press, 2003.

———, and Garrett A. Sullivan, eds. *Environment and Embodiment in Early Modern England.* Basingstoke: Palgrave Macmillan, 2007.

Flynn, Maureen. "The Spectacles of Suffering in Spanish Streets." In *City and Spectacle in Medieval Europe*. Eds, Barbara A. Hanawalt and Kathryn L. Reyerson. Minneapolis and London: University of Minnesota Press, 1994. 154–63.

Foakes, R.A. *Shakespeare and Violence.* Cambridge: Cambridge University Press, 2003.

Foucault, Michel. "Of Other Spaces." *Diacritics* 16.1 (1986): 22–7.

———. *The Order of Things: An Archaeology of the Human Sciences*. New York: Vintage Books, 1971.

Fraprie, Frank Roy. *The Castles and Keeps of Scotland.* Boston: L.C. Page, 1907.

Friedman, Alice T. *House and Household in Elizabethan England: Wollaton Hall and the Willoughby Family*. Chicago: University of Chicago Press, 1989.

Friedman, John Block. *The Monstrous Races in Medieval Art and Thought.* Cambridge: Harvard University Press, 1981.

Friedman, Susan Stanford. "Spatial Poetics and Arundhati Roy's *The God of Small Things*." In *A Companion to Narrative Theory*. Eds, James Phelan and Peter J. Rabinowitz. Malden: Blackwell, 2005. 192–205.

———. "Spatialization: A Strategy for Reading Narrative." *Narrative* 1.1. (1993): 12–23.

Frye, Northrop. *Anatomy of Criticism*. Princeton: Princeton University Press, 1957.

Fumerton, Patricia, and Simon Hunt, eds. *Renaissance Culture and the Everyday*. Philadelphia: University of Pennsylvania Press, 1999.

Garber, Marjorie, ed. *Cannibals, Witches, and Divorce: Estranging the Renaissance*. Baltimore: John Hopkins University Press, 1987.

García Santo-Tomás, Enrique. "Fortunes of the *Occhiali Politici* in Early Modern Spain: Optics, Vision, Points of View." *PMLA* 124.1 (2009): 59–75.

Garner, Stanton B. *Bodied Spaces: Phenomenology in Contemporary Performance*. Ithaca: Cornell University Press, 1994.

Geertz, Clifford. *Local Knowledge: Further Essays in Interpretive Anthropology*. New York: Basic Books, 1983.

Geremek, Bronislaw. *Poverty: A History*. Trans. Agnieszka Kolakowska. Oxford and Malden, MA: Blackwell, 1997.

Giglierano, Geoffrey J., and Deborah A. Overmyer. *The Bicentennial Guide to Greater Cincinnati: A Portrait of Two Hundred Years*. Cincinnati: Cincinnati Historical Society, 1988.

Gillies, John. "The Scene of Cartography in *King Lear*." In *Literature, Mapping, and the Politics of Space in Early Modern Britain*. Eds, Andrew Gordon and Bernhard Klein. Cambridge: Cambridge University Press, 2001. 109–37.

———. *Shakespeare and the Geography of Difference*. Cambridge: Cambridge University Press, 1994.

Goldman, Michael. "*Hamlet*: Entering the Text." *Theatre Journal* 44.3. (1992): 449–60.

Gordon, Andrew, and Bernhard Klein, eds. *Literature, Mapping, and the Politics of Space in Early Modern Britain*. Cambridge: Cambridge University Press, 2001.

Gorse, George L. "Christopher Columbus and Andrea Doria: The Two Worlds of Renaissance Genoa." *Mediterranean Studies* 16 (2007): 120–42.

Gowing, Laura. *Domestic Dangers: Women, Words, and Sex in Early Modern London*. Oxford: Clarendon Press, 1996.

Granville-Barker, Harley. "A Note upon Chapters XX and XXI of *The Elizabethan Stage*." *Review of English Studies* 1.1 (1925): 60–71.

Graves, R.B. *Lighting the Shakespearean Stage, 1567–1642*. Carbondale: Southern Illinois University Press, 1999.

Gray, J.C., ed., *Mirror up to Shakespeare: Essays in Honour of G.R. Hibbard*. Toronto: University of Toronto Press, 1984.

Grazia, Margreta de. *Shakespeare Verbatim: The Reproduction of Authenticity and the 1790 Apparatus*. Oxford: Clarendon Press, 1991.

Greenblatt, Stephen. *Hamlet in Purgatory*. Princeton: Princeton University Press, 2001.

———. *Renaissance Self-Fashioning: From More to Shakespeare*. Chicago: University of Chicago Press, 1980.

———. "Shakespeare Bewitched." In *New Historical Literary Study: Essays on Reproducing Texts, Representing History*. Eds, Jeffrey N. Cox and Larry J. Reyonolds. Princeton: Princeton University Press 1993. 108–35.

Greene, Gayle. "'This That You Call Love': Sexual and Social Tragedy in *Othello*." In Barker and Kamps, 47–62.

Gurr, Andrew. *The Shakespearean Stage 1574–1642*. Third Edition. Cambridge: Cambridge University Press, 1992.

———, and Mariko Ichikawa. *Staging in Shakespeare's Theatres*. Oxford: Oxford University Press, 2000.

Hall, Kim F. *Things of Darkness: Economies of Race and Gender in Early Modern England*. Ithaca: Cornell University Press, 1995.

Hallett, Charles A., and Elaine S. Hallett. *The Revenger's Madness: A Study of Revenge Tragedy Motifs*. Lincoln: University of Nebraska Press, 1980.

Hankins, John Erskine. *Source and Meaning in Spenser's Allegory: A Study of "The Faerie Queene"*. Oxford: Clarendon, 1971.

Harbage, Alfred, ed. *Shakespeare: The Tragedies: A Collection of Critical Essays*. Englewood Cliff: Prentice-Hall, 1964.

Harris, Jonathan Gil, and Natasha Korda, eds. *Staged Properties in Early Modern English Drama*. Cambridge: Cambridge University Press, 2002.

Hendricks, Margo, and Patricia Parker, eds. *Women, 'Race', and Writing in the Early Modern Period*. London and New York: Routledge, 1994.

Heninger, Jr, S.K. *A Handbook of Renaissance Meteorology*. Durham: Duke University Press, 1960; rpt. New York: Greenwood Press, 1968.

Hibbard, Howard. *Caravaggio*. New York: Harper & Row, 1983.

Hodgen, Margaret T. *Early Anthropology in the Sixteenth and Seventeenth Centuries*. Philadelphia: University of Pennsylvania Press, 1964.

Höfele, Andreas, and Werner von Koppenfels, eds. *Renaissance Go-Betweens: Cultural Exchange in Early Modern Europe*. Berlin and New York: Walter de Gruyter, 2005.

Holian, Heather L. Sale. "Family Jewels: The Gendered Marking of Medici Women in Court Portraits of the Late Renaissance." *Mediterranean Studies* 17 (2008): 148–82.

Homan, Sidney. *Shakespeare's Theater of Presence*. Lewisburg: Bucknell University Press; London and New York: Associated University Presses, 1986.

Hopkins, Lisa. *Shakespeare on the Edge: Border-crossing in the Tragedies and the Henriad*. Aldershot and Burlington: Ashgate, 2005.

Houaiss, Antônio, Mauro de Salles Villar, and Francisco Manoel de Mello Franco. *Dicionário Houaiss da Língua Portuguesa*. Rio de Janeiro: Editora Objetiva Ltda., 2001.

Howard, Deborah. "Venice and Islam in the Middle Ages: Some Observations on the Question of Architectural Influence." *Architectural History* 34 (1991): 59–74.

Howard, Jean E. "Shakespeare, Geography, and the Work of Genre on the Early Modern Stage." *Modern Language Quarterly* 64.3 (2003): 299–322.

Humfrey, Peter, ed. *Artistic Centers of the Italian Renaissance: Venice and the Veneto*. Cambridge: Cambridge University Press, 2007.

Hunter, G.K. "Flatcaps and Bluecoats: Visual Signals on the Elizabethan Stage." *Essays and Studies* 33 (1980): 16–47.

Ide, Richard S. "The Theatre of the Mind: An Essay on *Macbeth*." *ELH* 42.3 (1975): 338–61.

Jagodzinski, Cecile M. *Privacy and Print: Reading and Writing in Seventeenth-Century England*. Charlottesville and London: University Press of Virginia, 1999.

Jewers, Caroline. "Reading and Righting: Issues of Value and Gender in Early Women Poets". *Exemplaria: A Journal of Theory in Medieval and Renaissance Studies* 10.1 (1998): 97–121.

Johnson, Douglas L. *The Nature of Nomadism: A Comparative Study of Pastoral Migrations in Southwestern Asia and Northern Africa*. Chicago: Department of Geology Research Papers, 1969.

Jones, Emrys. *Scenic Form in Shakespeare*. Oxford: Clarendon Press, 1971.

Jones, Ernest. *Hamlet and Oedipus*. New York: W.W. Norton, 1976.

Jones, Paul V.B. *The Household of a Tudor Nobleman*. Urbana: University of Illinois Press, 1917.

Jorgensen, Paul A. *Our Naked Frailties: Sensational Art and Meaning in Macbeth*. Berkeley: University of California Press, 1971.

Joseph, Bertram. *Conscience and the King*. London: Chatto & Windus, 1953.

Kahn, Coppélia. *Man's Estate: Masculine Identity in Shakespeare*. Berkeley: University of California Press, 1981.

Kantor, J.R. *Tragedy and the Event Continuum*. Chicago: Principia Press, 1983.

Kernodle, George R. *From Art to Theatre: Form and Convention in the Renaissance*. Chicago: University of Chicago Press, 1944.

———. *The Theater in History*. Fayetteville: University of Arkansas Press, 1989.

Kiefer, Frederick. *Shakespeare's Visual Theatre: Staging the Personified Characters*. Cambridge: Cambridge University Press, 2003.

Kimbrough, Robert. "Macbeth: The Prisoner of Gender." *Shakespeare Studies* 16 (1983): 175–90.

King, Steven. "Chance Encounters? Paths to Household Formation in Early Modern England". *International Review of Social History* 44:1 (1999): 23–46.

Kinney, Arthur F. *Lies like Truth: Shakespeare, "Macbeth," and the Cultural Moment*. Detroit: Wayne State University Press, 2001.

———. *Shakespeare and Cognition: Aristotle Legacy and Shakespearean Drama*. New York and London: Routledge, 2006.

———. *Webs: Networks of Meaning in Renaissance Drama*. New York and London: Routledge, 2004.

Kipling, Gordon. *Enter the King: Theatre, Liturgy, and Ritual in the Medieval Civic Triumph*. Oxford: Clarendon, 1998.

Knapp, Ethan. *The Bureaucratic Muse: Thomas Hoccleve and the Literature of Late Medieval England*. University Park: Pennsylvania State University, 2001.

Knight, G. Wilson. *The Wheel of Fire*. 1930; rpt. Cleveland and New York: Meridian Books, 1964.

Korda, Natasha. *Shakespeare's Domestic Economies*. Philadelphia: University of Pennsylvania Press, 2002.

Kott, Jan. *Shakespeare Our Contemporary*. New York: Doubleday, 1966.

Kristeva, Julia. *Powers of Horror: An Essay on Abjection*. Trans. Leon S. Roudiez. New York: Columbia University Press, 1982.

Kronenfeld, Judy. "'So Distribution Should Undo Excess, and Each Man Have Enough': Shakespeare's King Lear-Anabaptist Egalitarianism, Anglican Charity, Both, Neither?" *ELH* 59.4 (1992): 755–84.

Lancashire, Anne. "The Emblematic Castle in Shakespeare and Middleton." In J.C. Gray, ed. *Mirror up to Shakespeare*. 223–41.

Lanzi, Abate Luigi. *The History of Painting in Italy*. Vol. 2. London: George Bell, 1887.

Lawrence, Roderick J. "Deciphering Home: An Integrative Historical Perspective." In *The Home: Words, Interpretations, Meanings and Environments*. Ed. David N. Benjamin, David Stea, and Eje Arén. Aldershot; Brookfield, VT: Avebury, 1995.

Levenson, J.C., ed., *Discussions of Hamlet*. Boston: D.C. Heath and Company, 1960.

Levey, Martin. "Medieval Arabic Toxicology: The Book on Poisons of ibn Wahshīya and Its Relation to Early Indian and Greek Texts." *Transactions of the American Philosophical Society*, New Series 56.7 (1966): 1–130.

Lévi-Strauss, Claude. *Tristes Tropiques*. Trans. John and Doreen Weightman. Harmondsworth; New York: Penguin, 1992.

Levy, Eric P. *Hamlet and the Rethinking of Man*. Madison: Farleigh Dickinson University Press, 2008.

Lewis, C.S. "Death in *Hamlet*." In Harbage, 71–4.

Loomba, Ania. *Gender, Race, Renaissance Drama*. Manchester: Manchester University Press, 1989.

———. *Shakespeare, Race, and Colonialism*. Oxford: Oxford University Press, 2002.

Loomis, Edward Alleyn. "Master of the Tiger." *Shakespeare Quarterly* 7.4 (1956):457.

Loomis, Roger Sherman. *The Grail: From Celtic Myth to Christian Symbol*. Cardiff: University of Wales Press; New York: Columbia University Press, 1963.

———. *The Spoils of Annwn: An Early Arthurian Poem*." *PMLA* 56.4 (1941): 893–4.

Lybyer, A.H. "The Ottoman Turks and the Routes of Oriental Trade." *The English Historical Review* 30.120 (1915): 577–88.

McAlindon, Tom. "Tragedy, *King Lear*, and the Politics of the Heart." *Shakespeare Survey* 44 (1992): 85–90.

McBride, Kari Boyd. *Domestic Arrangements in Early Modern England*. Pittsburgh: Duquesne University Press, 2002.

McGee, Arthur R. "*Macbeth* and the Furies." *Shakespeare Survey* 19 (1986): 55–67.

McJannet, Linda. *The Voice of Elizabethan Stage Directions: The Evolution of a Theatrical Code*. Newark: University of Delaware Press; London: Associated University Presses, 1999.

Mack, Maynard. "The World of *Hamlet*." In Harbage, 44–60.

Mackintosh, Iain. *Architecture, Actor and Audience*. London and New York: Routledge, 1993.

Mackenzie, James Dixon, Sir. *The Castles of England: Their Story and Structure*. 2 vols. London: W. Heinemann, 1897.

Maclean, Ian. "Foucault's Renaissance Episteme: An Aristotelian Counterblast." *Journal of the History of Ideas* 59.1 (1998): 149–66.

McNeill, William H. *Venice: The Hinge of Europe, 1081–1797*. Chicago: University of Chicago Press, 1974.

MacQuoid, Percy. "The Home: Furniture, Food and Drink, Christenings, Weddings, Funerals." In *Shakespeare's England: An Account of the Life & Manners of His Age*. Oxford: Clarendon Press, 1916. II: 119–52.

Malinowski, Bronislaw. *The Sexual Life of Savages*. 1929; Boston: Beacon Press, 1987.

Marrapodi, Michele, ed. *Italian Culture in the Drama of Shakespeare & His Contemporaries*. Aldershot and Burlington: Ashgate, 2007.

Marshall, Cynthia. *The Shattering of the Self: Violence, Subjectivity, and Early Modern Texts*. Baltimore and London: Johns Hopkins University Press, 2002.

Mason, H.A. *The Tragic Plane*. Oxford: Clarendon Press, 1985.

Maus, Katherine Eisaman. *Inwardness and the Theater in the English Renaissance*. Chicago: University of Chicago Press, 1995.

Meek, Richard. *Narrating the Visual in Shakespeare*. Farnham and Burlington: Ashgate, 2009.

Menzer, Paul. "Dislocating Shakespeare: Scene Locators and the Place of the Page." *Shakespeare Bulletin* 24.2 (2006): 1–19.

Merleau–Ponty, Maurice. *The Primacy of Perception*. Ed. James M. Edie. Chicago: Northwestern University Press, 1964.

———. *The Visible and the Invisible*. Ed. Claude Leffort. Trans. Alphonso Lingis. Evanston: Northwestern University Press, 1968.

Mertes, Kate. *English Noble Household, 1250–1600: Good Governance and Politic Rule*. Oxford: Blackwell, 1988.

Miller, Naomi J., and Naomi Yavneh, eds, *Maternal Measures: Figuring Caregiving in the Early Modern Period*. Burlington: Ashgate, 2000.

Miola, Robert S. "Othello *Furens*." *Shakespeare Quarterly* 41.1 (1990): 49–64.

———. *Shakespeare and Classical Tragedy: The Influence of Seneca*. Oxford: Clarendon Press, 1992.

Mowat, Barbara. "Nicholas Rowe and the Twentieth-Century Shakespeare Text." In *Shakespeare and the Cultural Traditions*. Eds, Tetsuo Kishi, Roger Pringle, and Stanley Wells. Newark: University of Delaware Press; London: Associated University Presses, 1991. 314–22.

Murphy, John L. *Darkness and Devils: Exorcism and King Lear.* Athens: Ohio University Press, 1984.

Mylonas, George E. *Eleusis and the Eleusinian Mysteries*. Princeton, NJ: Princeton University Press, 1961.

Neely, Carol Thomas. "Circumscriptions and Unhousedness: *Othello* in the Borderlands." In *Shakespeare and Gender: A History*. Eds, Deborah Barker and Ivo Kamps. London and New York: Verso, 1995. 302–15.

Neill, Michael. "Servant Obedience and Master Sins: Shakespeare and the Bonds of Service." In *Putting History to the Question: Power, Politics, and Society in English Renaissance Drama*. New York: Columbia University Press, 2000. 13–48.

———. "Unproper Beds: Race, Adultery and the Hideous in *Othello*." In *Shakespeare's Middle Tragedies: A Collection of Essays*. Ed. David Young. Englewood Cliffs: Prentice Hall, 1993. 117–45.

Newman, J. "Inigo Jones and the Politics of Architecture." In *Culture and Politics in Early Stuart England*. Eds, Kevin Sharpe, and Peter Lake. Stanford: Stanford University Press, 1993. 229–55.

Norberg-Schulz, Christian. *Meaning in Western Architecture*. New York: Rizzoli, 1980.

Oliver, Paul, eds, *Shelter in Africa*. New York: Praeger Publishers, 1971.

O'Neill, Stephen. *Staging Ireland: Representations in Shakespeare and Renaissance Drama*. Dublin: Four Courts Press, 2007.

Onions, C.T., and Robert D. Eagleson. *A Shakespeare Glossary*. Oxford: Clarendon Press, 1986.

Orgel, Stephen. "Shakespeare Imagines a Theater." *Poetics Today* 5.3 (1984): 549–61.

Orgel, Stephen, and Roy Strong. *Inigo Jones: The Theater of the Stuart Court*. 2 vols. London: Southeby Parke Bernet; Berkeley: University of California Press, 1973.

Orlin, Lena Cowen, ed., *Center or Margin: Revisions of the English Renaissance in Honor of Leeds Barroll*. Selingsgrove: Susquehanna University Press, 2006.

———, ed., *Othello: Contemporary Critical Essays*. Houndsmills and New York: Palgrave, 2004.

———, ed., *Elizabethan Households: An Anthology*. Washington: Folger Shakespeare Library, 1995.

———. "Gertrude's Closet." *Shakespeare Jahrbuch* 135 (1998): 44–67.

———. *Locating Privacy in Tudor London*. Oxford: Oxford University Press, 2007.

———. "Man's House as His Castle in *Arden of Feversham*." *Medieval and Renaissance Drama in England* 2 (1985): 57–89.

———, ed. *Material London, ca. 1600*. Philadelphia: University of Pennsylvania Press, 2000.

———. *Private Matters and Public Cultures in Post-Reformation England*. Ithaca: Cornell University Press, 1994.

———. "Spaces of Treason in Tudor England." In Orlin, ed. *Center or Margin*. 158–95.

———, and Miranda Johnson-Haddad, ed. *Staging Shakespeare: Essays in Honor of Alan C. Dessen*. Newark: University of Delaware Press, 2007.

Panofsky, Erwin. *Meaning in the Visual Arts: Papers in and on Art History*. Garden City: Doubleday, 1955.

Park, David. *The Fire within the Eye: A Historical Essay on the Nature and Meaning of Light*. Princeton: Princeton University Press, 1997.

Parker, Patricia. "Fantasies of 'Race' and 'Gender': Africa, *Othello* and Bringing to Light." In Hendricks and Parker, eds. *Women, 'Race', and Writing*, 84–100.

———, and Geoffrey Hartman, ed. *Shakespeare & the Question of Theory*. New York and London: Methuen, 1985.

Paster, Gail Kern. *Humoring the Body: Emotions and the Shakespearean Stage*. Chicago: University of Chicago Press, 2004.

———, Katherine Rowe, and Mary Floyd-Wilson, eds, *Reading the Early Modern Passions: Essays in the Cultural History of Emotion*. Philadelphia: University of Pennsylvania Press, 2004.

Paul, Henry Neill. *The Royal Play of Macbeth*. London: Macmillan, 1950.

Paul, Stephen de. "Phenomenological Criticism." *Encyclopedia of Contemporary Literary Theory: Approaches, Scholars, Terms*. Ed. Irena R. Makaryk. Toronto: University of Toronto Press, 1993. 139–44.

Pearson, Lu Emily. *Elizabethans at Home*. Stanford: Stanford University Press, 1957.

Pechter, Edward. "A Note on the Text." *Othello: A Norton Critical Edition*. New York and London: W.W. Norton, 2004. xiii–xvii.

Penrose, Boies. *Urbane Travellers 1591–1635*. Philadelphia: University of Pennsylvania Press, 1942.

Penrose, Valentine. *Erzsebet Bathory, la Comtesse Sanglante* [*The Bloody Countess*]. Trans. Alexander Trocchi. 1970; London: Creation Books, 1996.

Perry, Curtis. *The Making of Jacobean Culture: James I and the Renegotiation of Elizabethan Literary Practice*. Cambridge: Cambridge University Press, 1997.

Peters, Belinda Roberts. *Marriage in Seventeenth-Century English Political Thought*. Basingstoke: Macmillan Palgrave, 2004.

Platt, Colin. *The Great Rebuildings of Tudor and Stuart England: Revolutions in Architectural Taste*. London: UCL Press, 1994.

Pocock, Douglas C.D., ed. *Humanistic Geography and Literature: Essays on the Experience of Place*. London: Croom Helm; Totowa: Barnes & Noble Books, 1981.

Pound, John. *Poverty and Vagrancy in Tudor England*. Second Edition. London and New York: Longman, 1986.

———. "An Elizabethan Census of the Poor." *Historical Journal* 8 (1962): 135–61.

Purves, Dale. *Why We See What We Do: An Empirical Theory of Vision*. Sunderland, MA: Sinauer Associates, 2003.

Pugliati, Paola. *Beggary and Theatre in Early Modern England*. Burlington: Ashgate Publishing, 2003.

Pye, Christopher. *The Vanishing: Shakespeare, the Subject, and Early Modern Culture*. Durham: Duke University Press, 2000.

Rakoff, Robert M. "Ideology in Everyday Life: The Meaning of the House." *Politics and Society* 7 (1977): 85–104.

Ray, C. Claiborne. "Little Blue Lights." *New York Times*, August 7, 2007: D2.

Ray, Sid. *Holy Estates: Marriage and Monarchy in Shakespeare and His Contemporaries*. Selinsgrove: Susquehanna University Press; Cranbury, NJ: Associated University Presses, 2004.

Reiss, Timothy J. *Mirages of the Selfe: Patterns of Personhood in Ancient and Early Modern Europe*. Stanford: Stanford University Press, 2003.

Rey, Roselyne. *The History of Pain*. Trans. Louise Elliott Wallace, J.A. Cadden, and S.W. Cadden. Cambridge, MA and London: Harvard University Press, 1995.

Richardson, Catherine. *Domestic Life and Domestic Tragedy in Early Modern England: The Material Life of the Household*. Manchester: Manchester University Press, 2006.

———. "Home, Household and Domesticity in Drama in Early Modern London." In *Imagined Interiors: Representing the Domestic Interior since the Renaissance*. Eds, Jeremy Aynsley, Charlotte Grant, and Harriet McKay. London: V & A Publications, 2006. 50–63.

Roberts, Sasha. "'Let me the curtains draw': The Dramatic and Symbolic Properties of the Bed in Shakespearean Tragedy." In Harris and Korda, eds, 153–74.

Robertson, James. "Stuart London and the Idea of a Royal Capital City." *Renaissance Studies* 15 (2001): 37–58.

Romano, Dennis. "City-State and Empire." In Humfrey, ed. *Artistic Centers,* 9–30.

Rosenthal, Margaret F. *The Honest Courtesan: Veronica Franco, Citizen and Writer in Sixteenth-Century Venice*. Chicago: University of Chicago Press, 1992.

Rosmarin, Adena. *The Power of Genre*. Minneapolis: University of Minnesota Press, 1985.

Ross, Charles. *The Custom of the Castle: From Malory to Macbeth*. Berkeley: University of California Press, 1997.

Rybczynski, Witold. *Home: A Short History of an Idea*. Harmondsworth and New York: Penguin, 1986.

———. *The Perfect House: A Journey with the Renaissance Master Andrea Palladio*. New York: Scribner, 2002.

Sacks, Claire, and Edgar Whan, eds. *Hamlet: Enter Critic*. New York: Appleton-Century-Crofts, 1960.

Salgado, Gamini. *Eyewitnesses of Shakespeare: First-Hand Accounts of Performances 1590–1890*. New York: Harper & Row, 1975.

Sanders, Walter. "Terence at Newberry, 1470–1700: A Rough Checklist." *Research Opportunities in Renaissance Drama* 9 (1966): 62–75.

Sandler, Robert, ed., *Northrop Frye on Shakespeare*. New Haven, CT and London: Yale University Press, 1986.

Scarry, Elaine. *The Body in Pain: The Making and Unmaking of the World*. Oxford and New York: Oxford University Press, 1985.

Schoenfeldt, Michael C. "Fortifying Inwardness: Spenser's Castle of Moral Health." In *Bodies and Selves in Early Modern England: Physiology and Inwardness in Spenser, Shakespeare, Herbert, and Milton*. Cambridge: Cambridge University Press, 1999. 40–73.

Scolnicov, Hanna. "Theatre Space, Theatrical Space, and the Theatrical Space Without." *The Theatrical Space*. Themes in Drama 9. Ed. James Redmond. Cambridge: Cambridge University Press, 1987. 11–26.

Scott, William O. "Contracts of Love and Affection: Lear, Old Age, and Kingship." *Shakespeare Survey* 55 (2003): 36–42.

Shami, Jeanne, ed. *Renaissance Tropologies: The Cultural Imagination of Early Modern England*. Pittsburgh: Duquesne University Press, 2008.

Sharpe, Kevin, and Peter Lake. *Culture and Politics in Early Stuart England*. Stanford: Stanford University Press, 1993.

Shattuck, Charles H. *The Hamlet of Edwin Booth*. Urbana, IL: University of Illinois Press, 1969.

Shepard, Paul. *Man in the Landscape: A Historic View of the Esthetics of Nature*. College Station: Texas A & M University, 1991.

Shuger, Debora Kuller. *Habits of Thought in the English Renaissance: Religion, Politics, and the Domestic Culture*. Berkeley, CA: University of California Press, 1990.

———. "The 'I' of the Beholder: Renaissance Mirrors and the Reflexive Mind." In Fumerton and Hunt, eds, 21–41.

Skelton, R.A. *Explorers' Maps: Chapters in the Cartographic Record of Geographical Discovery*. London: Routledge and Kegan Paul, 1958.

Slights, Jessica. "'The 'Undividable Incorporate': Householding in *The Comedy of Errors*." In *Domestic Arrangements in Early Modern England*. Ed. Kari Boyd McBride. Pittsburgh: Duquesne University Press, 2002. 74–102.

Smuts, R. Malcolm. *Court Culture and the Origins of a Royalist Tradition in Early Stuart England*. Philadelphia: University of Pennsylvania Press, 1987.

Snyder, Susan. *The Comic Matrix of Shakespeare's Tragedies: Romeo and Juliet, Hamlet, Othello, and King Lear*. Princeton: Princeton University Press, 1979.

Soja, Edward W. *Postmodern Geographies: The Reassertion of Space in Critical Social Theory*. London and New York: Verso, 1989.

Sopher, David E. "The Landscape of Home: Myth, Experience, Social Meaning." In *The Interpretation of Ordinary Landscapes: Geographical Essays*. Ed. D.W. Meinig. Oxford and New York: Oxford University Press, 1979.

Sorensen, Roy. *Seeing Dark Things: The Philosophy of Shadows*. Oxford: Oxford University Press, 2008.

Sousa, Geraldo U. de. "Alien Habitats in *The Tempest*." The Tempest*: Critical Essays*. Ed. Patrick M. Murphy. New York and London: Routledge, 2001. 438–61.

———. *Shakespeare's Cross-Cultural Encounters*. 1999; London and New York: Palgrave, 2002.

———. "Unhoused in *Othello*." *Approaches to Teaching Shakespeare's* Othello. Eds, Peter Erickson and Maurice Hunt. New York: MLA, 2005. 133–40.

Stallybrass, Peter. "*Macbeth* and Witchcraft." In Brown, ed. *Focus on Macbeth*. 189–209.

———. "Marginal England: The View from Aleppo." In Orlin, ed. *Center or Margin*. 27–39.

———. and Ann Rosalind Jones. "Fetishizing the Glove in Renaissance Europe." *Critical Inquiry* 28.1 (2001): 114–32.

———. "The World Turned Upside Down: Inversion, Gender and the State." In Wayne, ed. *Matter of Difference*, 201–20.

———. "*Macbeth* and Witchcraft." In *Focus on Macbeth*. Ed. John Russell Brown. London; Boston: Routledge & Kegan Paul, 1982. 189–209.

States, Bert O. *Great Reckonings in Little Rooms: On the Phenomenology of Theater*. Berkeley: University of California Press, 1985.

———. *Hamlet and the Concept of Character*. Baltimore, MD: The Johns Hopkins University Press, 1993.

Strauss, Leo. *Xenophon's Socratic Discourse: An Interpretation of the Oeconomicus*. Ithaca, NY: Cornell University Press, 1970; South Bend: St Augustine's Press, 2004.

Sugden, Edward H. *A Topographical Dictionary to the Works of Shakespeare and His Fellow Dramatists*. Manchester: Manchester University Press, 1925.

Summer, William Graham. *Folkways: A Study of the Sociological Importance of Usages, Manners, Customs, Mores, and Morals*. Boston: The Athenaeum Press, 1913.

Swartley, Ariel. "Shakespeare, and the Wilds Found Indoors." *The New York Times*, October 4, 1998, 45.

Teague, Frances. *Shakespeare's Speaking Properties*. Lewisburg: Bucknell University Press; London: Associated University Presses, 1991.

Thorndike, Ashley H. *Shakespeare's Theater*. New York: Macmillan, 1916.

Thorne, Alison. *Vision and Rhetoric in Shakespeare: Looking through Language*. New York: St Martin's Press, 2000.

Thurley, Simon. "Elizabethan Whitehall, 1558–1603." In Thurley, *Whitehall Palace*, 65–74.

———. "The Domestic Building Works of Cardinal Wolsey." In S. Gunn and P. Lindley, eds. *Cardinal Wolsey, Church, State and Art*. Cambridge: Cambridge University Press, 1991. 76–102.

———. *The Royal Palaces of Tudor England: Architecture and Court Life, 1460–1547*. New Haven and London: Yale University Press, 1993.

———. *Whitehall Palace: An Architectural History of the Royal Apartments, 1240–1698*. New Haven and London: Yale University Press, 1999.

Tipping, H. Avray. *English Homes: Late Tudor and Early Stuart 1558–1649*. London: Offices of Country Life and George Newnes; New York: Charles Scribner's Sons, 1922.

Tobriner, Alice. "Almshouses in Sixteenth-Century England: Housing for the Poor Elderly." *Journal of Religion and Aging* 1.4 (1985): 13–41.

Torrens, H.S. "Mawe, John (1766–1829)." *Oxford Dictionary of National Biography*. Oxford: Oxford University Press, 2004. http://www.oxforddnb.com.www2.lib.ku.edu:2048/view/article/18391, accessed August 6, 2007.

Tuan, Yi-Fu. *Space and Place: The Perspective of Experience*. Minneapolis: University of Minnesota Press, 1977.

Turner, Henry S. *The English Renaissance Stage: Geometry, Poetics, and the Practical Spatial Arts 1580–1630*. Oxford: Oxford University Press, 2006.

Turner, Jack. "Spices and Christians." *Encompassing the Globe: Portugal and the World in the 16th & 17th Centuries*. Ed. Jay A. Levinson. Washington, DC: Smithsonian Institution, 2007. 45–53.

Turner, James. "Landscape and the 'Art Prospective' in England, 1584–1660." *Journal of the Warburg and Courtauld Institutes* 42 (1979): 290–93.

Turner, Richard. *The Vision of Landscape in Renaissance Italy.* Princeton, NJ: Princeton University Press, 1966.

Tydeman, William, ed., *The Medieval European Stage, 500–1550*. Cambridge: Cambridge University Press, 2001.

United States Department of the Army. *U. S. Army Survival Manual*. New York: Dorset Press, 1991.

Van Beek, Gus W. "Frankincense and Myrrh." *The Biblical Archaeologist* 23.3 (1960): 70–95.

Van Riel, Gerd. *Pleasure and the Good Life: Plato, Aristotle, and the Neoplatonists*. Leiden, Boston, and Köln: Brill, 2000.

Van Straten, Roelof. *An Introduction to Iconography.* Trans. Patricia de Man. Muiderberg: Gordon and Breach Science Publishers, 2000.

Varner, Eric. "Reading Replications: Roman Rhetoric and Greek Quotations." *Art History* 29.2 (2006): 280–303.

Varriano, John. *Caravaggio: The Art of Realism*. University Park, PA: Pennsylvania State University, 2006.

Vaughan, Alden T., and Virginia Mason Vaughan. "Before Othello: Elizabethan Representations of Sub–Saharan Africans." *The William and Mary Quarterly* 54.1 (1997): 19–44.

Vaughan, Virginia Mason. *Othello: A Contextual History*. Cambridge: Cambridge University Press, 1994.

———. *Performing Blackness on English Stages, 1500–1800*. Cambridge: Cambridge University Press, 2005.

——— and Kent Cartwright, eds. *Othello: New Perspectives* London and Toronto: Associated University Presses, 1991.

Vitkus, Daniel. *Turning Turk: English Theater and the Multicultural Mediterranean, 1570–1630*. London: Palgrave, 2003.

Wade, Nicholas J. *Perception and Illusion: Historical Perspectives*. New York: Springer, 2005.

Wall, Wendy. *Staging Domesticity: Household Work and English Identity in Early Modern Drama*. Cambridge: Cambridge University Press, 2002.

Warwick, Genevieve, ed. *Caravaggio: Realism, Rebellion, Reception*. Newark, DE: University of Delaware Press, 2006.

Wayne, Valerie, ed., *The Matter of Difference: Materialist Feminist Criticism of Shakespeare*. Ithaca, NY: Cornell University Press, 1991.

Webb, Jr., James L.A. *Desert Frontier: Ecological and Economic Change along the Western Sahel, 1600–1850*. Madison: University of Wisconsin Press, 1995.

———. "The Trade in Gum Arabic: Prelude to French Conquest in Senegal." *The Journal of African History* 26.2–3 (1985): 149–68.

Weimann, Robert. *Shakespeare and the Popular Tradition in the Theater: Studies in the Social Dimension of Dramatic Form and Function.* Ed. Robert Schwartz. Baltimore, MD, and London: Johns Hopkins University Press, 1978.

Weinber, Bernard. *A History of Literary Criticism in the Italian Renaissance.* 2 vols. Chicago: University of Chicago Press, 1961.

Wells, Stanley and Gary Taylor. *William Shakespeare: A Textual Companion.* Oxford, UK: Clarendon Press, 1987.

Welty, Eudora. *Place in Fiction.* New York: House of Books, 1957.

West, Russell. *Spatial Representation and the Jacobean Stage: From Shakespeare to Webster.* Houndmills, Basingstoke, Hampshire; New York: Palgrave, 2002.

Weyl, Herman. *Symmetry.* Princeton, NJ: Princeton University Press, 1952.

Wheale, Nigel. *Writing and Society: Literacy, Print and Politics in Britain 1590–1660.* London and New York: Routledge, 1999.

White, Martin. *Renaissance Drama in Action: An Introduction to Aspects of Theatre Practice and Performance.* London and New York: Routledge, 1998.

Whitney, Lois. "Did Shakespeare know Leo Africanus?" *PMLA* 37(1922): 470–88.

Wickham, Glynne. *Early English stages, 1300 to 1660.* 3 vols. London: Routledge and Paul; New York: Columbia University Press, 1959–81.

———. "Hell-Castle and Its Door-Keeper." *Shakespeare Survey* 19 (1966): 68–74.

Wigley, Mark. "Untitled: The Housing of Gender." In *Sexuality & Space*. Ed. Beatriz Colomina. Princeton, NJ: Princeton Papers on Architecture, 1992. 326–89.

Williamson, Claude C.H., ed., *Readings on the Character of Hamlet 1661–1947.* London: George Allen & Unwin, 1950.

Willis, Deborah. *Malevolent Nurture: Witch-Hunting and Maternal Power in Early Modern England.* Ithaca and London: Cornell University Press, 1995.

Wilson, Bronwen. "Venice, Print, and the Early Modern Icon." *Urban History* 33.1 (2006): 39–64.

Wiseman, John 'Lofty'. *The SAS Survival Handbook: How to Survive in the Wild, in any Climate, on Land or at Sea.* London: Harper Collins, 1999.

Wittkower, Rudolf. *Art and Architecture in Italy 1600–1750.* Revised by Joseph Connor and Jennifer Montagu. New Haven: Yale University Press, 1999.

Woodbridge, Linda. *Vagrancy, Homelessness, and English Renaissance Literature.* Urbana and Chicago: University of Illinois Press, 2001.

Wood, Robert E. *A Path into Metaphysics: Phenomenological, Hermeneutical, and Dialogical Studies.* New York: State University of New York Press, 1990.

———. "Space and Scrutiny in *Hamlet*." *South Atlantic Review* 52.1 (1987): 25–42.

Wright, George T. "Hendiadys and *Hamlet*." *PMLA* 96 (1981): 168–93.

Zamora, Lois Parkinson. "New World Baroque, Neobaroque, Brut Barroco: Latin American Postcolonialisms." *PMLA* 124.1 (2009): 127–42.

Index